CRAFTING FOR DOLLARS

CRAFTING FOR DOLLARS

Turn Your Hobby into Serious Cash

Sylvia Landman

PRIMA PUBLISHING

PRIMA PUBLISHING and colophon are registered trademarks of Prima Communications, Inc.

Library of Congress Cataloging-in-Publication Data

Landman, Sylvia.
Crafting for dollars: turn your hobby into serious cash / by Sylvia
   Landman.
   p.   cm.
   Includes index.
   ISBN 0-7615-0442-7
   1. Handicraft industries.   2. Home-based business.   3. Title.
HD2341.L27   1996
745.5′068—dc20   96-15836
                                                                      CIP

96 97 98 99 00 HH 10 9 8 7 6 5 4 3 2 1
Printed in the United States of America

HOW TO ORDER:

Single copies may be ordered from Prima Publishing, P.O. Box 1260BK, Rocklin, CA 95677; telephone (916) 632-4400. Quantity discounts are also available. On your letterhead, include information concerning the intended use of the books and the number of books you wish to purchase.

Visit us online at http://www.primapublishing.com

To the three most important men in my life:

Francisco Machón Vilanova, author, poet, mentor, and beloved grandfather;

Philip L. Landman, my husband, who supported me in every possible way . . . in life, in my career, and in bringing this book to reality;

My brother, Rick Matosich, whose pride in my work kept me going.

And to all those craft professionals who shared themselves so generously in this book so others may learn, I extend my heartfelt appreciation. You have enriched us all. Each of you affirms my belief that, indeed, crafting is a wonderful and special world.

CONTENTS

FOREWORD

There are many books in print on how to sell arts and crafts, but it has been almost twenty years since anyone has written a book on the topic of how to build a successful *career* around one's creative skills and talents. I'm happy to see that my friend Sylvia has finally done it. Given today's economy, with so many thousands of people either out of work or dissatisfied with the way they are making a living, this book could not have come at a better time.

There is a big difference between making a little money from one's hobby and building a career or business around it. As both Sylvia and I have learned from managing our own home-based businesses, a big secret to success is learning how to wear all the different hats involved. By structuring her book around the many responsibilities related to each of these hats—that of office manager, researcher, secretary, designer, seller, marketing agent, and so forth—Sylvia has given the reader a practical plan for building both a profitable business and a joyful career.

As beginning writers, both Sylvia and I took the advice of other professionals to write about what we knew. Here, Sylvia brings more than thirty years' experience to bear as she shares the lessons she has learned while building her own profitable career in crafts. Like everyone else, she began with a dream, then worked hard to achieve her individual goals. I have long admired Sylvia's business expertise and can-do attitude. Through her writing and speaking, she has inspired thousands of people to do something special with their skills and talents. Sylvia has continued to accomplish new goals one by one, always helping others along the way. With the publication of this book, she has realized yet another dream, while also proving that her career advice is right on the money. If you're looking for a good role model, you've just found her.

Barbara Brabec
author of *Homemade Money* (Betterway, 1994) and
Handmade for Profit (Evans, 1996)

PREFACE

Children love to fantasize but I reveled in it. The question, "What will I be when I grow up?" pranced in my child's mind tirelessly. My imagination searched for the perfect career while demanding answers to the perennial question asked by children everywhere. "What if . . . ?"

What if I could work in a chocolate factory? Perhaps someone would pay me to eat all the chocolate I could hold. Wouldn't it be wonderful if someone would pay me to sing and make music every day?

What if I could earn money to read my favorite books without my eyes ever growing tired? Maybe I could travel to far-off lands and come home and write about them.

What if I could bring beautiful, heavenly angels with silvery wings down to earth? And wouldn't it be fun to bring delicate fairies to life so we could see them all the time?

What if I could color everything around me using *my* favorite colors without caring what anyone else thought? I had always loved romantic, costume movies. Would anyone pay me to watch them on television?

What if I could have all the beautiful, feminine things I had always admired? How grand if only I could collect all the laces, ribbons, beads, fabrics, yarns, threads, clothes, quilts, and old doilies I wanted. No one would question their practicality. They would exist just to delight me. I would admire them and touch them lovingly every day!

Well, I'm a big girl now. Needlecrafts have been my full-time occupation since 1962. My passion for fiber, needle, and color still thrives unabated. And because I've nurtured them carefully, most of my childhood fantasies fill my adult life.

Many times I vowed not to take one more class in an untried technique. But, somehow, a book or magazine on the subject found itself in my hands. Their charm urged me on. Sooner or later, in spite of my resolve to limit my exploration, my passion drove me. Books persuaded me to continue exploring.

Today, my studio brims with fabric, quilts, thread, yarn, every conceivable needle, doll, bead, and lace along with a vast array of textile paints.

Angels no longer dwell only in heaven. Three live in my studio after their brief appearance in craft magazines. One, I crocheted in lace and trimmed with pearls and satin ribbons. Gracing my studio is my "Knitting Angel." Serenely, she watches over me in her fine gown of knitted lace and silver thread adorned with iridescent wings. She holds her own ethereal knitting worked on toothpicks from translucent filament.

Oh yes! Fairies who could be mistaken for flowers hover nearby. I attired each in a ruffled dress reminiscent of a flower. Each glitters with metallic threads. Tiny elfin shoes turn up at the toe showing off tiny bells. Lacy wings keep my fairies poised for flight. They, too, have graced the pages of craft magazines. I hope that readers follow my design patterns and use my instructions to make these angels and fairies, and I hope they enjoy their creations.

But no life is perfect. I must confess no one has made me a career offer in the field of chocolate. To salve my disappointment I've needlepointed chocolate samplers. Silver thread simulates chocolate kisses, attesting my love for them. Hand-painted T-shirts sport chocoholic idioms. Perhaps it's better that the chocolate calories reside on my clothing rather than in my body.

My dreams of yesteryear have become my vocation today. Indeed, I earn my living designing with my favorite colors, fibers, and techniques. Deadlines add a working dimension to even the most favored activity, yet I am still awed to receive payment for creating treasures I would gladly make for nothing. And when do I do all this? While watching romantic, costume movies of course!

Students teach me; their incessant curiosity never permits me to shirk continual research. Thanks to their endless thirst for information, my library overflows with books. Reading them contributes to my livelihood, just as I fantasized.

Editors educate me with their constructive criticism and suggestions. American manufacturers introduce me to the most wonderful products available anywhere in the world. Publishers continue to inspire me with magazines and provocative books to fawn over, read, and study. The learning process never ends for me.

My passion for needlecraft took me to Europe and Central America. Indeed, I returned home to receive payment to write about the wondrous crafts from other lands. Ideas flow in continuous streams in my head. Raw materials almost design themselves in my hands while I look on, ever amazed at the process.

Oh yes! Lest I forget to mention it, my music fantasy also thrives in my everyday life. Though I do not earn an income from music, happy hours spent at my piano each morning revitalize me. They prepare me for my workday of designing, stitching, painting, and writing.

What other career in the world allows one to evolve artistically, generate self-discovery, and express oneself endlessly? Few jobs are flexible enough to permit daily piano practice and healthy exercise. No other could make work seem like play. Crafts transformed my childhood fantasies into a satisfying, profitable career. If you read this book, perhaps the same can happen for you!

INTRODUCTION

"Craftspeople have one of the least stressful jobs in the United States," says freelance writer Lisa Schroepher. Independently, three job-stress experts agreed on this when Schroepher interviewed them for a recent article in *Men's Health* magazine.

Among hundreds of occupations, only forest rangers have less job-related stress than craftspeople. Schroepher's article explains the reasons behind the statistics. The summary of her premise? Craftspeople find it stimulating and rewarding to utilize their innate creative skill to develop their profession. Yet, they have the advantage of setting their own pace while they develop their talent into a full-time career.

Today's workplace features downsizing and cost cutting in place of secure, occupational opportunities. LINK Resources reports in its latest annual survey that forty-four million home-based businesses operated throughout the United States in 1995.

Ah! Working from home. A lifestyle once considered professionally questionable has become highly desirable. A person's home is no longer merely a castle in which to live. Now it doubles as a workplace. A career in crafts can be the ultimate joy for the creative personality, but doing so from home doubles the pleasure. Imagine staying home concocting beautiful articles while earning an income. What could be better?

Enjoying the comforts of working from home is not just for mothers of small children, either. Professional men in their prime income-producing years have joined the movement in record numbers, too.

Let's hope we've heard the last of such comments as, "You work at home—how cute!" "When will you get a *real* job?" "Don't you miss being out in the *real* world?"

Remember when society looked with pity upon women who took laundry or someone else's children into their homes to earn extra money? "Too bad," people thought. "The husband must be a poor provider and the family must be desperate."

Today, "desperate" means something else. Workers express downright despair when commuting for hours on congested roads. Mothers feel gnawing guilt when they leave their children in the care of another to take a job. Gasoline, parking, and car maintenance costs just to get to work continue to escalate. Where will it end?

Ah, the ten-second commute. Is it the perfect answer? Does it sound like heaven to go from a comfortable bed, walk through the kitchen, grab a warm breakfast, and head into the workplace in a mere ten seconds? No panty hose and high heels. No three-piece suits and too-tight ties. Sweat shirts and jeans have replaced them as unisex working outfits for everyone. Sound good? But how easy is it?

First, consider what constitutes a "home-office." Will a typewriter on a card table in the kitchen do? Successful companies such as Lillian Vernon and Land's End began this way, but these businesses evolved into corporate workplaces. Today's crafters prefer to curb growth. Most want to stay home and mind their own businesses—indefinitely.

Chapter 14 defines home-offices and studios based on guidelines from the ultimate authority—the IRS. For now, let's consider the practical. Full-time or part-time crafters need a workplace to work, think, plan, and create. A home-office or studio should be a well-equipped, sacrosanct area for work-related activities. It means having an efficient office and a well-supplied studio with tools and raw materials gathered in one place.

Faith Popcorn uses the term "cocooning" as an active, ongoing process. She predicted the '90's would cause Americans to burrow deeper inside as life grows more complicated outside. Cocooning feels safe, familiar, comfortable.

Americans continue to focus on the comforts of home. Witness the popularity of home entertainment centers, spas, computers, and exercise equipment. Today's shelter magazines meet the demand for ideas to restore, remodel, refinish, and redecorate our precious cocoons.

If a person's home is his or her castle in which to eat, sleep, rest, and play, why not work there, too? What a revolutionary idea! Except it is not new at all. Butchers, bakers, and candlestick makers worked from their homes for centuries. How quaint! How old-fashioned! How appealing! Let's do it again!

Though many career paths begin at home, a craft career can take up permanent residence. Home-based workers will find that crafts suit today's cocooning lifestyle perfectly. If working with your hands appeals to you, why not start a creative business from home? Once started, why not keep it there? This book will point out the advantages and the challenges you will face.

Child Care

Finding quality child care at affordable prices can cause frustration. Some facilities are downright harmful to children. Others serve as mere garages to park little people for the day. Excessive warehousing of children can make them feel lost in the shuffle. But the crucial issue is this: Can we expect others to love, nurture, and care for our children with the same level of devotion we offer them? Will you settle for less?

Do you enjoy delivering sleepy children to a sitter in the morning only to pick them up evenings and find them as tired and cranky as you? Child care costs can compete with mortgages and car payments in depleting hard-earned salaries.

Wait! Before assuming home-based crafters have a perfect solution to child care, take note. Successful entrepreneurs working from snug cocoons know adjustment is necessary. Interruptions from small children can sabotage deadlines and projects in progress. Children still have needs. Their demands still exist. While it's true you are home to meet those needs, can you do so without sacrificing your income-producing work?

Infants, sleeping peacefully nearby, offer little problem. Oh, if only they could stay that size for several years! Toddlers who nap and retire early consume time and energy, but there's plenty of time left for at least part-time work.

School-aged children leave large blocks of free time for home-based workers. Scheduling your day carefully while they attend school permits full-time earning capability.

Adolescents, with their rebellious attitudes, may require more time than you expect. Though past the stage of smearing jelly on your latest project, they can still cause you to lose your place when working.

I learned about this particular point of view when my teenage son, seeing me at my computer or at work in my studio, would begin a sentence with, "Mom, now that you're not busy . . . ."

Organizational tips and solutions to help you deal with "cocoon mates" appear in Chapter 4. Organizing is not limited to your desk and calendar. Managing a well-organized work schedule is even more critical. Enlisting the cooperation of people who live with you, large and small, will challenge you, but it's possible. Here's a hint to tide you over until you Chapter 4: Communicate!

Distractions and Interruptions

These two villains can wreak havoc on the productivity of home-based workers if not managed well. Children, pets, visitors, neighbors, and television may be precious to us, yet they can distract unwary crafters, cutting into valuable, productive time.

Card-carrying procrastinators unconsciously welcome such intrusions. "I just cannot get anything done," they lament, secretly happy to put off until tomorrow what should have been done today. Careful managers, on the other hand, handle intrusions practically, firmly.

Telephones lead the pack in business interruptus. Miraculous technology though they are, they can nag endlessly, demanding immediate response when we are busiest. Uninvited ringing intrudes into our concentration and we lose our place.

We must control, manage, and organize distractions and interruptions as we modify our lifestyles to work where we live. All we need is a moment to rethink and reorganize priorities from a new perspective.

Separate Personal from Professional Tasks when Working from Home

Working from home isn't a fad—it's here to stay. Books, newsletters, and catalogs nowadays dedicate themselves to the issues facing home-based workers. The tough question that always needs answering is: "How do you separate personal time from business tasks when you work where you live?"

Friends and relatives may ask, "Working with crafts sounds like fun, but is it really *work*?" "Isn't it more like play?" "How easy!" Craftspeople hear such comments often. Crafts are both fun and hard work. We love them yet we can incur an identity crisis working from home doing what others perceive as a leisure activity. How did it become so complicated?

Society programs us to associate home with family, rest, relaxation, and everyone's favorite—housework. Conversely, society programs us to expect that working from a job site means leaving home interests behind. With such a short commute from kitchen to studio, there's not much time to switch identities. No wonder we have a tough time determining who we are at any given moment.

Several generations have socialized us to a clear-cut separation. Relax at home. Work at the office. But reach back a little farther. Before the Industrial Revolution, most people knew how to work from home. It was the lifestyle of the time. Today, an entire new generation must re-learn these skills without the benefit of contemporary role models.

Once again, we feel drawn to work where we live, but often one of two extremes prevails: Home workers either relax too much, giving most of their attention to home/family issues, or become workaholics. Home workers find it easy to dedicate all their time to unrestricted domesticity while hurrying to squeeze in professional duties in too short a span.

Overzealous workers, on the other hand, find it hard to stop working at what they love. After all, craft work is so accessible at home. Computers and worktables beckon to us every day. Nights, weekends, and vacation times blend in with typical workweeks, blurring the distinction between "leisure" and "work time."

Neither extreme works well. Both cause guilt, frustration, and a sense of underachievement. Making a clear distinction between home and business obligations may not be easy, but it's essential.

Unattended, the problem can get out of hand, lower our efficiency, increase anxiety, and make us wonder if working from home is such a good idea after all. You bet it is! If we learn to balance our time obligations, a career in crafts is hard to beat.

The secret of success lies in identifying who we are and the task at hand. A little discussion with yourself is very helpful, but avoid doing so in the presence of others as you search for answers to important questions.

"Who am I for the next two hours? Homeowner or home worker?" If your "invoice" (my word for the inner self) quickly replies, "This is Sunday! Time to relax," do it! Read or watch television. Play with your children, work in your garden, or clean out closets, but do not work at your income-earning activity.

We must mix in a large dose of time management and self-discipline. We need a system to keep personal tasks separate from professional ones so we can get it all done with a minimum of stress. But how? You will find suggestions in Chapter 7.

Bear in mind that the goal in working from home is to lessen tension and generate income. The best way to do this is through efficient work habits and a clear distinction between the professional you and you relaxing in your cocoon. While you are "home" (as opposed to "at work") remember to take time for maintenance of your most valuable piece of machinery—your body. If you neglect it, where will you live?

Conscientious home workers may find it easy to forgo rest, exercise, and play. Take care not to overlook these essentials habitually. If this is a problem for you, solve it by including rest, exercise, or play in your written work schedule. (More about work schedules in Chapter 4.) Rest and exercise will keep you going and avoid burnout.

When in doubt about whether you should work or play, look to your "invoice" for answers. If Monday represents an important workday to you, discipline yourself to work as if you were doing so from an office. Pretend you are working for the best employer in the world. You are—yourself!

Working for the best boss in the world would bring out your best effort, wouldn't it? You would give your all. No stretching breaks and protracted meal times, no time wasted making personal calls or socializing. You would work at peak efficiency. You would want your employer to know how valuable you were. Show him or her how reliable and productive you can be. Impress upon your employer that you are absolutely irreplaceable. Bear in mind, *you* are that wonderful supervisor. Respect and love the person who holds your career in hand.

Make time for play. This means the activities you enjoy doing outside of work. Whatever your age, your inner child needs recreation.

Maintaining Motivation

Last, let's not overlook fifty-thousand-mile tune-ups. They keep your car in safe, working order so you will have reliable transportation. Why not do the same for what drives your career? Your creativity.

Driving yourself continually without tune-ups may cause burnout. You don't want to wear down your batteries, do you? Periodically, take time to refresh yourself. Take a vacation. Attend a retreat. On a daily or weekly basis, take a walk. Swim or run. Cherish your inner gifts.

Maintain your motivation and enthusiasm for your craft business. Attend trade shows regularly. Search out exhibitions and demonstrations. Visit with other artisans in your field. Read about your craft voraciously. Stay informed about the latest product materials, books, trends, and equipment. Read about others in the same field. Pour over trade journals. Keep growing. Join craft associations and business groups such as your local chamber of commerce. Stay fresh. Stay informed.

Don't let your career follow its own path. Take it in the direction *you* choose. Plan. Reach forward. With regular self-discipline you'll get where you want to go. Yes, you *can* support yourself and your family in a pleasurable way with a career in crafts.

Resources

Brabec, Barbara. 1994. *Homemade Money.* Virginia: Betterway Publications.

Popcorn, Faith. 1991. *The Popcorn Report.* New York: Doubleday.

Edwards, Paul and Sarah. *Making It on Your Own.* Los Angeles: Jeremy Tarcher, Inc.

Wurman, Richard. 1989. *Information Anxiety.* New York: Doubleday.

CHAPTER 1

YOU AS ANALYST

SALES OF CRAFT products surpassed video rentals, which, according to the *Official Guide to Household Spending,* were estimated at $9.6 billion dollars. These figures confirm the latest Hobby Industry Association (HIA) annual survey. Craft sales were nearly double that of movie box-office receipts, according to a $5.5 billion estimate published in the *Hollywood Reporter* for the same period. Fitch, Inc., a research firm working with HIA, states that sales in the U.S. craft industry totaled $9.8 billion for 1994. Researchers estimate the figure will rise to $10.9 billion for 1995 based on increases recorded in surveys from 1992 to 1994.

Critics who still insist that crafts is a passing fad or an unprofitable occupation need to study this survey. The size and magnitude of the industry reveals it to be a worthy enterprise for creative entrepreneurs.

Encompassing all the craft arenas, the survey provides details ranking each specific craft, comparing it with others. In the report, the total numbers of hobbyists across the country are further categorized by annual spending habits for craft materials, proficiency levels, preferences, and number of crafters per American household. Clearly, the crafts industry has come into its own and should be taken seriously.

Given that forty-four million people worked from home in 1995, and that crafts ranked third as Americans' recreation of choice (right behind dining out and going to the movies), crafting is an ideal home-based career. Creative work provides personal satisfaction and worthwhile income when entrepreneurs prepare well. *Crafting for Dollars* teaches you how.

Crafting beautiful objects offers people of all ages the opportunity for creative play. Hobbyists enjoy creating items of lasting interest, charm, and beauty. Most craft to give personalized gifts that say, "I cared enough to make this for you, myself."

Professional crafting requires a different mind-set. Though you may still consider crafting enjoyable, profit making requires you to treat as a business what you once considered a pastime. Let's explore the many advantages of crafts as a profession.

First, a career in crafts makes an ideal home-based business. It satisfies the need to cocoon, to work where you live—a strong '90s trend.

Second, working in artistic media gratifies the creative instinct. Crafts, with its diversity and increasing technological advances, literally commands its artists to grow and develop, offering continual opportunity for creative self-expression.

Third, the recreational appeal of crafts delights professionals even more than hobbyists. Enthusiastic "oohs" and "ahs" fill convention halls, seminars, and major trade shows when career crafters encounter innovative designs. Serious artisans find themselves constantly motivated and stimulated by exposure to new products, raw materials, and the imaginative ideas of their peers.

Last, home-based business owners must wear many hats. The variety of tasks required prevents boredom and humdrum working conditions. Marketing, writing, manufacturing, choosing materials, reading, and designing offer the professional crafter a constant change of pace.

Hobby to Business: A Good Idea?

"You have such talent! Why continue giving away your lovely creations when you can sell them? Go into business! Turn your skill into cash!"

Many professional crafters started their career urged by this familiar advice from friends and family. Affirmations and encouragement such as this are valuable to all of us. We treasure important people in our lives who sincerely praise and appreciate our skill. Yet, to succeed, we must understand the difference between "hobby" and "business."

Entrepreneurs who believe that passion for their craft will substitute for business skills are in for a surprise. A quilter who opens a shop armed only with her love of fabric or the jeweler turned shopkeeper to surround himself with gems may be heading for trouble. While enthusiasm for your craft is important, it takes business skills to turn your hobby into a profitable business.

Can you make the transition to see your craft as an income-earning opportunity rather than a pleasant hobby? Can you set aside your personal tastes and preferences while you observe industry trends objectively? The most crucial question to ask yourself is, "Will I make a sincere effort to learn business essentials like marketing, bookkeeping, customer service, and product information?"

The IRS has something to say about every aspect of one's livelihood. They demand proof that profit making is the goal of your craft business. They do not allow taxpayers to take deductions merely to support a hobby.

The IRS advises anyone who begins a business that others perceive as a hobby to follow good business practices. Their literature explains that while you do not have to work in a field you dislike, you'd better focus on profitability if you want the IRS to take seriously a business that others consider recreational.

Guidelines state that you must show a profit at least three out of five years. Further, IRS statutes define you as self-employed when you net more than $400 per year. This minimum earning requires you to file a Schedule C, declaring your self-employed income when you file your federal income tax return each year.

Prepare yourself, from the moment you turn professional, to prove a profit motive. Anytime the IRS declares your business as a hobby, they can disallow otherwise legitimate business deductions. (For additional details about establishing a profit motive to satisfy the IRS, see Chapter 14.)

How do you prove a profit motive? By the existence and proper order of books and records. Face an audit with receipts, invoices, canceled checks, a general business ledger, customer records, and a bookkeeping system. Thus prepared, your battle to prove that you are a professional rather than a hobbyist is half over. Answer the following questions to help define your status as craft hobbyist or professional.

- Does your business make a profit?
- Do you have a comprehensive bookkeeping system?
- Do you have the necessary business licenses and permits?
- Do you advertise your service or product?
- Have you filed the proper tax forms to show your personal and business deductions?
- Do you have a working relationship with wholesalers and vendors?
- Does your work space pass muster as a "business office"?
- How much time do you spend operating your business?
- Can you prove recent business growth?
- Do your business documents establish you as a professional? Business cards, letterhead stationery, brochures, business bank accounts, credit cards, and invoices will do the trick.

Isolation: Curse or Blessing?

Some home-based businesspeople become lonely working by themselves, while others view isolation as one of the primary benefits of a creative, solitary occupation such as crafts. Business books and newsletters advise us against burying ourselves in our home-offices and studios. "Join groups!" "Get out regularly!" they suggest.

As you analyze crafts as your business, examine your personality, too. While some miss the companionship of others in the workplace, many prefer solitude.

Assess your workplace preferences. Do you need the stimulation of others to keep going? Do you seek the approval of other artisans, family members, or friends about your business? Do you need reassurance to validate your artistic talents and design skill? Do you consider feedback from others essential to your professional development?

If the above paragraph describes you, take steps to provide yourself with outside stimulation and reassurance. Without it, you may smother your creativity in self-doubt. Joining groups of other crafters may help. In fact, it helps to participate in non-craft groups and associations as well.

Invite others into your studio regularly. Listen to their response to your work, but guard against creating just to please onlookers rather than to satisfy your inner self. Develop your own style and preferences to nurture artistic growth.

But wait! What about those of us who seek and prefer solitude? Many creative personalities enjoy seclusion and deliberately avoid crowds. Personally, I prefer a workweek when I don't need my car. I like working at a steady pace with few phone calls and other interruptions.

Only you can decide if you find isolation a problem. Ask yourself this question: "Do I have too much or too little solitude?" Evaluate yourself carefully. Strive to balance time alone with companionship, based upon your own personal preference. Low stress levels are one of the principal advantages of a craft career. You have no one to blame but yourself if you develop a stressful work environment that does not suit your temperament. How you apportion solitude versus companionship depends on whether you are an extrovert or an introvert.

Extrovert or Introvert: Which Are You?

Carl Jung, world-famous behaviorist and psychologist, proved that everyone has one of two basic personality characteristics. We prefer to function either as introverts or extroverts.

Authors David Keirsey and Marilyn Bates describe the differences in their informative book *Please Understand Me,* based on Jung's worldwide studies. Introverts feel energized by solitude. Extroverts become bored by it. Persons who prefer extroversion make up 75 percent of the population. Only 25 percent of individuals prefer introversion.

Extroverts crave outside stimulation. When they're alone, they often turn on the television or radio to simulate having company. They are usually gregarious and outgoing. They take the initiative in social situations. They feel compelled to start conversations with strangers. Others see them as the life of the party.

Introverts reach within themselves as their primary point of reference. They motivate themselves. Their direction and ideas come from within. They daydream and visualize. Rarely do introverts seek ideas from others. Their seemingly endless creative flow satisfies them most of the time.

Do not assume all introverts are shy or soft-spoken. Many seek and find careers as articulate public speakers. According to Jung, this personality type produces most of our craftspeople, artists, writers, teachers, musicians, thinkers, and philosophers. Introverts need generous amounts of solitude to work and to renew themselves. The party that stimulates the extrovert exhausts introverts. They prefer intimate groups of two or three people at a time in contrast to the large social gatherings extroverts enjoy.

Introverts and extroverts do well to try to develop more of the other side of their personalities. Ideally, we should strive to balance both aspects, though we may favor one over the other.

Extroverts need to learn to look inward—to focus on the self at times. If you strongly prefer extroversion, learn to look to yourself for solutions to problems. Try to diminish your dependence on the ideas of others.

Introverts need to learn to look at the outside world more often. This helps them to avoid chronic self-absorption. Though highly self-motivated, they may need to make an effort to maintain contacts outside their own world. (See Chapter 19 for more about personality preferences.)

Right or Left Brain Dominance?

Think about how your brain functions as you consider entering the craft marketplace. Why? Because your preference of working from the left or right sphere of your brain will help you head off potential trouble spots. Understanding how the brain works helps the hobbyist convert a pastime into a profitable enterprise.

In his book *Use Both Sides of Your Brain,* author Tony Buzon illustrates how the brain operates. The left part of the brain functions differently from the right. The left hemisphere deals with logic, numbers, and sequence. It seeks order and analysis, mathematical calculations, and linear thought. The right hemisphere deals with music and rhythm, imagery and conceptualization, visualization, daydreaming, color, pattern, and harmony—in short, all the elements we consider the essence of creativity.

Everyone prefers to use one side of the brain or the other. We choose based upon how we function most naturally, effortlessly, and efficiently. Unconsciously, we hone this preference, developing those skills that come naturally to our way of thinking.

People who function best from their left brain usually choose professions requiring the skills it best performs. They often choose to be bookkeepers, accountants, engineers, or scientists. They collect data and statistics. Researchers and computer programmers usually prefer to engage their left brain. Such individuals have an innate need to create order around them. Recognize them when they interrupt a conversation with the question, "OK, what's the bottom line?"

Creative personalities usually resist functioning this way. Right-brained people prefer activities that left-brained people have trouble comprehending.

Those of us who rely most heavily on our right brain can see color, texture, shape, and design in our minds. We use imagery and visualization to work out projects in our head. We need space to daydream, conceptualize, and give our right brain the opportunity to create.

Thus, our left brain gets less of our attention as we place a higher value on the artist within. Conflicts may arise when creative people enter the competitive business world. We must not limit our functions to creative thinking.

Artistic individuals tend to put off left-brained tasks such as bookkeeping, correspondence, and maintaining records. "Those chores bore me," they lament. "I prefer to use my time to design, craft, and create!"

Do you recognize yourself here? Artists and crafters have earned their reputation as poor bookkeepers and business managers. Naturally, they prefer to do what they do best—create.

Some feel they compromise their creative ethic as they perform marketing or bookkeeping chores, for example. They may resent time spent shuffling paper when their hearts yearn for "real work." Their fascination with pattern, color, design, creativity, and beauty seems endless. They "hear" brushes, paints, needles, and clay clamoring for their attention.

Most artisans do not consider bookkeeping to be as much "fun" as creating designs or working in a favored medium. Yet, we must discipline ourselves to learn all we can about accounting, advertising, and marketing if we want to generate income from our artistic talents. Crafters must become entrepreneurs to become profitable.

Here is an idea to help you strike a good balance between the creative and the business aspects of your career. Schedule a *regular* time for business chores. Set aside an hour per day or assign Tuesday afternoons for bookkeeping, for example. Set a time limit to avoid feeling overwhelmed by endless correspondence. Setting a timer will help you "see the light at the end of the tunnel" rather than intimidate you (more on this in Chapter 4).

Make your work environment as pleasant as possible. Sip a delicious tea as you work. Play your favorite music in the background. While busy with bookkeeping, do not sabotage yourself by welcoming interruptions.

Design Ideas—Your Bread and Butter

Artistic individuals usually have more ideas than time to implement them. Most of us begin planning our next project while working on the current one.

But let's go back to preferred brain dominance. Left-brained people prefer single tasks. "Don't bother me with anything else until I finish this," they declare. Right-brained thinkers always have ideas bubbling up. You recognize them by the number of unfinished projects they have. "I'll finish them someday," they say. "But I couldn't wait to try out my new idea, now."

People who prefer single tasks reap their own reward. They follow through. Generally, they perform a task from start to finish.

While they may envy the single-mindedness of their left-brained counterparts, right-brained people think ahead. Before completing a project in progress, they waylay themselves. You hear them say, "I know I haven't finished this, but I couldn't resist shopping for materials for my next design," or "I just had to take time off before finishing this to make preliminary sketches for something new I have in mind."

Ideally, though these two groups of thinkers differ considerably from one another, they complement each other well. Collaborate with a left-brained partner, spouse, or family member. Together, you can fill in one another's gaps and get more done as a team.

Resources

Copies of the Hobby Industry Association's "1995 Size of Industry Survey" are available by writing to:
HIA
319 East 54th St.
Elmwood, NJ 07407

Bates, Marilyn and Keirsey, David. 1978. *Please Understand Me.* Del Mar: Prometheus Nemesis Books.

Buzon, Tony. 1983. *Use Both Sides of Your Brain.* New York: E. P. Dutton, Inc.

Stuart and Ellen Quay
Qualin International, Inc.
P.O. Box 31145
San Francisco, CA 94131
Phone: (415) 333-8500   Fax: (415) 282-8789

INTERNATIONAL SILK IMPORTERS

Both Stuart and Ellen Quay bring strong financial backgrounds to their international mail-order importing business. Both worked as systems analysts and held other financially related jobs for big city banks such as Bank of America and Wells Fargo.

Though well paid, both Stuart and Ellen came to dislike the pressures and demands of the corporate workplace. They, like the other craft professionals in this book, yearned to become their own bosses. For a time, they didn't know what direction to take.

Ellen, a native of Hong Kong, has family members there and in China. Finding her bilingual skills valuable, the Quays began their self-employment as tour group leaders to China. Manufacturers of high-quality products and native crafts were always on their itinerary. Easy conversationalists, the Quays always stopped to chat with factory managers and owners, asking about their interest in exporting to the United States.

Fascination with unique Chinese craft products continued to interest the Quays on each trip. Their business began when they imported stunning double-sided silk embroideries and hand-crafted floor screens.

In 1985, the Quays attended their first U.S. trade show. They also began taking classes on small business, customs regulations, and international trade prerequisites between trips to China.

I met the Quays when they enrolled in several college courses I taught on how to operate small craft businesses. I ask students in every class to introduce themselves and to describe the particular craft arena they find of interest.

One student introduced herself as a designer and painter of silk scarves. Ellen Quay jumped up, responding that she was importing these items from China. Networking after class, the artist became the Quays' first steady customer.

Stuart and Ellen became trade-show exhibitors for the first time in early 1986. Here, they displayed double-sided embroideries, lacquer screens, and hand-painted silk scarves.

Show sales disappointed the Quays, but the business they did with silk painters also exhibiting launched Qualin International, Inc. Skilled silk painters agreed that their problems were threefold:

1. Consistent high-quality, undecorated silk garments were not available in the U.S.
2. Supplier inventory levels abroad were erratic.
3. Responsive service was frequently lacking.

"We recognized our niche on the spot," said Stuart. "We vowed to be the first to solve these problems."

To tackle the first, the Quays had to initiate intensive quality-control measures for their imported silk items. Both Quays spent months painstakingly inspecting each piece of imported silk. In the beginning, as much as 60 to 70 percent had to be returned to China as inferior.

Ellen went to China and personally explained what American silk painters wanted. Factories began meeting Quay standards and, at last, brought them recognition as quality providers. Backbreaking quality control paid off— today, their reject rate is only 1 percent.

To resolve the second problem, the Quays now receive most of their silk shipments from China by air. Today, they emphasize service to solve the final problem. Personal friendships with customers have become their prized reward.

Crafts Brief

Business founded: 1986

Legal form of business: Began as a sole proprietorship; incorporated in 1995

Home-office? Today, Stuart and Ellen still operate their business from their home without outside help, though they recently acquired space for their inventory two miles from home. Wholesaling provides the Quays' major income, followed by retail selling at consumer shows and mail order.

Hours: Both Quays find working ten- to fifteen-hour days tolerable since they don't commute and thoroughly enjoy dealing with creative people.

Best part of craft career: Stuart describes his feelings about his business this way: "To me, the professional craft world is like a big creative sandbox. I love dealing with artists and crafters because they are always so happy in their own work."

Least favorite: Calls from East Coast beginning as early as 5:30 A.M. Phone traffic becomes difficult when people call in orders so close together that neither Quay can write up previous orders. Busy mornings can bring up to two hundred requests for price lists (especially after returning home from a trade show).

Strengths: The Quays credit their business acumen and financial expertise with their success.

Weaknesses: Lack of time to experiment with new products, dyes, and colors they wish to add to their line.

Professional organizations: The Quays belong to HIA, ACCI, and The Society of Decorative Artists.

Professional journals: Both Quays read and advertise in *Threads, Fiber Arts, Decorative Artist Workbook, Sew News, Surface Design, The Crafts Report,* and others.

CHAPTER 2

YOU AS OFFICE MANAGER

To PROFIT FROM your craft business, you must take it seriously. Plan your home-office with an eye to detail. Though a few well-known entrepreneurs launched their businesses from home-offices equipped only with a card table and folding chair, think of this romantic notion as a temporary—and inefficient—setup.

Your Office: Make It an Efficient Work Space

Maximize your efficiency by *designing* your office—not merely assigning it leftover space. Give it *prime* space. Consider these two ideas: The bedroom our youngest child vacated when leaving home today houses my working studio. Our former double garage is now a spacious home-office.

THE EXTRA BEDROOM

A spare bedroom makes an ideal home-office or studio. Consider rearranging living space in your home so you can claim an entire room for an office. You can redesign bedrooms inexpensively and easily into efficient work spaces.

Recent studies show that offices with windows offer important benefits to workers. Rachel Kaplan, psychology professor at the University of Michigan, states that people who gaze away from work often relax more and concentrate better. They experience less frustration during hard work sessions and experience more job satisfaction. Though you need not place your desk directly in front of a window, try to place it where you can glance outside frequently.

Next, consider proper lighting. Nothing produces more physical discomfort than straining to see and focus. Install the best lighting you can afford.

Before discussing furnishing your new office, let's turn to another conversion possibility in your home—the garage.

THE GARAGE

Relax! Your car will not be traumatized by losing its home. Converting a garage takes more effort and money than a bedroom conversion—but then you usually get more space! Over the years, many clients and students have expressed surprise when they realize they are standing in what used to be our garage.

Begin by adding walls and a ceiling to transform your garage into a room. Indoor-outdoor rugs installed over a thick pad transform a cold cement floor into a soft, carpeted one. Consider windows here, too. We decided to install a lovely, stained-glass window in the office wall that faces the street. It offers several benefits. Not only is it an attractive addition to the office interior, but visitors can use it as an exterior landmark to find my home-office easily.

Additionally, I have a beautiful, restful place from which to gaze as I work. The window ushers in light in a charming way. Its frosted background permits me to see out while preventing passersby from seeing in.

DESKS . . . WHAT DO YOU REALLY NEED?

Once you have a room, be it a garage or a bedroom, it's time to furnish it. Choosing a comfortable desk should be a top priority. You can spend a fortune on a new, modern desk from an office furniture company, but consider saving a little money by customizing older desks. Choose the place for your desk carefully because it will be the heart of your work space. Make sure it receives the best available light.

Select a desk with drawers on each side of the center knee well if possible. Try on your desk for size. Sit at the desk *before* you buy. Make sure the space between the columns of drawers accommodates your knees and legs comfortably, for you will spend many hours here.

A common mistake people make when choosing a desk is to select one with an inadequate working surface. You need space to place essential equipment such as a typewriter, computer, and phone, but you also need open space on which to work.

One of my first remodeling mistakes was to select a desk with a surface area that was too shallow. I found myself fumbling around trying to turn pages of books I had balanced on my lap since there was no room to lay them on the desk. There was no place to make handwritten notes or to shuffle papers. Here's a simple, inexpensive solution if you already have a desk you find too small: Purchase a sheet of plywood or fiberboard. Cut it wider and deeper than the surface of the desk. Cover it with inexpensive adhesive shelfpaper or wallpaper, or paint it. Place it on top of the existing desk and, voilà—you have expanded your desk's work area.

CHAIRS

The chair is an essential element that is too often overlooked. Humans did not always spend most of their lives in a sitting position. And today, a myriad of low-back problems attest to the body's resistance to this position. Skimp on purchasing anything else for your office before you choose an inadequate chair. Your mind will function better if your muscles remain relaxed and comfortable in the sitting position.

Physical therapists offer valuable tips about how to sit. From them, I learned the value of an ergonomic chair. Tilt mechanisms that vary the slant of the back rest and seat pan with the push of a button are indispensable.

Reposition the back rest and seat of the chair often as you work. Even a slight change in position will realign your body's pressure points, lessening pain and stiffness that can result from prolonged sitting.

Take a book with you when you shop for a chair. That's right—try a chair on for size before you buy. Select a chair because it fits your body, not because it fits your budget. Sit and read for at least fifteen minutes when testing a chair. Evaluate its features carefully, for you will spend many hours sitting. Chairs with arms offer additional upper-body support. Choose one with a five-wheel base to provide stability when you swivel.

Note the depth of the seat pan. People with long legs require a deeper seat than those with short legs. If the seat pan is too short, your thighs will not receive adequate support. A seat pan that is too long will impede circulation behind your knees.

Last, look for a chair with a back rest that rocks back and forth, enabling you to lean forward. Also, try to find a chair that permits you to raise and lower the back as well.

TO YOUR GOOD HEALTH: ARRANGING YOUR OFFICE

It is smart to arrange your office according to tips from occupational and physical therapists. These professionals know best how you can use your body most efficiently at your work situation. I will be forever grateful to the capable person who visited my home-office for a "makeover." Below you will find a few of the tips she suggested as she observed me at work.

Sit in your chair in front of your desk. Extend your arms out sideways at shoulder level. Your prime space lies between your outstretched hands. Place important tools and equipment within this area. Right-handers benefit when they place the phone at the tip of their outstretched *left* hand, leaving their dominant hand free to write. Lefties, do the opposite.

Arrange pencil/pen holders, floppy disk boxes, and other essentials within the prime space of your arm's reach. Next, stand in front of your chair. Stretch your arms out again. Before you is your second level of prime space.

Consider installing a book shelf here for items that should remain within reach. Your back will thank you each time you stand from a sitting position to reach for dictionaries, manuals, and other such items.

Sit and open the drawers of your desk. Place items used most often in the top drawers. Put those of less importance in middle drawers, and place objects least used in the bottom drawer. Keep the space in front of your desk free and open for writing and study. Do *not* allow clutter to gather here. Reserve this as a sacrosanct work space. This way, you will keep your body facing straight ahead, avoiding the tendency to twist your spine.

Now, take a look *under* the desk. How much space lies beneath the knee well? To position myself correctly in front of my computer screen, I must elevate my chair. This, in turn, causes my feet to dangle as I sit—an unacceptable situation. I use a slanted footrest to support my feet and legs. Do you need such an aid?

If space remains beneath your desk beyond what you need for your legs and feet, consider using the area for storage. Cardboard file boxes often fit these spaces well. Use them to store files and papers you reach for occasionally. You can even use the file box itself as a footrest!

Copiers and computer printers need not take up valuable prime space. Position them farther away from the desk area. That way, you have a chance to stand up and stretch your legs and back when you have to make a copy or send a fax.

Here's another valuable tip learned from an occupational therapist: Low-back problems prevent me from sitting for long periods of time. When she spied my electronic typewriter sitting on a second small desk nearby, she suggested I consider a stand-up work station. Today, the typewriter sits on a sturdy, adjustable drafting table in the corner of my office, providing an alternate working position.

To further enhance stand-up work stations, add a small footstool beneath the table. Alternately rest each foot on the lowest rung. Consider placing a bar-stool to lean back upon without actually sitting. This makes typing or writing in this position comfortable and restful.

Think and plan before installing your telephone. If you use a computer or typewriter at your desk, you will find it helpful to have the phone within reach. Speaker phones free your hands, enabling you to type or write during important business calls. Telephones that automatically dial frequently called numbers eliminate wasting time looking up numbers you call regularly.

Position the phone within reach of file cabinets, too. You need only swivel in your chair to search for information from file drawers when needed. No need to put callers on hold. More tips about business phones in Chapter 7.

COMPUTERS

Chapter 18 deals with selecting hardware and software in detail. For now, let's focus on locating the computer in your office. Home-based businesspeople who work with computers recognize them as the star of the show. Those of us who use them daily recognize them as "willing slaves."

Computers require thoughtful consideration as you select proper office space for them. Take care to place them so nearby windows and light fixtures will not create glare as you sit in front of the monitor.

Problems that arise for people who sit many hours in front of a computer monitor are common knowledge nowadays. Position the screen so you see it straight ahead. Good ergonomics dictate that the top of the monitor line up with your forehead. This position lessens neck strain and headaches. Do not permit yourself to hang your head downward to read a screen that is too low, or tilt backward to gaze at one too high.

Keyboards should line up as closely as possible to your elbows. Wrists are especially prone to repetitive motion injury. Use a padded rest to position hands and wrists correctly. You can also buy specially made Lycra therapeutic gloves, which offer added wrist support.

COPY MACHINES

Office copiers do more than save you precious time driving to and from copy centers. I rate my office copier second in importance to my craft business. Only the computer takes precedence.

The reduction and enlargement capability of an office copier offers many benefits to a crafts designer. Consider the following possibilities:

Choose any line drawing, sketch, design, or other copyright-free clip art. Enlarge or reduce as needed to create your own logo and letterhead stationery design. Enhance instructional materials with clip-art figures, cartoons, and borders.

Dover Publications, Inc., listed in the resource section of this book, offers a large array of copyright-free clip art, alphabets, borders, and other visual materials.

Make graphs for publication using easy-to-see, large grids. Reduce when completed to accommodate available space.

Update instruction sheets easily. Rather than redraw or retype, use cut-and-paste techniques on your copier. Today's machines all but eliminate shadows caused by edges of cut paper.

One computer plus one office copier perform many if not all desktop publishing tasks. Fashion your own project booklets, catalogs, and newsletters.

Design with your copier! For example, I photographed my own stained-glass window. I enlarged the photo on my copier. Once enlarged to proper size, I had an accurate pattern sheet to use in designing a quilt replicating the stained-glass design.

Listed below, you will find features you want to consider in selecting an office copier:

- Will it enlarge and reduce?
- Will it make acceptable two-sided copies?
- Do you need the machine to sort and collate pages?
- Will the machine make copies from books?
- Will the copier make oversize copies such as legal size and larger?
- Is the machine easy to maintain, and easy to refill with toner and developer?
- Have you found a good provider to perform regular servicing?
- Have you determined how many copies you purchase from a copy store and how many weekly/monthly trips you make there?
- Will purchasing a copier pay for itself in convenience and economy?

Last, consider leasing a copier for a month or two. Give it a trial run. Also, think about buying used copiers from reputable office supply dealers. You too may find yourself wondering how you ever managed without one.

FAX MACHINES

Facsimile machines offer valuable technology to any business, but a word of warning is in order. Economizing by combining your fax with your phone line does not work well. Too often, when home-based workers shut down their computer or leave home or retire, they forget to switch on their fax line. Frustration awaits customers and colleagues who fruitlessly try to send a fax only to find you "closed down."

Consider, instead, a dedicated phone line. This means installing another phone line so you can send or receive faxed messages day or night. Dedicated lines keep your communication facility available twenty-four hours a day. Many clients prefer to call during evening or early morning hours to take advantage of lower phone rates. Try not to frustrate them by making your fax unavailable.

Working moms, take note. Your business contacts will have a hard time taking your craft business seriously if you allow small children to interrupt fax messages by answering the phone during a fax transmission. Callers must spend more time and money to redial—a situation you want to avoid.

YOUR FILING SYSTEM: ONLY AS GOOD AS YOUR RETRIEVAL METHOD

Magazines and newspapers provide valuable information, but how do you find exactly the specific publication containing an article you read three months ago? Saving publications in a random pile courts disaster. All you can be sure of is frustration as you search through all of them for specific research material.

Make storage and retrieval of information from magazine and newspaper articles simple. Every time you read a publication, note on the cover what you found of value within.

Try steel-tipped pens that will write on the heavy, coated paper stock used on magazine covers. Below, you will find a few shorthand codes you may find helpful in creating a retrieval system.

Code Word		Example
Copy	p. 21	about setting fees
Write	p. 34	to request information about a product
Do	p. 42	call the 800 number and order this book

Save	p. 61	refer to this ad for color ideas
Study	p. 75	good article about storing painting equipment
Idea	p. 84	for possible future quilt design
Refer	p. 92	to bookkeeper in case my business qualifies
Tear	p. 103	to design binder

This system helps you know immediately why you saved a publication. End wasting time thumbing through countless issues looking for an idea you remember but can't locate.

Toss magazine issues that have no such notations on the covers. This tells you you found nothing worth saving after the initial reading. Of course, if you are collecting all issues of a particular subscription, you can make an exception.

The key to success is to place a tear sheet *immediately* into its binder. Don't allow small bits of paper to collect on your desk. Assign them a place from the beginning. Consulting your idea binder frequently becomes its own reward. Design idea binders are discussed more in Chapter 12.

What if you want to catalog specific information but prefer not to tear up a valuable publication? Photocopy what you need and store it in the appropriate binder or file. But first a special note here about copyrights.

When you buy a book or magazine, you may make photocopies for your personal use. The copyright law calls this "fair use." Buyers do not violate copyright law or deprive an author of earned income because they have already purchased the book.

However, you may not copy, sell, trade, or even give away photocopies under present copyright law. Copies made for storage or used as reference when away from home when you find a book too cumbersome to carry, for example, also constitute "fair use." Find extensive details about copyright restrictions in Chapter 15.

Your Working Studio

Like your home-office, your working studio requires proper equipment, supplies, and arrangement to make your job—crafting—go as smoothly as possible.

EQUIPMENT

Let's define equipment as the larger implements and machinery you need to perform specific tasks in your craft business. Some examples:

- Sewing machines
- Ceramic kilns
- Electric table saws
- Silk-screening equipment
- Drills

All equipment required to manufacture your craft items is 100 percent tax deductible. Details listing these and other deductions appear in Chapter 14. Selecting equipment for your studio constitutes a business investment. Choose the best you can afford. Let go of hobbyist thinking such as, "How can I spend the least to do the job?"

Instead, think like a professional. Select only the most efficient, durable equipment that will help you produce high-quality goods. Study warranties and service contracts. Keep precious office space in mind. Choose items that will serve more than one function when possible.

Preserve storage space. For example, why not purchase an office copier stand that includes shelves to store paper? How about lamps with side clamps rather than space-consuming table bases? Footrests that double as storage containers? Floppy disk boxes that serve double duty as bookends? Got the idea?

TOOLS

Think of tools as hand-held implements that perform specific tasks. The cliché, "The right tool for the right job," applies seriously to all crafters choosing tools for a studio. Professional tools selected for performance eliminate wasted time trying to "make do" with a tool not up to the task. Proper tools increase the quality of products you create.

I recently violated this principle to annoying—though not totally disastrous—results. Though primarily a fiber artist, I became fascinated with bead jewelry. Thus, I found myself needing jewelry-making tools. Books on the subject recommended *both* round-nosed and flat-nosed pliers.

Since beading is a hobby for me, I opted to buy only one set of pliers. Naively, I hoped one tool could do the work of two. Not so! After trying to form round loops on head-pins, I realized the difficulty had resulted from my use of the incorrect tool. Most decidedly, flat-nosed pliers could not achieve the round shapes I was trying to create.

Fortunately, my career was not on the line. I was only playing with beaded jewelry, not trying to create quality products for sale or publication. I shudder to think about raw materials spoiled and time lost had I been on a deadline or struggling to meet a customer's need. Though similar, the two types of pliers do not perform interchangeable tasks. My decision to economize at the expense of proper tools was unwise.

WORK SURFACES

Plan carefully. The space you need to work is important—allow plenty. If you have room, consider placing an older dining room table in the middle of your studio, permitting you to walk, reach, and work from all four sides.

For those of you needing more room for your sewing machine than available table models permit, consider this idea: Buy an old-fashioned, heavy office desk. Give it a facelift by sponge painting or tole painting it with designs. Cover the top surface with leftover floor tiles. You may also consider the modern-style tiles with peel-off adhesive backing.

Over the center knee well of the desk, cut an opening to accommodate the base of your machine so it will sit flush on the new desk top. I remodeled an old army desk this way and discovered an extra bonus. The middle shallow drawer meant for pencils and small office items was exactly the right depth to store spools of thread.

Thus, the machine sits flush on the table while the drawer beneath provides valuable storage. The large double drawer on one side meant for hanging files is perfect for filing sewing patterns. We paid $5 for the desk, $8 for floor tiles, and spent a day or two sanding and painting. Voilà! A custom work space permitting easy sewing on even the largest quilts.

Investigate today's collapsible, heavy cardboard work and cutting tables. They enable you to cut, draft, and lay out large projects, yet, when not in use, these temporary work spaces fold to hide under tables and beds.

Also consider camping tables with folding legs if studio space is at a premium. Set them up when you need them— take them down when you are finished working.

New Shelves in Old Corners

Utilize room corners in busy studios. Stack trays and shelves from floor to ceiling. Open bins nesting into one another are practical. Contents remain in view, yet all but the top bin receive protection from dust from the bin above.

Excellent storage buys become available when small stores in your area close their doors. Look for notices advertising fixtures for sale. Adjustable shelving, bins, and cubbyhole shelving to display goods in shops work well in home-studios, too. Some are even designed and shaped for corner placement. Plant stands work well also. Many corner styles offer half-circle shelves arranged in tiers from floor to ceiling.

Check out open board shelving that rests on wall-supported brackets and notches. These units cost little, yet remain adjustable and moveable. Fit them nearly anywhere you find spare wall space. For storage or display, make every inch count!

CLOSETS: THE PERFECT STORAGE SPACE

Regard the closet in a converted bedroom studio as a treasure. Take command by removing the door to create a walk-in storage closet. Sturdy shelves should already be in place overhead. Consider adding one or two more above the existing shelf to expand storage to the ceiling of the closet.

Remove the clothes bar. Build shelving inside the closet. Better still, buy used bookcases and fit them in. These can be plywood, compressed fiberboard, or unfinished wood. By the time you fill them, they will not be visible. Nothing beats a walk-in closet with shelves from floor to ceiling.

Vary the space between shelves—they need not be of equal depth. Reserve a few narrow spaces for patterns, blueprints, albums, and items not easily stacked. Allow some large spaces, too! Compress batting and other bulky items here.

Clear, plastic boxes filled with small items stack easily on shelves. They permit both viewing of contents and easy retrieval. Such boxes act like drawers, enabling you to pull out exactly the one you want and eliminating the need to remove and look into each box.

Old chests of drawers also come in handy. Though contents are not visible, traditional dressers offer prime storage space. Why not paint or decorate all pieces of old furniture with a common theme to furnish your studio? Give it a unified look.

BOOKS AND PATTERNS

The value of your own reference library is only as good as the system by which you can find what you need. Bookshelves, of course, are the ideal place for books, but why shelve them in random order? Organize your books by topic.

Make a list of all your book titles by topic. Each time you buy a new book, add it to your list. Whenever you attend seminars or visit bookstores, take your list along. You will always know what you already have in your collection, thereby avoiding duplicate purchases.

Group the books together on the shelf as they appear on your list. Consider making another list of titles you would like to add to your library. Carry it with you, ever ready to enrich your collection in a planned way, not on impulse.

Storing patterns presents a different challenge. Remove patterns from their original envelopes. Sewing patterns, large graphs, and schematic patterns for wood cutting are like road maps. Folding and replacing them in their original envelopes tries anyone's patience.

Make your patterns uniform and easy to store. Tape or paste the cover of the pattern envelope on the outside of a manila folder. Refold and press the pattern sections to fit inside the folder. Label the folder.

Purchase inexpensive cardboard file boxes that accommodate manila folders perfectly. Remember, if you have no room to store the box, use it as a footrest beneath your desk, work table, or computer.

Slip cases sold by magazine publishers to hold a year's subscription can be both expensive and bulky. Consider instead plastic magazine holders. What humble gems! These three-hole punched plastic strips come in sets of twelve for less than $4.

Place them in a binder labeled with the magazine's name. Open each magazine to its centerfold. Slip each magazine, annotated as described previously, through the plastic slit. That's all there is to it. No need to punch holes in magazines. Remove them when necessary, replacing them easily to store your collection neatly and permanently.

Last, keep all your supplies in good order. Searching for what you need is a waste of time. Returning everything to its proper place when finished with it saves time in the end.

Resources

Edwards, Paul and Sarah. 1985. *Working from Home.* Los Angeles: Jeremy Tarcher Publications.

Suzann Thompson
Suzann's Designs
2704 Del Curto Road
Austin, TX 78704
Phone: (512) 441-8769

KNITTING PLUS JEWELRY EQUALS A PROFITABLE CRAFT CAREER

Suzann Thompson combines diverse crafts in her successful full-time career. Knitting had always fascinated her as a hobby. It also began her career when she self-published her first booklet, "Continental Style Knitting: A Beginner's Manual," in 1985. Innovative as a designer from the beginning, she began offering her original garment designs to knitting magazines.

Becoming a published designer bought the young, energetic crafter local teaching assignments. Before long, she was in demand to teach for national craft seminars and conventions, sharing her techniques with eager students.

Writing instructions for consumer publications came next, followed by designing for yarn manufacturers. Valuable contacts within the industry led Suzann to freelancing as a craft demonstrator at national trade shows and seminars, where she continued to broaden her own craft education.

Suzann's designs appear in more than fifteen craft and knitting publications. Though selling designs and well-researched articles still provides Suzann's primary income, her earnings from freelancing as a teacher and demonstrator continue to increase.

Today we find Suzann publishing not only knitting designs but those for beaded jewelry as well. Jewelry by Suzann regularly appears on the cover of *Jewelry Crafts* magazine.

Crafts Brief

Business founded: 1985

Legal form of business: Sole proprietorship

Home-office? Suzann converted a spare bedroom into a studio. She added wall shelving, a work table, bookcases, knitting frame, sewing machine, filing cabinet, and "yarn supplies and beads everywhere!"

Like many crafters, Suzann lists her computer and laser printer as most important to her business. Always planning ahead, she looks forward to adding a copy machine and a fax modem to her growing office/studio.

Hours: Suzann began her business part-time as a professional knitting designer. Working full-time for an employer, she could only devote two to ten hours weekly to developing her business. Finally, in January 1993, she left her day job to dedicate herself to crafts full-time.

Anna Thompson, Suzann's mother, helps with the business. Suzann also hires contract knitters as needed. Together with a friend and partner, she is currently exploring the potential of selling crafts by mail order.

Daily routine: Suzann begins her day at 9 A.M. and works until 5:15 P.M., when she attends her exercise class. After dinner, she relaxes, as many designers do, by crafting for up to three more hours.

Whether designing knit garments or making Fimo beads for her jewelry designs, Suzann has a lot of "stick-to-itiveness." She tries to stay with one task until she completes it. When correspondence piles up, she may consume an entire day working on it until she is completely caught up.

Though once exclusively a knitter, Suzann now spends increasing amounts of time on her fascination with jewelry crafting. Ever watchful for trends, Suzann recognized this

popular medium as a worthwhile pursuit early. "I've under-
gone a shift in my attitude trying to decide which craft will
take most of my time. It's no longer as important to indulge
my personal favorite as it is to make a living."

Best part of crafting career: "I like the flexible work hours
and being my own boss. Making business decisions without
consulting anyone else satisfies me. I enjoy the reward system built into the job. When I've judged my client correctly
and come up with a good design, I earn my pay! It's up
to me!"

Least favorite: "The publishing time frame! After I complete a design, it takes months to see it published and I
don't get paid until then. Also, I don't enjoy writing tedious
instructions."

Strengths: "I am a good designer, able to present myself and
my work very professionally. I feel this is important."

Weaknesses: "Stubbornness! I think I'm right most of the
time, but find that this also can be a strength. Second, I'm
too easily distracted by new ideas before completing current projects."

Professional organizations: "The Society of Craft Designers is the best networking group, offering excellent relationships with manufacturers and editors. Membership in
the Professional Knitwear Designer's Guild helps me keep
up with knit design news."

Professional journals: "*Craftrends & Sew Business* and *Craft
& Needlework Age* inform me about products and craft
trends and help me scope out potential new clients."

Goals: "I plan to build this business into one that will support family members and several employees. I strive for
maximum gain from every idea. Becoming well known and
sought after by the fiber art and craft community inspires
me. I love my work and would knit and craft even if it were
not my occupation. I'm glad I recognized I could develop
a new career without spending a lot of time and money to
formally reeducate myself."

Advice: "Decide what you *will* do and do it. Remain open to all possibilities within those boundaries. Decide what you will *not* do and don't do it! For example, as a fast typist, I could earn extra money typing manuscripts for others. However, since I dislike this, I elect not to spend time and energy here.

"Take advantage of every opportunity that comes your way! Always be polite and professional. Follow up on every lead. Spend money on your business when it will help you earn more later. *Never* apologize or belittle your successes. Even when those around you sound pessimistic, do not add your voice to destructive chatter. Dare to dream of all possibilities."

CHAPTER 3

YOU AS BUSINESS CONSULTANT

IMAGINE DRIVING ACROSS the United States from coast to coast—alone. Would you start your trip merely by backing your car out of the driveway on any random day? Do you find the destination so exciting that planning seems unnecessary?

What does "cruise control" mean to you? Does it mean your car will take you where you want to go, automatically? Do the terms "positive thinking" and "hope for the best" sound like appropriate travel guides to you? Should you lose your way during your journey, how confident do you feel that someone will come to the rescue? Will all good Samaritans who offer help be experts about your needs? Would you begin a long auto trip such as this prepared only with this mind-set?

Incredible though it sounds, many crafters start a new business with this concept as their only tool. They begin their careers prepared only with a passion for their art and the wish to make a profit. Their love for their craft and the joyful prospect of working at that craft daily exhilarates them. They feel confident their dedication will see them past any obstacle. Such dreamers feel positive they will make a good living without taking the time to research the *business* of crafts. They just can't wait to begin!

Evaluating your business realistically and accurately as outlined in Chapter 1 requires more thought than a cross-country trip. Driving from coast to coast will take only a week or two out of your life. A successful craft career can last a lifetime.

To succeed in *any* business, especially one that others perceive as recreational, you must take control. Choose your own route. Make your own decisions. Leave nothing to chance. Three wonderful tools will help point you toward success—an Action Board, a Monthly Action List, and a Business Plan.

The Action Board helps you gather and organize information. A Monthly Action List helps you maintain realistic schedules. A Business Plan becomes your customized road map to success.

Your Action Board

Begin your business with this effective tool and bring your ideas to life. Though the technique helps you start your business, you can also use the system for problem solving later. Action boards help you define goals and organize priorities. They are simple and they work!

Start with a small tablet of gummed notes and a bulletin board. Think about all the chores your business requires. Consider every possible task it will entail, large and small. Set a two-week time limit for intensive introspection. Take the little notepad everywhere you go, day and night. Each time you think of an idea important to your career, write it on *one* sheet of the notepad. Don't jot down two or more thoughts on one sheet. The reason for this will become clear later.

Read as many business books as you possibly can during this period. Study craft magazines. Peruse consumer publications and trade journals. Listen to business programs on radio and television. Talk to experienced businesspeople both in and out of the crafts field. Attend classes, work-shops, and seminars. Immerse yourself in your subject. Stimulate your mind in every possible way.

Aim to tap all available sources as you search for information. Consider every possible notion or activity that can contribute to the success of your new enterprise.

For best results, avoid prejudging ideas. Do not consider any concept trivial or impractical. Set no limits on the number or nature of ideas. Listen to suggestions from others, but place a greater importance on delving into your own imagination. Consider *everything*. Later, you will have time to weed out the impractical.

Do not try to place the notes in order of priority, yet. Instead, use this time to rack your brain, looking for every possible idea that can lead your business toward success. End each day by randomly affixing the little notes to your board.

If someone else will work in your business with you, encourage him or her to carry a notepad, too. Do not discuss the project with one another during the two-week period. Give each person complete latitude to brainstorm options and possibilities, uninfluenced by the opinions of the other. As you draw deep within your creativity unhampered by judgments, more ideas and solutions will surface.

Now, the fun begins. When those two intense weeks end, look over all the notes. Eliminate duplicates and nothing else! Moving the notes around, place the most important tasks at the top of the board. Relegate the least important chores to the bottom.

The advantage of those gummed little notes should now become apparent. Do you see why I suggested you assign only one idea per page? You can arrange and rearrange the sticky notes as much as you like. Continue organizing until all notes appear in order of importance.

You may be surprised by the way seemingly unrelated ideas become a cohesive plan. Respect them all. Compliment yourself on the innovative thoughts and concepts you may never have considered before.

Next, consider time sequence. Rearrange the notes as needed, placing at the top tasks that must precede others. For example, did you know you cannot obtain a Seller's Permit to purchase raw materials at wholesale prices until you have filed a fictitious name form? Thus, on your finished list of priorities, you would need to choose a name for your business *before* applying for a Seller's Permit.

Stand back and look over your Action Board. Study it for a few days. Move the slips of paper around as you continue to think ideas through. When the final sequence makes sense, get ready for the next step. Before you is a rough draft of . . .

Your Monthly Action List

Convert your Action Board into a Monthly Action List this way: Go over the notes with a pencil. Assign completion dates, allowing adequate time for each chore. Continue until every task on your board has a firm, practical date.

Now, go back over each slip. Note who will actually accomplish the task. Place the word "self" on those for which you will be responsible.

You may need help from others. For example, beside the task, "Set up a bookkeeping system," perhaps you plan to consult a certified public accountant (CPA). On that slip jot down "CPA."

If others help you in your business, encourage them to choose chores from the list for which they will be responsible and to initial them. Keep an eye on the expertise of each person. Will your spouse do the banking? Will a grown child run errands? Or perhaps yours is a solitary undertaking and you plan to manage everything yourself.

Set a starting date to begin the entire process. When every task has someone's name and a starting date beside it, transfer the information from the notes. Type or write the list on 8½-by-11-inch sheets of paper.

At the bottom of the sheet, enter an ending date. This is the deadline when *all* tasks must be completed. Have other participants sign and date the document. Your new system for growth and improvement is now in place.

Place the Action List where you will see it. Refer to it often. Post copies on the refrigerator door, on your studio door, on cupboards and bulletin boards. Make sure others who help in your business study it, too. This way, the success of your business will be on everyone's mind. Whether you prefer to work alone or as a part of a team, stay fixed on the goal. Work toward it steadily.

As each person completes a task, allow the person who completed it to initial and date it. Do not do this for them, as this deprives them of the opportunity for self-recognition. Maintain a positive attitude. Compliment each other on accomplishments. What remains undone will be obvious to everyone who looks at the list.

My husband/business partner and I used the technique to decide whether to expand my craft business by adding a mail-order catalog. The enterprise was new for us. Separately, we jotted down ideas on our little pads. At this point, I must make a small confession. As the creative one in our relationship, I smugly expected to be the chief "idea person" when my husband and I worked together on our Action Board.

What a surprise I had in store! My husband's perspective on my business was entirely different from mine. His multicolored notes appeared on the bulletin board in greater number than mine! Since we had agreed not to curb each other's flow of ideas by reading or commenting about them, we pinned our notes face down on the cork board. We began a friendly competition to see who could post the most gummed notes.

My curiosity grew as he came home each night with a fresh batch of notes. What suggestions could he have that I hadn't thought of? Would his contributions be practical? Did he know enough to have this much input? (He did!) Difficult though it was, I decided to trust his good judgment. I resisted peeking at the notes, though the temptation was strong.

After two weeks, we were eager to see what we had accomplished. When we turned our sticky notes face up and eliminated duplicated ideas, there were still plenty of surprises. Each of us proposed suggestions for launching the new project that the other had never considered.

Based upon careful study of our mutual ideas, we decided to forge ahead with the catalog. My mail-order catalog continues to bring added income to my craft business.

We used our Action Board to answer the question, "What must we do to expand Sylvia's Craft Studio to include a mail-order catalog?" Here is a copy of our Action List, which resulted from our Action Board project and became the first draft of our Business Plan. Note the outline format we used to help rank tasks and priorities.

I.   Make a draft copy of proposed catalog. We will offer for sale:
   A. Hard- and soft-cover craft and entrepreneurial textbooks
   B. Reprinted copies of my articles
   C. Copies of workbooks distributed in my college classes
   D. My audio cassette tapes based on my college and seminar lectures
   E. A series of my original design project booklets
II. Compile our first house mailing list to include:
   A. Present and past students and clients
   B. All former customers of craft items
   C. Students who sign our mailing list
   D. Look into renting a list from a broker (see Chapter 10)
III. Implement an advertising plan
   A. Consider classified ads in local newspapers
   B. Contact magazines for which I write; offer to write free articles in exchange for display ads

    C. Send out press releases announcing the new catalog to craft colleagues and national magazines and newsletters

    D. Write to local newspapers announcing the expansion of my business from teaching and design studio to a home-based catalog business

IV. Seek advice from business consultant with mail-order expertise

V. Distribute *free* copies of the catalog in all classes, workshops, and seminars

VI. Other areas to explore:

    A. Write to local civic organizations; offer to present brief programs or trunk shows about my craft and distribute catalog

    B. Consider contacting local radio and TV talk shows

    C. Donate an hour's free consultation to PBS fundraising

    D. Create a new brochure listing availability of catalog

    E. Contact printing companies for bids to produce the catalog

    F. Look into getting a bulk-mail permit

    G. Write publishers to request review copies of books for possible inclusion in our catalog

We used our list to integrate catalog chores into our regular Monthly Action List. Remember to think of the list as a daily "itinerary" to keep you on track, leading to your ultimate destination—a successful career in crafts.

Your Action List provides a monthly "to do" schedule. Tasks and chores appearing on the list should lead to both short- and long-term goals. Refer to it often. See at a glance what you have accomplished and what remains.

Update your monthly list faithfully and you will never have the dilemma of remaining undecided about what to do next. Since your list ranks tasks by priority, you will always be able to decide immediately how to best spend your time and energy.

I store and update my Monthly Action List on my computer. Each month, I delete completed chores. I carry those left undone into the new month and print out a new copy. It sits on my desk in plain sight.

During the month, I date each task as I finish it to indicate "mission accomplished." Indeed, this type of self-awareness and recognition bolsters self-esteem. Think of each task you complete as a promise made and kept. Keeping promises you make to yourself results in self-assurance.

Procrastination means breaking promises made to oneself. If we indulge in it regularly, the resulting disappointment damages our self-esteem. Regular procrastination makes us feel as though we have failed. We lose self-confidence. We begin to question our ability to conduct a successful business. We weaken our sense of self-reliance. Inside, we feel "ripped off." We become our own worst enemies.

Like many of you, I already had many commitments in my business when the catalog idea came up. You can't stop everything else and give 100 percent of your time to a new project. To manage your business and watch it grow, you must assimilate new projects into your *existing* schedule.

Your Business Plan

Alice in Wonderland asks the Cheshire Cat, "Would you please tell me which way I ought to go from here?"

"That depends on where you want to go," replies the cat. "Otherwise it does not matter which way you go." Another definition I like is: "The difference between a dream and a goal is a plan!"

Sadly, this is the typical response I often receive from students and clients when asking about their business plan: "I am too busy to write out a business plan, and I don't need to! It's in my head," they explain. Here are some of my interpretations of the real meaning behind that statement:

- "I do not *want* to take time from money-making opportunities for this unimportant paperwork."
- "My business is small—only part-time. Business plans do not benefit me."
- "Business plans require writing. I don't like to write. I am in business to make money with my craft. After all, I am an artist."
- "*Organize* my business on paper? What does that accomplish? I have no need for a loan, so why waste time writing all that detail? Who will read it anyway?"

My reply? "The most important reader of your plan, the one who must scrutinize it regularly, is *you!*" There are three reasons for making a business plan:

1. The invaluable experience of imprinting a picture of your business in your mind. Researching, gathering and organizing information, putting it into logical sequence, typing it, and editing it will all affect your conscious and subconscious. You will have an easier time making decisions when guided by the goals and priorities in your plan.
2. If you need a loan to start your business, you *must* have a business plan to present to the loan officer. And the one "in your head" is not acceptable.
3. Employers, clients, agencies, and others who want to hire you may ask to see a Business Plan. Your CPA will use it to assess your business.

A Business Plan is a detailed guide to plot the course of your business and prepare for problems before they arise. A good plan states goals and direction. Use it to measure your business' actual performance when you compare what you planned with what actually happened. Business Plans should:

- Assess business ideas
- Develop your point of view and marketplace niche
- Help you set reachable goals in logical sequence

Let's go back to the analogy of the coast-to-coast auto trip. Let's say you plan to attend an important craft convention in New York and you live in California. Further, let's say you will serve on a panel to speak about your craft upon arriving.

Let's use the scenario of a person armed only with a mental Business Plan. You would begin your trip with no road maps or advance reservations, just a travel plan—in your head. No sense wasting time and paper planning.

No time for choosing routes or locating overnight lodging. Instinct will guide you. Merely point your car east. Not to worry, you'll "feel" your way as you go. Allow yourself several days to travel leisurely. If your first scheduled appointment looms forward too suddenly, you can drive faster. You want to be flexible, don't you? Just cut back a little on sleep and motivate yourself to cover more miles for the last day or two. Things will take care of themselves, won't they?

Attitude is the important thing, you tell yourself. Expect the best and "fly by the seat of your pants." There will be plenty of time to solve problems when they occur. Why worry in advance?

Now, how many people would undertake a cross-country trip this way? Not me! How about you? Let's make a plan. In fact, let's dust off what we learned in junior high school about making formal outlines to organize ideas. You thought you'd never need them in real life? Think again! The classic outline system is the perfect tool for creating a Business Plan for your new career. Let me show you.

OUTLINE FOR YOUR BUSINESS PLAN

I.   Table of Contents
        After completing your plan, arrange and number all pages. Include copies of articles, documents, and letters. Organize information according to the outline format below. Begin with a cover page. Identify each section by its heading and Roman numerals in the table of

contents.

II.   Executive Summary

In one or two pages, present a brief overview of the entire plan.

III.   Mission Statement

Explain why you chose your business and how you feel about it. Express enthusiasm about your craft.

IV.   Legal Structure

State whether you plan to run your business as a sole proprietorship, a partnership, or a corporation. If you chose a fictitious name for your business, note it. You must use *both* your first and last name in your business name or file a fictitious name form with the County Clerk's Office in the county in which you reside. See Chapter 13 for more on this.

V.   Owner Information

State who owns your business and list that person's address and telephone number.

VI.   Personal History

List your qualifications and experience here. Include a copy of your résumé in this section.

VII.   Type of Business

"Crafts" is too general a term to describe your business. Explain whether you are manufacturing, wholesaling, retailing, exhibiting, designing, or writing about crafts. Describe the nature of your business completely. Crafts may be your passion, but many readers of your plan need to know what craftspeople "do."

VIII.   Product Description

Describe your product. Include photographs, color ads, and fliers. Crafters who will perform services may conclude that this section does not apply to them. But it does. Your service *is* your product.

IX.   Company Background
        If you are starting a business from scratch,
        delete this section. However, if you are expand-
        ing or modifying an existing business, provide
        background information about the company,
        followed by the proposed changes.

X.   Business Objective
        Don't be tempted to write, "Make a profit,"
        as your objective. Every business wants a
        profit. Perhaps your goal is to create a new ad-
        hesive. Maybe you have a new system for writ-
        ing knitting instructions. State your purpose
        clearly.

XI.   Product Benefits
        Completing this section will be of tremendous
        importance when you begin to write advertis-
        ing copy for your new business. It is *critical*
        to state the benefits of your product or service
        from the point of view of consumers. Will learn-
        ing become easier for them? Will your new
        paint dry faster? Are your patterns easier to
        follow?
        People buy benefits, not products. Frozen
        dinners offer convenience as their prime bene-
        fit over price and culinary delight. Answer the
        question, "Why should someone buy my prod-
        uct or service?"

XII.   Industry Data
        Support the wisdom of starting your new busi-
        ness by offering an overview of the industry. I
        remember a client who asked me to prepare her
        business plan to sell beaded products. I asked
        who else was making this specific bead item. She
        replied that no one else had thought of her idea
        (not true!) and that *everyone* would want to buy
        her product (far from true!). The woman knew
        nothing about the industry she was entering.

She was beginning a new business venture with only one thought in mind—how much *she* loved the product. Lack of knowledge leads to lack of preparation, which in turn leads to failure.

XIII. Statistics

Show your preparation with industry awareness. How many people craft in the United States? How many magazines are published in your field? Perhaps you can find figures on how many crafters purchase their raw materials from mail-order catalogs. Do many crafters in your field teach classes? How big is the industry? You don't know? Study the trade journals in your field and find out!

XIV. Other Supporting Data and Attachments

This is the place in your Business Plan to insert photocopies of articles about your industry. Choose a variety from business magazines, trade journals, and consumer publications.

XV. Marketing Plan

A. Customer Profile: Describe your target customers. Learn all you can about them, including:

1. What are their income levels?
2. What are their social and educational levels?
3. What are their occupations?
4. How will they learn about your product/service?
5. Why should they buy your product?
6. How do you know they want or need your product/service?
7. Will they pay your price? How do you know?

B. Marketing Strategies: How does your product/service fit into the present market?

1. What system did you use to arrive at your price?
2. Is there risk in trying your product?
3. Will consumers require training to use the product?
4. Are there government regulations relevant to using the product?
5. What follow-up customer-service method will you use?
6. What sales strategy will reach your target market?
7. How will you get the product to the customer? Mail? UPS?

C. Marketing Research Techniques
    1. Interview your customers. Ask them about the strengths and weaknesses of competitors. Listen to reactions.
    2. Talk to other businesses with related interests.
    3. Try to visit with direct competitors. (This is more easily said than done.)
    4. Read and talk with others in the industry. Interview others who belong to pertinent trade associations.
    5. What makes your product different from others?
    6. What can you offer that is not available elsewhere?

D. What About Your Competition?
    1. Where are they located?
    2. What benefits will you offer that will be better than those of your competitors?
    3. What are their strengths and weaknesses?
    4. What are yours?
    5. What can you learn from their vendors and distributors?

XVI. Budget Proposal
A. Be specific. List everything you need to purchase.

   B. Monthly expenses. If yours is a start-up business, estimate a budget.

   C. List cash-flow statements from past years if you are expanding an existing business.

XVII. Proprietary Rights (see Chapter 15)

   A. Copyrights. Place a copy of your copyright form in this section.

   B. Trademarks and logos. Do you want exclusive rights to use your trademark and/or logo? Include a copy of the document here.

   C. Does any part of your creativity require a design or utilitarian patent? If so, include a copy of your patent here.

XVIII. Significant Contracts

If you require a licensing agreement with another company to reproduce a design element in your product, list that company here. Conversely, if you have granted license for another to reproduce a portion of your intellectual property, list the company now. (See Chapter 15 for more on this.) Other contracts such as leasing agreements, rental contracts, studio fees, etc., should be listed here.

XIX. Plan for Future Growth

Describe your plans for the future in general terms. If successful, are you thinking of expanding into selling by mail order, writing, or selling out of state? State your hopes for the future of your business.

XX. Attachments and Appendices

List and number documents you are inserting into your business plan such as:

A. Photocopies

B. Articles from newspapers and magazines

C. Brochures

D. Résumés

E. Professional references

F. Testimonials

G. Endorsement letters

H. Letters of recommendation
I. Photos of products
J. Published information
K. Market studies
L. Questions to help you gather information for your business plan:
1. How much time are you planning to spend? Full-time or part-time?
2. Are you working alone? Who will do what jobs if there are others?
3. How much planning and start-up time do you need to begin?
4. How will you remain financially solvent while meeting the start-up phase of your new or expanding business?
5. Under what circumstances will you alter your plan?
    a. If you don't earn more than $10,000?
    b. If you don't have a given number of customers by a specific date?
6. If you present your plan to a bank as part of a loan request, and that request is rejected, ask for specific reasons. Understanding them will help you improve your business plan. Was your plan
    a. Easy to understand?
    b. Incomplete? Too many critical items missing?
    c. Credible?
    d. Under- or overstated?
    e. Lacking financial analysis?

After you complete your Action Board, Action List, and Business Plan, you have served as your own business consultant. Get ready for the next title you will earn—that of Organizer.

Resources

Brooks, Julie K. 1987. *How to Write a Successful Plan.* New York: AMA COM.

King, Jan B. 1994. *Business Plans to Game Plans.* Berkeley: Nolo Press.

Rodenkirch, John J., CPA. 1985. *Prepare Your Own Financial Plan.* Virginia: Betterway Publications.

Bonnie Boots
330 28th St. North
St. Petersburg, FL 33713
Phone and fax: (813) 323-6810

FIRST THINGS FIRST

Bonnie Boots spent a year of intense business preparation before beginning her full-time doll business . . . the second time. "Good planning and organization are vital," stresses Bonnie, a writer and designer. Bonnie has published her work in several specialty doll magazines. She emphasizes that since doll making is a *business,* not a hobby, she avoids non-profit-generating activities.

Immediately after graduating from high school, Bonnie began her first craft business. She admits she soon became a "starving artist." Though editors, publishers, and manufacturers praised her design ability, her business failed. Finally, she gave up, not knowing why her plans had not worked.

Bonnie still wanted to run a business of her own. She started a service business unrelated to crafts. "I knew little about running a commercial business," she admits. "I threw myself into a frenzy of self-education. I attended SCORE (Service Corps of Retired Executives) and Small Business

Administration workshops. I read every business text I could find. I subscribed to trade journals and attended programs provided by manufacturers." Bonnie created a successful cleaning business that she sold at a profit after ten years.

Reentering the crafts world remained in her mind. Bonnie frankly admits, "I found the reason I hadn't succeeded as an artist earlier in my life was because I had not taken an interest in business matters. Business to me had meant boring, dull, analytical tasks unsuited to one with artistic gifts. In my ignorance, I decided business matters were for others, not an 'artiste' like myself."

When Bonnie began her service business, she prepared thoroughly. She studied cash-flow, profitability, marketing, and payroll procedures. In short, she learned how to manage her business, something she had neglected in her first craft enterprise.

Valuable insight was hers after selling her service business. She explains, "I approached my writing and design business exactly as I did in my service business. I met with equal success. A change in attitude made all the difference.

"Today, I work from a business plan," she states. "I believe in the axiom, 'Plan your work and work your plan.' Now, I know the exact status of my business." Bonnie insists upon doing all her bookkeeping herself so she knows what business activities generate the most income. Now, she belongs to trade organizations, using them to make connections and promote her business. She maintains a regular sales and marketing program.

Novice crafters seek her advice, feeling as she once did. One person questioned her advice about becoming attentive to business matters. This hopeful crafter said, "If I have to do all that, I may as well become a bookkeeper, not an artist." Bonnie responded, "Working as an artist or craftsperson is every bit as competitive as any business. Become familiar with business basics and use them to your advantage."

Bonnie gave good counsel. She wants others to become successful, independent craftspeople, not starving artists. "If you organize well and project a professional image, people will trust you with assignments," she advises.

Today, Bonnie derives most of her income from selling her designs to clients, magazines, and manufacturers. Like many professional crafters, she also sells her doll designs by mail order. She attributes her success to her business savvy.

Crafts Brief

Business founded: 1990

Legal form of business: Sole proprietorship

Home-office? Yes. Bonnie lists her computer and quality photography equipment as her most important tools.

Hours: Forty hours per week.

Daily routine: Bonnie spends at least an hour a day on the phone with clients, editors, and other artists. She sets aside time *every* day for correspondence and bookkeeping. The remaining five to six hours per day she spends in actual production—sewing, drawing, making samples, and filling orders.

Best part of craft career: "The opportunity to earn good money doing what I love; the constant variety and working alone."

Least favorite: Being responsible for *all* aspects of the business.

Strengths: Highly disciplined and high level of creativity.

Weaknesses: Tendency to take on too much at once.

Professional organizations: The Society of Craft Designers and Florida Craftsmen.

Professional journals: *Craftrends & Sew Business, The Crafts Report,* and *The Popcorn Report* are essential for following trends and industry news. "Stay current or else!" advises Bonnie.

Advice: "The most important step in starting a craft business is to have a Business Plan. Ask yourself the following: Do I need income immediately? How much can I spend? What type of business do I see myself having? Plan the route that takes you where you want to go! Be realistic about your needs and abilities. Preparation and personal examination before you start will save stress and headaches later."

CHAPTER 4

YOU AS ORGANIZER

$L_{ET'S}$ $_{GO}$ $_{BACK}$ to the scenario of that cross-country trip to give a craft demonstration described in the previous chapter. Your destination is the long-term goal. Prearranged stops for rest, food, and fuel are the short-term goals. Think of priorities as road markers guiding you toward your ultimate destination.

Goal Setting

Effective goals inspire you to reach ahead—to do your best. They must be realistic and achievable. Open-ended goals invite procrastination. Goals with measurable deadlines motivate action. Determine your long-term goals by answering these questions:

- What do you want from your craft business?
- Do you want part-time or full-time income?
- What aspect of crafting motivates you?

Designing? Teaching? Demonstrating? Retailing? Joining the craft fair circuit? Perhaps you want to write a book or teach your craft at national seminars. Maybe conducting regular craft classes in your home-studio appeals to you.

Begin to organize your business in a notebook. List every goal you hope to attain. Time for setting priorities will come later.

List specific goals rather than generalizations: "Sell at least two original designs to a craft magazine each month," for example, rather than "Sell designs to magazines."

"Earn enough to make monthly payment on computer and kiln," rather than "Make enough money to pay bills."

Once you define your long-term goals, rank them. What must be done first? What's next? Review this list monthly to maintain the life of your business.

Check to see if you reach your goals much of the time. If not, determine the reason. If the plan was too ambitious, modify it. If you were not motivated enough, why not? What got in your way? How can you improve next month? For more ideas on how to make things happen in your business, review "Your Action Board" in Chapter 3.

SHORT-TERM GOALS

Short-term goals guide our activities day by day, helping us focus on our long-term goals. Begin a second list in your notebook to see how you spend your time now. Over a week's time, list all the activities that fill your day. Include everything—chores, meetings, recreation, paperwork. After one week, categorize each activity under one of the four following headings:

Sheet A: Top priority. "Must do list." These items lead directly to your goals.

Sheet B: Important but not crucial. Must do, but time frame can be flexible.

Sheet C: Mundane things you wonder why you do at all. Some are habit, some decided by others. Their value to your goals is questionable.

Sheet D: Tasks or activities you strongly dislike.

Study your list. Do you find items on your A list important to you but rarely completed? Do you tackle chores from your C list before completing those on the A list? From the D list, do you sit through meetings for an organization that means nothing to you and does not relate to your goals, for example?

Plan a work schedule by rearranging the chores and activities on each sheet. Make sure everything on your A list leads directly to your goals. Include deadlines whenever possible.

Jump to the D list. What can you eliminate here? Did you list housework? Consider hiring a housekeeper. Can't afford one? What profit-making activity will earn enough to hire someone? Move that activity to the B list.

End memberships in groups you find boring and unrelated to your goals. Reduce or eliminate activities that you dislike, provoke stress, waste your time, or derail reaching your goals. Tasks on the first three sheets become short-term goals.

Ask yourself each evening, "How did I do today? Did I spend most of my time aiming where I want to go? Can I do it any better tomorrow? Did I become preoccupied with an activity that had nothing to do with my goals or the priorities to help me reach my objective?" Answering these questions will help you stay on the road, making decisions with deliberation and control.

A word of advice. Do you experience getting "waylaid" when you work at home? Perhaps you established a system to complete tasks leading to your goals. You leave your workplace for a cup of coffee and a distraction grabs you. You stop to water a plant, or play with the dog. Ask yourself if such an interruption is justified or if it constitutes self-sabotage.

Break the habit of getting sidetracked. As soon as you realize you've lost your place, tell yourself you no longer break promises to yourself. Immediately return to work. Talk to yourself. Praise yourself for getting back on track. Do this enough and your subconscious will get the message that positive feedback from the self can redirect old habits, creating more efficient ones.

Priorities: How to Budget Your Time

Before prioritizing tasks, why not prioritize your body's "prime time"? Most of us have a physical prime time—the time of day when we function at maximum energy and alertness.

Never tackle C list jobs during your body's prime time. Save them for when your energy is low. Assign prime goals to physical prime time. Do not attempt important chores when you are tired.

Learn to consider your body as you schedule work. Plan your day so you alternate sitting and standing jobs, active with sedentary tasks, physical with mental. Your energy will last a lot longer.

When you set a schedule for yourself, stick with it as if you were punching a time clock. You are—only now, it's your own. Consider using a double-faced desk calendar that provides two pages for each day separated by a center post. List professional, income-generating tasks on the left side, personal and home chores on the right.

One of the greatest advantages for home-based workers is flexibility. You can alternate business tasks with personal tasks as long as you keep moving toward your stated goals. In fact, such shifting can refresh you and lengthen your work day. Why not work at your business all morning, for example, followed by aerobic exercise then return to professional activities? Or, craft all morning followed by grocery shopping then return to business correspondence, for example?

Use the double-faced calendar to set a week's priorities at a time. List tasks that will achieve your goals in order of importance. If you set 8 to 9 A.M. to work out a design, use the entire time for that task until it is completed. Do not read newspapers or make phone calls. Work as if you were in a traditional office. Let anyone who interrupts you, even inadvertently, know you will be working until 9 A.M. Those around you will learn to take your work seriously when you demand respect for your time.

It is vital to your self-esteem to cross out each item on your list as you complete it. This gives you a sense of accomplishment—a pat on the back and needed recognition—to and from yourself.

Here is another problem home-based workers may encounter. When someone asks you to take on something new, ask yourself, "Will this new activity lead me to my stated goals?" If not, ask yourself, "Will I have time for it without sacrificing my goals and priorities?" Avoid taking on new responsibilities just because you cannot think of a way to refuse when asked. Limit activities that may derail your goals by being frank to those who ask for your time. "Thank you for thinking of me, but I have a previous commitment to my career at this time. Please ask me again." Who can argue with that?

Time Management Skills

Think of organization and time management skills as tools to help you balance your personal life and professional life. You feel less stress and more sense of accomplishment when you manage your time well.

All we can do to become better managers of our lives, our schedules, our possessions, and our goals is to rearrange the time we already have by gathering up what we have been wasting. No one can *make* new time, but we can find unproductive time and make better use of it. Time management experts agree that good management begins with the steps below.

1. Recognize how you currently spend your time.
2. Determine how you *want* to spend your time.
3. Measure how effectively you can use your time.
4. Control and plan your time.
5. Eliminate time wasters and distractions.

Committed, self-employed crafters must motivate themselves. Try out your new schedule based upon your goals, priorities, and physical energy for a month. If you find you cannot accomplish everything on your list, you may be expecting too much from yourself. Modify your list. Delete the least important task for each day.

"I cannot," you say. "I must do them all to succeed." If this is the case, your schedule is telling you something. Answer the questions below. Do you:

- Need help? Hire someone, trade, or barter.
- Need less rest or recreation and more self-discipline?
- Find you are wasting time?
- Work at low-energy periods?
- Ignore priority tasks during high-energy periods?
- Allow too many interruptions?

Effective schedules should represent realistic weekly goals. Modify them until the list is tailor-made for your energy level, lifestyle, and work requirements. Sticking to it helps avoid leaving something undone at the end of the week only to have to ignore something else as you try to squeeze in too much.

Last, post your finished work schedule. I suggest the refrigerator for housemates to see, and another copy in your work area. Educate those around you. This includes friends and family who drop in unannounced since "You are home anyway." We must speak up for ourselves if we want respect from others for our work.

Watch "time wasters." Frequent, nonproductive consumers of time are:

Talking on the phone   *Solutions:* Keep materials for mundane tasks near the phone. Give them your attention only when the phone rings. Complete mindless tasks as you talk. Save calls you have to make for one time of day. Long phone cords and a phone shoulder rest are invaluable. Hands are free for mundane tasks.

Watching TV empty-handed   *Solution:* Save mindless chores like sealing/stamping envelopes, collating, folding laundry, etc., for this time, too.

Waiting   *Solutions:* Write postcards or checks while waiting in lines. Go through your "must read" magazines. Tear out articles of interest and take them with you to read while waiting. Let professionals who serve you know your time is valuable. Tell receptionists you only have a limited time for a medical or dental appointment, for example. If you are still waiting at the end of that time—leave. Apologies are unnecessary.

Indecision   *Solutions:* Don't waste time wondering what to do with an unexpected free hour or two—it may disappear while you are deciding. Post a wish list. List activities you'd like to do "whenever you have time." These can be "work," such as weeding, filing, or organizing a cupboard, or recreational, such as reading or visiting the newest craft mall in your area. When unexpected free hours show up, be ready. Make use of every minute. Don't squander precious gifts of time wondering how to use them.

Sometimes a feeling of being overwhelmed can become a time waster. To help shake the feeling, break a large chore into sections. Organize one shelf of books at a time; don't expect yourself to deal with the entire bookcase. Maybe you put off doing a job because you need a bigger block of time without interruptions. Barter with your own calendar. Redistribute other chores from your weekly list to free up one day. Then, tackle the big job during prime-time hours.

Fear can factor into time management, too. Sometimes procrastination stems from feeling fearful. Analyze your fear. List and number every horrible outcome you can imagine if you undertake the proposed task. Give yourself a few days to dig out every possible idea that intimidates you.

Next, take a second sheet of paper and list contingency plans. Devise an alternate plan for every eventuality listed. Plan what you would do if the feared event happened. Fear diminishes when you have an actual plan to counteract each possibility.

Learn to delegate. You don't want to be bossy or sound harried or everyone will learn to hate your work, including you. Delegating means letting others know you need help now and then. Try bartering with a child: "If you clean the stove for me today, I'll cook your favorite meal when I finish this paperwork." Keep your promises, of course.

Ask your spouse in an assertive tone for help—don't try delegating tasks to him or her. Say, "I really need your help with this project. Would you prefer to file my handout sheets or start dinner so we can have more time together later?" Clear, assertive statements go a lot further than complaints.

Flexibility counts. Learn to listen to your body's signals for food, exercise, and rest. Schedule recreation times if you tend to be a workaholic. Take time to play, and rest when necessary. Plan time for emotional growth, always. Take a day off every now and then and go somewhere to relax, especially if you work from home. Redistribute the day's chores to the other days in the week.

Keep an eye on important relationships in your life. Too much stress in favor of work may not be a good plan for your overall life goals. Build in prime-time togetherness with those you love so your life and work will be worthwhile to you.

Guidelines for Workaholics

Workaholics, take note. You represent the other extreme of the personality type we've discussed so far. If your family comes to resent your work, set definite "open" and "closed" hours for your business. Here are some ideas:

- Buy a small plastic clock with moveable hands similar to those shop owners use. Start to work on time. Set the hands to your closing time. Let everyone in your family know exactly when you will be available. Stop at the promised time.
- If a real emergency exists, working from home enables you to respond. But too many "emergencies" signal an unfocused or unrealistic work schedule. Work on weekends or late into the night only when needed or risk burnout.

- Set up a particular room in which to work, if possible. Assume the attitude that you work there, and you are working for someone important. You are! Yourself!
- Wear a particular piece of clothing such as coveralls or jeans when you work. Or put on an apron or place a towel in your back pocket. This "uniform" announces to the world and to you that work has begun. Take it off when you leave the workplace. This becomes a sign that you are taking time to eat lunch or rest. But be clear and focused about it. How long is lunch? Set a time and stick to it.

Designate a few rooms in the house where work is neither done nor discussed. Start with your bedroom and the dining room table. Save these places for relaxation and family or personal activities. Perhaps you prefer to set a quitting time, too. We choose to work Saturdays in our studio-office, but quitting time comes much earlier than on weekdays.

Set a regular time for exercise and physical fitness. Do it days or evenings, but do it at least three times per week. Workaholics tend to neglect their bodies' needs in favor of working more.

Consider establishing a reward system for yourself. Remember, there is no employer to offer you incentives. If you finish earlier in the day than expected, don't go straight to the next day's duties. Take the extra time for something pleasing and relaxing. This helps you enjoy being at home when you have finished your work-for-pay.

Resources

Fanning, Tony and Robbie. 1979. *Get It All Done and Still Be Human.* New York: Ballentine Books.

Hemphill, Barbara. 1988. *Taming the Paper Tiger.* New York: Dodd, Mead & Co.

Webber, Ross A. 1980. *A Guide to Getting Things Done.* New York: Free Press.

Winston, Stephanie. 1983. *The Organized Executive*. New York: Warner Books.

Debi Linker
The Cotton Ball Shop and
Creative Beginnings
475 Morro Bay Blvd.
Morro Bay, CA 93442
Phone: (805) 772-9030   Fax: (805) 772-5845

BUSINESSWOMAN EXTRAORDINAIRE

"I entered the craft arena because I enjoy combining crafting and fabric," Debi Linker explains. "My store changed focus as I added craft items to my existing fabric line. Though we began as a designer fashion fabric store in 1969, we now are known as a quilting, home decorating, and crafts shop. Our store is a pace setter within the industry."

I asked Debi a tough question: "Which craft is your personal favorite?" She responded that changes and trends renew her enthusiasm, but she cannot leave sewing for long. Selling charms, the focus of Creative Beginnings, her wholesale business, inspires her to incorporate them into her designs. "I love them," confesses Debi.

Debi explains her perspective as a business owner: "Deciding which craft to work in results from my exposure to consumer magazines, trade journals, TV, trade shows, and product availability. I prefer to work with products that are relatively new and in which I see development possibilities to appeal to my customers. I like to present new products and product usage to consumers. Good response from them leads to additional product designs and usage."

Debi's designs have appeared in many leading consumer and trade craft magazines. She has designed for Butterick Pattern Co., authored several books published by Design Originals, and appeared many times on "Aleene's

Creative Living" and "Start to Finish," both daily TV shows for craft consumers.

Crafts Brief

Business founded: Debi opened her retail store, the Cotton Ball Shop, in 1969. The wholesale portion, Creative Beginnings, began in 1982.

Legal form of business: Corporation. Debi's two companies, both family operations, employ about 125 people. Her son, Erik, president of Creative Beginnings, runs the company. Jason, his brother, is vice president in charge of operations. Jim, Debi's husband, is vice president in charge of trade shows. Sylvia Cook, Debi's mother, still helps in the store.

Daily routine: Debi begins her day at 6 A.M., making business calls to the East Coast. Most days, she spends the day in the design studio directing work in progress by her staff of designers. Other days, she works in the Cotton Ball Shop or is on the road working with buyers and merchandisers.

Debi's days dealing with employees, store buyers, salesmen, designers, publishers, and editors last until 5 P.M.—a full eleven-hour day. Saturday, Debi devotes the entire day to working in her store.

Best part of craft career: Debi credits the success of her craft career with the opportunity to work with her husband and sons. She also enjoys encouraging others in their craft endeavors. She loves the constant challenge of creating new designs and seeing her designs published and put into kits.

Least favorite: Debi's juggling so many craft-related business chores leaves her very little personal time.

Strengths: "Business acumen," to quote Debi, is her clear-cut strength. Debi also lists her ability to anticipate craft trends as vital.

Weaknesses: It's not hard to see that Debi's tendency to overextend herself can be a problem. She says she prefers to complete a design and go on to the next ones without having to spend time doing repetitive tasks.

Professional organizations: Debi belongs to the prime craft organizations: HIA, ACCI, and AHSCA. She also belongs to SCD, as do most of the crafters listed in this book. Debi affirms that the latter gives her the opportunity to introduce designers to her company products.

Professional journals: Reading *Craftrends & Sew Business, Craft & Needlework Age, Toy News,* and *Art Materials and Gift News* helps keep Debi informed about new products, trends, and people in the industry.

Goals: For her store manager to become her business partner. She also plans to keep her company, Creative Beginnings, a leader in innovative products in both marketing and service.

Advice: Debi's suggestions are appropriate for all readers of this book.

"First, take business classes to learn concepts, controls, and practices before starting. Understand bookkeeping and accounting and study merchandising and marketing.

"Be versatile, flexible, and willing to change. Market trends move quickly. To succeed, you must be adaptable. When even the smallest opportunity knocks, take it! You never know where it may lead.

"Never stop reading, learning, networking, and asking questions about your market and those related to yours. Knowledge is essential to longevity. Join SCD for good contacts, for networking, and to meet other designers. Many opportunities await."

CHAPTER 5

YOU AS RESEARCHER

SEVERAL CRAFT PROFESSIONALS share details about their individual businesses in the Crafts Briefs at the end of each chapter. You will find successful editors, publishers, designers, importers, teachers, and craft producers describing their day-to-day activities.

Each person provided answers to questions I posed in a questionnaire. Though their answers vary for many questions, all respondents agreed on one issue. All stated they read several trade journals regularly to stay informed about the craft industry. They find this critical to their business success. I could not agree more.

Craft trade journals keep you informed about the industry. Announcements about new products appear in craft trade journals first. Here are just a few topics contained in a monthly issue of a leading trade magazine:

- How to use the Internet to advance your craft business.
- A report from The Color Marketing Group predicting next year's color trends.
- Latest styles in the floral industry.
- A listing of wholesale craft shows around the country.
- Professional tips on how to photograph craft items.
- Benefit from using a craft sales representative.
- Recent mergers of several large craft chain stores.
- How to get the most from the next national trade show you attend.

- A report on the national craft survey explaining "what's hot—what's not!"

Do not look for trade journals on newsstands. Since they are not intended for consumers, most are available by subscription only. Two top trade journals, *Craftrends & Sew Business* and *Craft & Needlework Age* offer *free* subscriptions to crafters who can prove their professional status. (See resources at the end of this chapter for address listings.)

The Crafts Report, a prestigious publication in fine crafts, offers professional artisans information unavailable anywhere else. In it you can find important information concerning you as a crafter in business for yourself. *The Crafts Report* includes listings of consignment shops seeking specific crafts as well as monthly calendars of upcoming trade shows, workshops, exhibits, and scholarships.

The magazine also features interviews with full-time crafters from every segment of the industry. Other helpful items include marketing, advertising, and selling tips, and explanations of legal and tax issues full-time craftspeople face.

Subscribe to several trade journals to remain up-to-date on the craft industry. I recommend that you also subscribe to at least four craft consumer magazines as well. Choose two that feature craft projects and instructions from all segments of the industry. Select two or more industry-specific titles that relate to your work.

Do you intend to write about your craft, including project instructions? Subscribe to one of the leading magazines for writers such as *Writer's Digest* magazine, *The Writer,* or *Writers' Journal.* To sell your original designs to magazines, you will need to polish your writing skills. More on this in Chapter 22.

Stay informed on what customers across the United States want to buy or make. Trends continually shift. To stay on top of developments in the industry, you need to know what's selling and why. Is Southwestern decor in or out? Why do Victorian craft styles sweep the country periodically? What colors are in demand? Which are passé?

Pay attention to letters from readers in consumer craft magazines. Readers write in to state their preferences, voice complaints, and make requests. These sections help you keep in touch with consumer demand.

Keeping up with the external marketplace will help you remain aware of trends in the entire craft industry, not just your specialty. Take care to avoid developing a myopic view, focused only on your preferences. If you don't want to find yourself working in a vacuum, out of touch with what's going on in the industry, you must set aside time to read and research regularly.

Organize and store your craft magazines. You will need continual inspiration and information. Why not set up your own research library at home? (See Chapters 2 and 4 for organizing tips.)

There is yet another type of magazine you need. Choose one or more magazines devoted to business in general—not just the craft business. Magazines such as *Home Office Computing* and others offer reinforcement of good business practices, ideas, and contacts.

Newsletters such as the "Self Employment Survival Letter" and "Home Office Opportunities" reach out to those working from home, helping them compete in the marketplace. Look to magazines and newsletters like these for valuable networking contacts, pertinent small-business issues, and practical suggestions.

So far, we have focused on periodic publications. Books about small business, general crafts, and industry-specific topics should appear on your bookshelf. They, too, will demand some of your research time.

Libraries offer maximum information, but personally, I prefer to own my books. I read and reread them. I fill their pages with highlighter pen marks to help me find strategic information at a moment's notice. I annotate the flyleaf with page numbers and one or two words that will guide me to important information contained within.

On the next page you will find a list of topics you should have represented in your personal business library.

- Marketing
- Advertising
- Record and bookkeeping
- Writing
- Selling (retail and wholesale)
- Time management
- Mail-order selling
- The craft business in general
- Books about your particular craft field

Read every book you can find about the business of crafts. You will find many titles in the Resources section at the end of this chapter. Organizations such as the Hobby Industry Association, the Society of Craft Designers, or the Association of Crafts and Creative Industries are devoted to supporting crafters. These groups provide critical information with their frequent updates. They publish regular newsletters containing business tips, contacts, and information about the industry. You will find more information about networking through national organizations in Chapter 16.

Last, consider a few self-improvement books. Read any title by Paul and Sarah Edwards, particularly *Making It on Your Own*. This book helps develop a mind-set that will lead toward entrepreneurial success.

Books by Dr. Wayne Dyer and Nathaniel Branden have a lot to offer. These experts address issues of self-esteem, taking control of your life, assertiveness, and self-direction. I also found the book *Talking to Yourself* by Pamela Butler helpful. Her self-talk suggestions keep me focused, positive—heading toward personal and business success. Ms. Butler says a lot to those of us who start unsure of ourselves or carrying self-defeating attitudes from the past into our business' future.

Digest two business books by Barbara Brabec. *Homemade Money* provides a wealth of information as you research business matters. Her recent book, *Handmade for Profit—Where and How to Sell What You Make,* focuses on the craft business.

"But, I don't have time to read," you say? Make time. Do not confuse reading and research time aimed at craft success with reading for entertainment. Recognize it as a business activity. Even a half-hour per day will make a difference. Remaining informed and educated about your craft career leads to success and profit.

Resources

BOOKS

Brabec, Barbara. 1996. *Handmade for Profit—Where and How to Sell What You Make.* New York: Evans.

Todd, Alden. 1972. *Finding Facts Fast.* Berkeley: Ten Speed Press.

MAGAZINES

American Craft
40 West 53rd St.
New York, NY 10019

Byline
Box 130596
Edmund, OK 73013

Craft & Needlework Age
Box 420
225 Gordons Corner Plaza
Manalapan, NJ 07726

Craft Supply Directory (aimed at professional crafters looking to contact suppliers)
Box 420
225 Gordons Corner Plaza
Manalapan, NJ 07726

Craftrends & Sew Business
6201 Howard St.
Niles, IL 60714

The Crafts Report
Box 1992
Wilmington, DE 19899

Home Office Computing
730 Broadway
New York, NY 10003

The Writer
120 Boylston St.
Boston, MA 02116-4615

Writer's Digest
1507 Dana Ave.
Cincinnati, OH 45207

Writers' Journal
Box 25376
St. Paul, MN 55125

NEWSLETTERS

"Craft Marketing News"
Front Room Publishers
Box 1541
Clifton, NJ 07015

"Home Office Opportunities"
Box 780
Lyman, WY 82937

ORGANIZATIONS

American Craft Association
21 South Eltings Corner Road
Highland, NY 12528

Association of Crafts & Creative Industries
1100-H Brandywine Blvd.
Box 2188
Zanesville, OH 43702

Hobby Industry Association
319 East 54th St.
Box 348
Elmwood, NJ 07407

The Society of Craft Designers
6175 Barfield Road, Suite 220
Atlanta, GA 30328

Pat Maloney
Director, research and development, New Berlin Company
S 85 W 18716 Jean Drive
Muskego, WI 53150
Work phone: (414) 679-0700
Home: (414) 679-2379   Fax: (414) 679-3281

CRAFTS RESEARCH AND DEVELOPMENT

Pat Maloney joined the New Berlin Company in 1987. Within six months, she discovered her niche—research and development. The New Berlin Company manufactures needlework kits, primarily for counted cross-stitch and beadwork. She moved up to her current position of director in 1989.

Pat feels the advantages outweigh disadvantages in working for a small company. She likes the way everyone participates in every facet of the business. At times, this opportunity is lacking in larger companies. Working with a team brings satisfaction to Pat. She explains, "We must work together to design, produce, and market a fresh, new product."

Crafts Brief

Business founded: 1983 by Bill and Tracey Holmes

Legal form of business: Corporation. The company employs twenty to sixty workers, depending on the time of year.

Hours: Pat works long hours—forty-five to seventy per week, depending on the season of the year.

Daily routine: Mornings find Pat working closely with owners Bill Holmes, company president, and Tracey Holmes, national sales manager. Using this time because there are fewer interruptions, the team develops new designs and works with individual accounts.

Best part of craft career: Pat's enthusiasm rises in reply to this question. "I have the best job in the world. I draw, paint, and dream up new ideas . . . getting paid to 'play'!"

Least favorite: Dealing with disorganized people and those who procrastinate.

Strengths: Artistic ability and organizational skills.

Weaknesses: Not delegating some work to others and not taking adequate personal and rest time.

Professional organizations: "Our company is a corporate member of the Society of Craft Designers. In this position, I receive input as to what's happening in the industry. The job provides me the opportunity to see firsthand the new, fresh ideas submitted to us by designers."

Professional journals: *Craft & Needlework Age* and *Craftrends & Sew Business* provide perspectives on the direction of the craft industry as well as ideas.

Goals: Pat expresses such satisfaction with her work that her long-range goal is to remain at the New Berlin Company until she retires.

Advice: "Have faith in yourself and your ideas. If an idea doesn't work, don't assume your design is not valuable. Consider every idea and explore it, otherwise you'll never know what you can do."

CHAPTER 6

YOU AS PURCHASING AGENT

TAKE CHARGE OF supplies for your office. By "taking charge" I mean start your business by choosing what you want to use rather than making do with leftover products.

Purchasing agents for large companies stay informed about the best products, sold by the best companies at the best prices. Good purchasing agents make sure they never run out of needed items or pay more than necessary for them. They also maintain systems to keep track of purchases. You are the purchasing agent for your business. Here is a partial list of what you need in your office:

- Promotional Supplies:
  business cards, letterhead stationery, brochures
- Desk Supplies:
  invoice and receipt forms
  pens, pencils, highlighter pens, marking pens
  stationery, envelopes
- Mailing/Shipping Supplies:
  shipping boxes, manila envelopes, cellophane tape, transparent tape
  sheets of postage stamps in every denomination up to $1
  postage scale to prevent over-paying postage
- Office Supplies:
  file cabinets and file folders
  storage boxes
  bookcases or shelves

- Equipment Supplies for:
  typewriter, computer, copier, fax machine

Today, you can make your purchases in three different ways:

1. You may buy locally, in person.
   Plus side: You can network and establish local business relationships in your community.
   Minus side: You will pay the highest prices.
2. You may prefer deeply discounted items from large business supply chain stores.
   Plus side: Here you will find the lowest prices.
   Minus side: You may not always find preferred brands and styles.
3. Consider buying and replenishing office supplies by mail order. (Names and addresses of such companies are listed in the resources section at the end of this chapter.)
   Plus side: A great time saver and largest product selections.
   Minus side: You must anticipate your need and allow for shipping time.

The Well-Stocked Craft Studio

Creative people become frustrated when they rush into their studio bursting with a new idea only to find they do not have basic supplies to begin. Avoid this situation by keeping your craft area stocked with materials you rely on most.

Painters, why keep only a few paint brushes on hand when you can stock one in each size and shape you need? You can accumulate every conceivable color you may need, but why not keep five colors always on hand? White, black, and the three primary colors enable you to mix any color you need at a moment's notice.

My craft business consumes yarns and threads at an alarming rate. I used to feel frustrated when an idea came to me and I did not have a desired color. I learned to dye my own fibers. Today, I keep white yarn and threads on hand plus basic dye stuffs. At a moment's notice, I can dye yarn or thread in that elusive color immediately. This saves me from jumping into my car and driving all over town to look for what I need.

Craft tools are our stock and trade. We need the proper tool for the proper job. Keep your supplies in view, together and organized in clear, plastic boxes.

Looking for what you need wastes valuable time better spent crafting. Fabric addicts and quilters understand this dilemma. They regularly pick up several yards of fabric in assorted colors and prints just to have them on hand when creativity strikes.

How to Find Manufacturers That Sell at Discount or Wholesale

Contact craft supply manufacturers before you become desperate for supplies. When you become a regular subscriber to trade journals such as *Craftrends & Sew Business* and *Craft & Needlework Age,* you will receive annual product directories. Use this valuable resource to order craft products for your own use and for reselling to your clients, students, and customers.

The *Thomas Register of American Manufacturers* is the principal resource for locating wholesalers in all industries. You will find these encyclopedia-like books in the library. You may also order a CD-ROM version of this comprehensive resource for your computer. Look under a specific item, say, "acrylic paints," and you will find *every* manufacturer that produces them plus company name, address, and phone number. If you know the name of the company you want to deal with, find it under "American companies" to see if it stocks, distributes, or manufactures the brand you need.

How to Buy Wholesale

You must have a Seller's Permit, also known as a "resale license," "wholesale license," and "buyer's permit." State

Boards of Equalization in each county across the United States issue Seller's Permits to enable businesses to buy at wholesale prices what they will resell for a profit.

There is no fee to acquire a Seller's Permit. However, at times, the State Board of Equalization *may* ask a new business with no previous record of collecting and paying sales taxes to post a bond. This amount can vary from $50 to several hundred dollars. The Board of Equalization will hold the fee for one to several years as security against prompt payment of collected sales taxes. The board returns the money when the business establishes a good sales tax paying record.

Technically, a Seller's Permit authorizes you to buy only what you will sell to the ultimate consumer—the person who takes the item home. You may not purchase office supplies, machines, and other equipment used to produce your items. These items are for business use and not for resale. This is usually the first misconception a new entrepreneur has about wholesale buying. Seller's Permits provide three advantages:

1. The permit allows you to buy at wholesale prices without paying state sales taxes. Only the end consumer pays sales tax. If you buy art supplies from a wholesaler for resale to students, for example, you are a distributor, not a consumer. Customers buying from you are the consumers and only they pay the sales tax.
2. Generally, the difference between retail and wholesale prices in the craft industry ranges from 40 percent to 50 percent. Thus, a Seller's Permit enables you to buy goods for approximately half price. The difference between your buying cost and the selling price to the customer becomes your profit.
3. Having a Seller's Permit enables you to attend professional trade shows to see the latest materials in your field and to place orders. Such shows are excellent gathering places for wholesalers to display and explain their merchandise to potential retailers. Consumers are not allowed to attend. Your permit identifies you as a business inter-

ested in buying. Most trade shows require a copy of your permit to qualify you for the benefits of attending.

Remember, you can only buy at wholesale what you intend to resell. If you teach dressmaking, for example, you cannot buy your sewing machine at the wholesale price because you don't intend to resell it. But you may buy fabric, threads, and patterns that you will make up into kits to sell to consumers. (More about how to record and pay sales taxes in Chapter 14.)

After granting a permit, the State Board of Equalization requires a business buying wholesale and selling at retail to collect state sales taxes on every dollar earned from direct sales of products. The amount varies from state to state. Each county branch office provides free information about the amount to collect. Since you will add sales taxes to the retail price customers pay for a product, keep sufficient funds on hand to pay these taxes on a quarterly or yearly basis.

New businesspeople assume that having the permit assures that all wholesalers, also called distributors, will want to sell to them. At times, a wholesaler you want to buy from will refuse to deal with you. Don't take this as a personal affront, for it is rarely personal. Some wholesalers may have a contract with a shop in your area that guarantees that no other business within a certain radius will be able to sell the same merchandise.

Another reason wholesalers may not want to do business with you is that your orders may be too small for them. At times, they discourage owners of small businesses from buying by instituting high minimum orders. So, a wholesaler's minimum order may be too high for a home craft business. If this happens to you, consider teaming up with another home-based crafter nearby so, together, you can afford to meet minimum-order requirements.

Wholesalers may also refuse you if you approach them in a nonprofessional manner. If you write on personal stationery rather than business letterhead and use cute or folksy language in a formal letter, this may create an impression you are merely a hobbyist seeking wholesale buying power for personal use—the wholesaler will surely refuse you. Prepare for refusals by contacting more distributors than you need at your disposal. Then you can still choose from those who respond.

When you write to a wholesaler, make your letter very brief. In three paragraphs, do the following:

1. Inform the company you are familiar with its product line. Give a few specifics about products of theirs that you have used in the past.
2. Tell the company how you plan to use the product in your retail business activity now (quilt batting to stuff your teddy bears or lacquer to create decoupage boxes).
3. Ask the company about its "terms of sale." This means you are requesting literature containing minimum-order amounts, shipping locations, time requirements, credit information, etc. Study terms of sale information carefully. Select companies based on what is most suitable and profitable for your business.

Once you establish a buying record and good credit with a few wholesalers, you will find it easier to find more. To increase the number of companies you deal with, to give yourself a wider range of goods from which to choose, contact manufacturers you would like to add to your list. Express your interest in dealing with them. Include the names and addresses of companies with whom you have established good relations when requesting this company's catalog or other information. This way, your older contacts generate new ones. Honor your commitments to wholesalers and treat them fairly and you will find that they, too, are eager for your business to grow.

There may come a time when you can receive many craft products at no cost at all. Writing instructions for craft magazines may entitle you to complimentary supplies as well as endorsement fees. This means some manufacturers may not only send free supplies but pay you an additional fee if your materials list mentions their product by name.

This payment is in addition to the fee paid to you by the editor of a magazine for your design. For more information about this, see Chapter 22.

Resources

NEBS: The Small Business Resource
500 Main St.
Groton, MA 01471
(800) 225-6380

Personal Office Catalog
1 Crutchfield Park
Charlottesville, VA 22906
(800) 521-4050

Quill Office Supplies
100 South Schelter Road
Lincolnshire, IL 60197

Mickey Baskett
Prolific Impressions, Inc.
160 South Candler St.
Decatur, GA 30030-3740
Phone and fax: (404) 377-2512

INSTRUCTION BOOK EDITOR

Mickey Baskett began her craft career immediately after college. "I have worked for the same company for twenty-five years," she says. David Cunningham of Cunningham Art Products hired her in 1969 to write ads and product label copy.

Six years later, Cunningham formed Plaid Enterprises, a company to publish craft instruction booklets.

Established as a successful editor for Cunningham's first company, Mickey took on a new challenge with Plaid.

She was instrumental in launching *Craftrends* magazine, one of the most prestigious craft trade journals in the industry. Though Plaid no longer owns the publication, its continued success today is a tribute to Mickey's hard work getting it started.

Mickey has seen many craft trends come and go over the years. "Crafts that were popular twenty years ago are making a comeback," she observes. "Techniques don't change much, but products are updated." Spotting hot trends and translating them into instruction booklets is one of the skills that marks her success.

Prolific Impressions, Inc., is Mickey's production company that produces Plaid's line of craft instruction books. She works closely with each designer, planning craft projects that will eventually become a Plaid instruction book.

Mickey edits each book manuscript. After a copywriter reviews it, Mickey is responsible for the final copy edit. Planning the photography and formatting for each booklet are tasks Mickey and her staff take seriously.

Crafts Brief

Business founded: 1983

Legal form of business: Corporation

Home-office? Yes

Hours: Mickey puts in sixty hours per week and has the help of three copywriters, two artists, a photo stylist, and an office manager.

Best part of craft career: The opportunity to express creativity.

Least favorite: Like many crafters—paperwork!

Strengths: Good organizational skills and an innate sense of design. Anticipating craft trends that will become popular is a skill Mickey appreciates having.

Weaknesses: Mickey admits she needs to be more detail-minded.

Daily routine: Correspondence begins Mickey's workday. Mickey coordinates publication schedules and editorial calendars for the company. Dealing with designers' contracts, creating layouts for how material in each book will appear, is of prime importance to Mickey's company.

Professional organizations: As with many people interviewed for this book, the Society of Craft Designers heads Mickey's list of networking groups. She also belongs to the Hobby Industry Association and the Association of Crafts and Creative Industries.

Professional journals: *Craftrends & Sew Business* and *Decorative Woodcraft.*

Goals: Mickey is clear about her long-range goals: She wants to be the leading publisher of craft books in the market.

Advice: "Jump at every opportunity to hone your skills. Strive for perfection. Enjoy your work and stick to your principles, and success will surely follow."

CHAPTER 7

YOU AS SECRETARY

CORRESPONDENCE IS ESSENTIAL for home-based crafters to communicate with the world. Answering letters promptly projects a professional image that declares we take our work seriously. Often, the timeliness with which we respond makes the difference between being hired or passed over when submitting proposals, articles, designs, and business contracts. Procrastination can be detrimental to business.

Winning the Paper War

Control your correspondence by handling incoming mail efficiently, only *once*. Begin with a system for sorting mail *before* it arrives. Choose only one place to screen your mail. Sit at your desk with the wastebasket nearby. As you come across pieces you are sure are of no interest to you, drop them in—unopened.

Next, eliminate the pieces addressed to others in your household. Place these in a prearranged place for your housemates. Open what remains. I keep six folders at my desk. I labeled the first "Personal Correspondence." Letters from family and catalogs from which I may order gifts are examples of what goes in this file immediately after opening. No time to lose anything this way. This file gets my attention later.

I labeled the second folder "Craft Business." It contains business correspondence only. "Design and Writing Ideas" appears on a third folder. This folder gets not only my scribbled notes, but also tear sheets from magazines I don't intend to keep, drawings, photos, and ideas for future projects.

The fourth folder is labeled "Mail Order." This file contains orders to fill along with requests for brochures and information. This type of mail is critical. Store it carefully until you enter the order information into your computer. In our office, we consider this priority paperwork to be recorded and filled within two days. Filling orders promptly demonstrates your professionalism and builds your reputation as a competent businessperson. Don't delay here!

The fifth and sixth folders are actually small boxes inside the top drawer of my desk. One is labeled "Household Bills," the second "Business Bills." Both checkbooks and a smaller box containing canceled checks and bank statements for each account also live in here. All bills we must pay go into one of the two bill boxes. It is more efficient to write checks once or twice per month rather than whenever you think about it or someone reminds you you are overdue . . . again! Assign yourself a regular day or days of the week/month on which to manage finances.

A necessity for storing opened mail is a file cabinet. If you do not have an metal office file, buy an inexpensive cardboard file box. Keep it under your desk if space is at a premium. Purchase manila folders for the box.

Each time you come to something you want to keep as you open mail, open the box and add it to an existing file. Start new files as needed, carefully labeling them. Organize the file folders alphabetically at first. After filing your paper this way for a while, you can decide to keep this first system or start another. Give yourself a few months using the alphabetical system to see if it meets your needs over time.

If you follow the steps above, you will find that when you finish opening your mail, you have dispensed it all immediately—no piles remain. The last step in handling correspondence is to set aside a regular time each week to respond to it. View this task as a routine, essential part of your business—not an intrusion—and your attitude toward it will become positive. After all, no correspondence signals no business.

Here's another idea to speed up an essential part of your business. When the designated time for bill paying and answering correspondence arrives, spread out receipts and letters on your desk. Stack them according to priority. Work through the stack steadily. As you seal and stamp an envelope containing payment for an expense, enter it in your computer spreadsheet program or business ledger.

Immediately, pick up the next piece of paper from the stack so you don't break the momentum. Discipline yourself to use this time to work your way through the stack efficiently.

Paperwork never ends, so don't feel guilty if you cannot finish all of yours in one sitting. When correspondence time is up, stop! Don't push yourself unless you feel the momentum you have going will spur you on in a positive way. Rather than resent record or bookkeeping, believing it takes time away from your "real work," think of paperwork as a sign that your business is alive and healthy.

If you have a paper backlog and want to gain control, set a timer. Don't stress yourself trying to catch up all at once. Work diligently. Stop when the time is up. After working on it for the given time, rearrange it into priority order until your next "correspondence period" arrives. Eventually, you will catch up using this system of moderation. Your ultimate goal is to remain current.

The Phone: Your Link to the Outside World

Two elements link you and your business to the world—your mail delivery and your phone. Home-based workers may not use a personal phone line or extension as a business deduction. If you have but one phone in your home, the IRS permits you to deduct *only* long-distance calls if you itemize them.

To deduct the costs of monthly telephone bills and answering machines, you must have a business phone. This means you need a *second* phone number, not a mere extension of your personal number. Telephone companies object to your using personal phone lines to conduct business. They will probably contact you to make it clear that you must install a second line.

Modify your love-hate relationship with telephones with three pieces of equipment. Phones should not control their owners; owners should control their phones. After all, you pay the bill. Here are a few tips:

- Invest in an extra long cord for your phone. It permits you to walk around more freely in your office while on the phone. You may reach bookshelves, files, and documents as you speak without putting your callers on hold.
- Keep your hands free while you talk. Consider either a speaker phone or a shoulder rest. Physical therapists warn against habitually cradling the receiver between neck and chin. Such a position produces neck and back pain and can bring on TMJ, or temporomandibular joint syndrome, a painful stiffness of the hinge joint in the lower jaw and temporal bone. The best shoulder rests are the old-fashioned U-shaped ones. They straddle your shoulder without causing neck pain.
- Do you consider answering machines friend or foe? Home-based workers divide themselves into two camps regarding answering machines. Some prefer never to answer the phone when it rings. They simply leave the speaker volume turned up so they can monitor recorded messages as they come in. If they decide the call is important, they pick up the receiver and begin to speak. If they don't want interruptions, they allow the machine to record the message so they can return calls later.

Business books and articles, however, tell us the promptness with which we answer our business phone reveals a lot about our efficiency. They advocate using answering machines to record messages only when you are truly unavailable. They encourage entrepreneurs to keep in mind that phone calls link us to the outside world. Think of them as opportunity—not annoyance.

Personally, I want my business contacts to perceive me as a busy, responsive home-based worker. I always answer my phone promptly when it rings. I believe it hurts business if callers feel routinely monitored by a machine. You decide.

Frustrated by too many calls interrupting your work? Chapter 4 offers tips on organizing your time and minimizing interruptions. Allowing children to answer your business phone is always a mistake. I don't mean competent teenagers who understand the importance of your work. I refer to small children who yell, "Mommy, it's for you," into a caller's ear. Not much professionalism here. In this case, an answering machine is preferable to a toddling receptionist!

Here is another problem: We may feel beholden to "stay on the line," allowing the caller to determine the length of the conversation. We want others to judge us as cooperative, communicative, and friendly. We fear being perceived as rude if we excuse ourselves before the talker is finished.

Use these precious minutes for mundane tasks left by the phone waiting for your inattention. Fold laundry, sort mail, hem, rip, or clean. Got the idea? When the call ends, the task ends. Allow it to wait for the next call. It's surprising how many mindless chores you can complete during one day's calls without ever giving them your complete attention.

Resources

Lakein, Alan. 1973. *How to Get Control of Your Time and Your Life.* New York:Signet Books.

Mackensie, R. Alec. *The Time Trap.* New York: McGraw-Hill.

Joan Green
Designs by Joan Green
6345 Fairfield Road
Oxford, OH 45056
Phone: (513) 523-2690   Fax: (513) 523-1520

RETAILER TO FULL-TIME DESIGNER

Joan began her crafts career in 1979 as part owner of a
needlework shop in Nebraska. She painted needlepoint
canvases and made charts for counted cross-stitch when customers requested designs not readily available.

Led by customer demand, Joan and her partner decided to manufacture and market complete kits. Established mail-order companies included several of Joan and
her partner's kit designs within their pages. This gave her
enough confidence for the next step—renting booth space
at trade shows.

Joan believes successful crafters must show a sensitivity
to the market. Today, she makes time to spot design and
color trends by "devouring magazines and gift catalogs," as
she puts it.

This busy home-based designer is a frequent contribu-
tor to fifteen national consumer magazines. She has written
more than eighty pattern booklets for counted cross-stitch
and plastic canvas needlepoint, working for ten different publishers. Her monthly column in *Crafts* magazine
boasts a loyal reader following. Joan also sells her kits by
mail order.

Joan shows her marketing awareness when she says, "I
prefer to do seasonal/holiday designs because it's what
most editors want." Like many crafters, Joan remains flexible as craft trends shift. She began when country designs
drove the market. During the quilt revival in the late '70s,
she designed needlepoint and cross-stitch patterns that
employed quilt motifs. Later, ever sensitive to the market,
she developed her own line of "elegant" designs by upgrad-
ing her craft to use finer materials and upscale colors.

Crafts Brief

Legal form of business: Sole proprietorship

Home-office? Yes. Joan writes and designs in a fully equipped office with a fax, copier, and computer.

Hours: Joan devotes fifty to seventy hours per week growing her business. Her husband accompanies her to some trade shows and does all her photography. Her grown son and daughter helped with kit manufacture while they were still at home.

Best part of craft career: Creative opportunity, artistic expression, flexible schedule.

Least favorite: Negotiating fees and not being paid promptly at times.

Daily routine: Walks in mornings, followed by design time and business matters. After lunch, the ever important correspondence followed by trips to the post office. Her time for "serious crafting"? Evenings and late night.

Strengths: Ability to budget time well enables her to meet deadlines. Joan feels she must keep up with market research to determine consumer needs.

Goals: Joan hopes to write a full-length book and to design in other areas such as greeting cards.

Advice: Always stay in touch with the consumer market!

CHAPTER 8

YOU AS FORECASTER

EXISTING MARKETS FOR any product rise and fall in open markets. Fashion preferences come and go. Economic and societal conditions affect national and international markets, influencing trend-following consumers everywhere.

Craft professionals who prepare for the buying public's changing tastes find it easier to remain financially solvent. Though most crafters achieve proficiency in a specific area, wise artisans also recognize that styles, trends, colors, and fads are transitory. Shifts in women's fashions create a continuing demand for updated wardrobes. So it is with craft trends.

What's Hot and What's Not?

During a recent national craft conference, a group of craft magazine editors presented a joint lecture titled "What's Hot and What's Not?" They defined the following terms:

Fad: A general preference enjoying intense popularity lasting less than two years.
Trend: Of popular interest lasting at least five years.
Tradition: A preference maintained for at least twenty years.
Heritage: An enduring preference lasting longer than twenty-five years.

Pet rocks and hula hoops were fads. The sunflower craze in the mid-'90s became a trend. Quilting and knitting remain long-lasting traditions. Fine woodcarving falls into the heritage group. Many craft styles begin as fads, become trends, and fade, reappearing every so often. Our present interest in Victoriana is an example.

To maintain steady incomes, artisans must not only recognize these various levels, they must *expect* them. Only then can craft professionals offer consumers what they want *when* they want it. The principal questions are these: How do you remain informed? Where do you look for the latest news on fads, trends, and traditions? How can you learn "what's hot and what's not"?

Remember the emphasis in Chapter 5 on reading trade journals? To keep up with the external marketplace, you must not only read, but study, research, and organize information. Once you have committed to making time for this critical activity, the resource guide that follows will help you get started:

1. Craft trade journals such as:
   American Craft
   Artist
   Crafts Report
   Craft Supply Directory
   Craftrends & Sew Business
   Craft & Needlework Age
2. Newsletters and seminars provided by professional craft networks:
   Society of Craft Designers (SCD)
   Hobby Industry Association (HIA)
   Association of Craft and Creative Industries (ACCI)
   Industry-specific national conferences, seminars, and workshops
3. Industry-specific organizations. Here is a partial list:
   American Home Sewing and Craft Association
   Craft Yarn Council of America
   Doll Artisan Guild
   Glass Art Society
   International Ceramic Association

Miniatures Independent Association of America
National Quilting Association
National Society of Tole and Decorative Painters
Professional Association of Custom Clothiers
Society of Glass Beadmakers

4. Library resources:

National Trade and Professional Associations of the U.S. An excellent resource to find trade and professional associations related to your field.

Business Organizations, Agencies and Publications Directory. Gale Research Co. In libraries, or you may purchase copies from Gale.

Directory of Information. A reference periodical covering all types of directories, lists, and guides.

Encyclopedia of Associations. Gale Research Co. Lists more than sixteen hundred American associations that publish newsletters or trade journals pertinent to a specific interest.

Guide to American Directories.

Standard Rate and Data Service. A quarterly publication listing TV stations, radio stations, newspapers, magazines, and trade and business publications alphabetically by category. Includes name and owner of publication, address, publishing schedule, and advertising rates.

Cumulative Book Index. A listing of books in a given subject.

Reader's Guide to Periodic Literature. Articles published in magazines listed by subject matter.

Concern yourself with national trends as well as those in your particular craft field. Keeping up with the broader market is critical if you want to create relevant designs acceptable to consumers. For example, let's assume you are a freelance knitting designer. It is not enough to understand trends in yarns and fibers. Successful knitting designers study:

- Fashion trends such as current styles, fit, and color
- Accessories to accompany popular fashion styles
- International fashion trends. Do they affect U.S. markets?

- Home decorating trends and styles
- Economic conditions in the United States

When considering the last item, ask yourself some pertinent questions. Is our country in a conservative, serious mood or enjoying moderate affluence and security? Do you remember how gas shortages affected the styling and size of automobiles during the 1980s? Fur coats were the rage in the 1940s, but were no longer considered environmentally correct by 1980.

Attend trade shows and conventions. Read books and newsletters unrelated to your craft field. Subscribe to at least two magazines focusing on American business and the economy. Magazines such as *American Demographics* provide current marketing data, trends, fads, and information about consumer preferences.

Color Wheels: The Ultimate Color Forecasters

What do color wheels have to do with forecasting? When influential sources like craft trade journals and the Color Marketing Group announce color forecasts for the next two years, pay attention.

Artisans of all types rush to follow the forecast, reinforcing it. Why not do likewise? However, if you study color trends and vary from the forecast just a little, you may stand out from the crowd.

For example, at this writing, purple and lavender are popular due in part to the substitution of pansies for sunflowers. Clothing, jewelry, flowers, and home decor show purple and its variations as current popular colors.

Color-wheel students recognize yellow as the direct complement of purple. Yellow will both enhance purple and soften it. If you observe an overuse of these two colors, why not turn to your color wheel for help? Yellow-green and yellow-gold are *near* complements of purple. Consider using them instead. Why not add a fresh touch to your next creation and avoid the overdone in favor of subtle variations?

You can carry this idea further by reversing the process. Yellow's complement is indeed purple, but red-violet and blue-violet are its near complements. Rather than repeat exactly what you see around you, vary your color choices this way.

Though many color wheels and books about color exist today, none can surpass the work of the world-renowned master of color Johannes Itten. His book, *The Art of Color*, leads the field. For a shorter version, read his treatise, *The Elements of Color*. Another marvelous color aid by Itten is *The Color Star*, a unique system of solving color problems.

I still remember a lesson I learned the hard way. During the 1970s, I began a Bargello needlepoint canvas in various shades of rust, cream, and black. I planned to keep it permanently "in progress" so students could see the step-by-step design procedure. As a visual aid, the piece served me well for two decades.

Finally, needlepoint waned and demand for classes trickled to a halt. "What an opportunity," I thought. The 1990s would be the perfect time to complete the piece and turn it into a stunning evening bag. I finished the bag and added a special touch. Beads were just beginning their phenomenal rise to popularity. Painstakingly I added them to enhance the design. Last, I created an unusual shoulder strap of strung beads. "Can't miss," I thought confidently.

Editors examined it after I completed it. They praised the work and finishing yet refused to buy the design. Even a magazine that had formerly bought everything I offered refused.

"What is wrong with this piece?" I asked. The answer? "Rust and cream were hot in the '70s, but not anymore. Would you be willing to reproduce this evening bag in today's jewel-tone colors? How about changing the color of all the beadwork and sending us the bag on speculation?"

Becoming Versatile

Successful craft professionals know they must develop skills in more than one area to remain self-supporting. The popularity of specific crafts rises and falls like everything else. Thus, the wise artisan develops sidelines early. Quilters often branch out into sewn wearables when quilting's popularity wanes. Potters may dabble in stained glass, or fine artists in decoupage. The important issue is to remain flexible and adaptable—always open to new ideas.

Learn to read the craft market. If new to the professional side of crafts, you've probably developed expertise in one area. Watch for signs of that area's decline. Remain alert for signs of a saturated market in your specialty. Prepare for the inevitable by choosing one or more alternate fields. Explore their potential.

This way, when your favored craft slows, you will be ready. Take classes, experiment, and read about related fields. Thus, you can continue writing, designing, or mass producing ready to meet changing consumer demand. Bear in mind that as surely as a specific craft declines, it will return.

Witness the intensity of the quilting movement displayed by our nation's biennial celebration in 1978. Every quilter, it seems, made red, white, and blue quilts, wall hangings depicting flags and their interpretation of the Statue of Liberty. A slower quilt market followed in the '80s only to accelerate again in the mid-'90s.

Remember the decoupage boxes of the '60s and '70s? Craft trade journals report a resurgence of interest in this art form. And today's greater variety of paints offers more diverse design possibilities than before.

Even the popularity of knitting, a traditional craft that has endured for centuries, rises and falls. British designers such as Kaffe Fassett and Sasha Kagan created a strong market for multicolored knitting in the 1980s. Though knitting remains popular in the United States, by 1994, crocheting surpassed knitting, according to the biennial

HIA survey. But knitting enthusiasts should relax: Their craft will return—again!

Market to More Than One Age or Ethnic Group

Another way to remain versatile is to market your craft business to different age groups. For a time in the late 1970s, the American birth rate fell. Women had fewer children and bore them later in life. Schools closed all over the country.

Had you been in the business of producing craft items for infants, you may have found yourself feeling the pinch of lessening demand. During this time, a proliferation of mail-order catalogs targeted senior citizens. Magazines such as *Modern Maturity* became very popular. Craft items for homes became fashionable. The age of "home deco crafts" had begun.

During the first three-quarters of the twentieth century, craft patterns and instructions appeared in English. Strong immigration trends during the last quarter of the century brought us Asian "Yellow Pages" in phone books across the land. Multilanguage instructions appeared on sewing patterns. If you can read and write in more than one language, now may be the time for you to offer bilingual craft skills.

Design in More Than One Style

Developing your craft in more than one style is yet another way to remain versatile. Do you prefer things Victorian? This enduring mode is with us once more. But what were crafters creating twenty years ago, when Victoriana was at rest?

Would you have been able to branch out into European styles when Russia opened its cultural doors to the world? Could you have been part of the Southwest trend? Learn to translate your media, skills, materials, and mood to popular trends and styles to remain steadily employed.

When Should You Diversify?

- When you feel you have exhausted the potential of a particular style or trend.
- When the consumer demand for a particular craft or style slows noticeably.
- When you find an unexpected niche in your market.
- When customers repeatedly request products and services you do not yet have available.
- When increasing numbers of your competitors add a particular service or product to their businesses.
- When you need to generate more income.
- When a new trend, style, or market excites you.
- When you scrutinize your business and find you are profiting more than expected from an area you previously considered a sideline.
- When serendipity strikes—learn to recognize and act on it.

Leave nothing to chance. As forecaster for your business, find out "what's hot and what's not"! Avoid a frequent error made by novices. They tend to produce what they like and find stimulating without a thought to what *consumers* want to buy. Choose a path to success by remaining sensitive to the whims of the marketplace.

Resources

Color Marketing Group, a nonprofit international association of twelve hundred design and color professionals dedicated to forecasting and tracking color/design trends in the United States, meets twice yearly. Reach them at:

4001 North Ninth St., Suite 102
Arlington, VA 22203
(703)528-7666

Itten, Johannes. 1974. *The Art of Color.* New York: Van Nostrand Reinhold.

Itten, Johannes. 1986. *The Color Star.* New York: Van Nostrand Reinhold.

Itten, Johannes. 1970. *The Elements of Color.* New York: Van Nostrand Reinhold.

Eileen Ternullo
Eileen Ternullo Textiles
786 St. Francis Ave.
Novato, CA 94947-2872
Phone: (415) 897-0438

FASHION WEAVER

Eileen Ternullo began her weaving business while working part-time as a seamstress for a leather designer. Producing her own clothing designs for local boutiques was Eileen's entrance into the professional craft world. Two years later, she began working with a sales rep who broadened the field for Eileen's designs. The ensuing exposure increased her production time to forty to sixty hours, making Eileen a full-time weaver.

Crafts Brief

Business founded: 1980

Legal form of business: Sole proprietorship

Home-office? Eileen describes her studio, a separate 12-by-24-foot room in her home: "I have overhead lighting and two large windows. Three walls contain floor-to-ceiling shelves for supplies and woven fabric. Production equipment fills the remaining wall. My invaluable working equipment consists of two large floor looms, cutting table, sewing machines, and pressing equipment." Eileen makes the most of her space. "My cutting table doubles as a desk with file cabinets and drawers below," she explains.

Daily routine: Eileen describes her typical workday, dividing it this way:

- Business paperwork: supply ordering and bookkeeping.
- Phone calls to: sales rep, contractors, and retailers.
- Product development: trend analysis and fabric design.
- Fabric preparation: loom dressing and weaving.
- Garment preparation: washing, cutting, sewing.
- Filling orders: quality control, packing, and shipping.

Wholesale sales provide the majority of Eileen's income, but she also profits from gallery displays, retail sales, and teaching classes and workshops.

Best part of craft career: "I enjoy being my own boss, responsible for my own success or failure," says Eileen. She enjoys her flexible work schedule and the recognition her work provides.

Least favorite: "Uncertainty of new designs and how retailers will accept them challenge me most. Bookkeeping, off-hour phone calls—especially on weekends—can be bothersome, too."

Strengths: Problem-solving skills and self-motivation serve Eileen well.

Weaknesses: Eileen acknowledges (as do most crafters interviewed in this book) that she must push herself to do bookkeeping and remain diligent about managing her time well.

Professional organizations: Belonging to the Tamalpais Weaving Guild and the Sonoma Art Guild provides Eileen with networking and supply resources and feedback about her new design ideas.

Professional journals: *Women's Wear Daily* and *Handwoven* magazine keep her abreast of fashion and weaving news. *The Crafts Report* provides Eileen with tips for managing her craft business and offers retail and wholesale opportunities.

Goals: Eileen affirms the emotional satisfaction of crafts as a career: "I want to continue past retirement in the textile field. I plan to continue designing, publishing, and teaching. I want recognition in the textile and clothing design world."

Advice: "Do what you love—it makes the hard work and hours bearable. Take classes pertaining to your craft as well as those relating to small business. Ask questions and investigate everything. Do not jump into a full-time venture; the pace can overwhelm beginners. Move slowly, gradually increasing business volume. Search out apprenticeships, continue to learn. Stay close to those who support you technically and emotionally—networking is important. Above all, keep a sense of humor!

CHAPTER 9

YOU AS DESIGNER

W*HAT IS AN* original design? *Webster's College Dictionary* defines the word "original":

1. Arising or proceeding independently; inventive; novel: an original idea.
2. Capable of or given to thinking or acting in an independent, creative, or individual manner: an original thinker.
3. Created, undertaken, or presented for the first time.

From the same source, the word "design" means:

1. To prepare the preliminary sketch or plans to execute a work.
2. To plan and fashion artistically or skillfully.
3. To intend for a definite purpose.
4. To form or conceive in the mind; contrive; plan.
5. To make drawings, preliminary sketches, or plans.
6. To plan and fashion the form and structure of an object, or work of art.
7. Organization or structure of formal elements in a work of art; composition.

Manufacturers, magazine editors, and buyers eagerly seek designs from talented newcomers. However, submitted designs *must* be original. An item is *not* original if it is:

- Made from a kit or variations
- Made from a commercial pattern or variations

- Made as a workshop project with input from a professional craft teacher
- Made following instructions from a magazine
- Copied from a copyrighted design, pattern, or displayed work of another
- Copied from an existing project
- Copied from a pattern, object, or instructions but containing different colors, dimensions, or other changes

Originality means so much to editors who buy designs that early in negotiations they ask you to sign a document verifying that the work in question originated with you. Changing one or two elements of an existing design does not constitute an "original" design.

In fact, literature on copyright infringement defines this practice as making "derivative copies." Only the original designer who copyrighted his or her work may profit from slight modifications of the original design. Copyright law prevents others from doing so. Penalties can severely damage the career of crafters who deliberately violate these statutes.

Look around you for ideas for original designs. Nature overflows with them. Start your next project from the very beginning as defined by *Webster's*. Begin with your own drawings, charts, or photos—not the work of others.

Patents and trademarks must be exclusive in order to be registered, but not so with designs protected by copyright. Artisans who have similar designs may copyright them even if they look like yours. The copyright office calls this "simultaneous discovery." Two people, unknown to one another, may execute a similar work. However, if each designer proves origination with drawings, sketches, photos, and other supporting evidence, both may apply for copyright. (More about copyrights in Chapter 15.)

Editors and manufacturers who buy your work often buy "all rights." This means you cannot sell an original design a second time without permission. When possible, try to sell only "first rights." This means the writer offers a publication the right to publish the design for the first time.

After that, all other rights revert to the writer. However, you *can* profit from a single, successful design many times without violating an "all rights" agreement.

Below, you will find twelve ways in which I profited from a pair of geometric designs embroidered on canvas. From the time I began work on these 12-by-12-inch projects, reactions from others indicated they might become very popular.

I call them "Warm as Gold, Cool as Silver." Both pieces are embroidered with silky floss and metallic threads. Both star burst designs feature an unworked background backed by foil paper. Both use identical stitching patterns and are exactly the same size.

"Warm as Gold" begins with gold thread in the center followed by the gradated, warm colors of the color wheel. I worked on yellow canvas, with gold foil peeking through the canvas holes to create a moody glow. Finally, I mounted the work in a gold frame.

"Cool as Silver," conversely, begins with silver thread followed by cool colors. Its frame is silver and silver foil glows through the unworked canvas.

This design pair generated more income than any other work I have created before or since. Each piece cost $12 for threads and canvas plus $8 for the frame. Revenues exceeded $4,000.

Here is how I extracted all the profit potential from a solitary design:

TWELVE WAYS TO PROFIT FROM ONE DESIGN

1. Write a how-to article so readers can make the project themselves. The magazine that purchased the design for "Warm as Gold, Cool as Silver" bought only "first rights." After the design appeared in color in a needlepoint magazine, I was free to use it again.
2. Write an article about an aspect of your design process. Many craft magazines feature in-depth articles about a single aspect in a work without publishing a complete

set of instructions. In my case, I wrote a second article about how I used a color wheel to select the careful gradations used in the project. I offered hints on how to prepare the threads and how to blend slightly different colors in one needle to create special effects.

3. Place a classified ad in craft magazines and sell the item in a kit format by mail order. Many excellent crafters across the country do not have an interest or inclination to design their own projects. They prefer work designed by others. Additionally, many people do not have access to sufficient materials and colors in local shops. Selling your kit by mail order is convenient for buyers because they have exactly what they need to complete a project while they provide you with a fair profit. Consider ordering enough supplies to make up craft kits for a successful design. Each kit should contain everything a crafter needs to duplicate your design. Protect yourself by listing items that are *not* included such as frames, batteries, etc.

4. Manufacture and sell the completed item by mail order to customers who do not craft. Home decor items appeal to a broad market. Many people prefer to buy ready-made crafts. Prepare for an unexpected but welcome surge of orders. Should it occur, enlist the help of people who can help you produce enough products in a timely manner to satisfy demand.

5. Sell your item at craft or trade shows, or fairs. Once you find that one of your designs pleases others, rent a booth at a small, local fair. You can either sell completed projects or take orders to do custom work.

6. Give demonstrations to interested groups to generate interest in your work. Show your best designs. Distribute brochures listing your line of goods and services.

7. Attend a street fair so others can observe you at work. With hesitation, I accepted an invitation to participate in a special outdoor craft fair. The show, billed as "Art in Action," featured local artists and crafters at work. I displayed my pair of matched designs as I worked on another. Passersby stopped and asked questions. I invited a few brave souls to try a stitch or two. This experience resulted in both teaching assignments and custom orders.

8. Give a workshop to help others make their own version of the item, teaching them basic skills. Craft instructors need sound, appealing designs to inspire others who want to learn a specific technique. (Read Chapter 21 about how to find teaching positions.)

9. Write a project booklet giving complete instructions to recreate the item. Sell the booklet in shops, in classes, or by mail order. Enhance your project booklet by fixing a color snapshot of the work on the cover page.

10. Enter successful craft designs in exhibits and fairs. Many allow you to advertise that your piece is for sale or to state that you will take orders. Winning cash awards and ribbons, of course, adds to your profits.

11. When you feel a design has no more income earning potential, give it as a gift or as a deductible donation in a raffle or as a door prize. Such visibility becomes a profitable marketing tool.

12. Wait several years and do it all over again. In the example I have used, the designs were first published in 1979. Later, in 1992, the needlepoint magazine asked permission to reprint the original article and instructions for a slightly reduced price. Why not?

Sell Your Designs to Craft Magazines

Writing for craft magazines offers freelance designers additional income. Join the Society of Craft Designers (SCD) to receive the most comprehensive education available about this process. Membership in SCD permits you to attend national seminars, where you will learn to write instructions, photograph your work, and market yourself on a professional level.

Learn what editors need and how to submit original designs to them. Remember, you sell only the design. Projects are returned after they are photographed. This means you still have the original item for resale later on. (More about writing for craft magazines in Chapter 22.)

Writing the How-to Magazine Article

Speaking of writing, take a few courses in the subject. Read a few of the excellent books published by Writer's Digest Books if writing appeals to you. Selling designs is just one way to profit from contributing to monthly publications.

Many magazines, such as *Threads,* for example, prefer articles about process over step-by-step how-to's. Recent issues featured quilters sharing their techniques for dyeing fabric and the art of appliqué, for example. Share your expertise to help readers improve their skills. Tell how you choose, collect, and store fabrics and notions for a special quilt, for example. Or, write articles about an aspect of your design process. Get paid to share your tips.

Resources

Howard, V. A., Ph.D, and Barton, J. H., M.A. 1986. *Thinking on Paper.* New York: Morrow.

Newcomb, Duane. 1987. *How to Sell and Re-Sell Your Writing.* Cincinnati: Writer's Digest Books.

The Society of Craft Designers
6175 Barfield Road, #220
Atlanta GA 30328

Maria Nerius
Nerius House Crafts and
Nerius House Designs
141 Salmon Drive Northeast
Palm Bay, FL 32907
Phone: (407) 725-0792

FROM CRAFT HOBBYIST TO ADVISER AND EDITOR

Maria Nerius' interest in crafts began as a hobby in 1985. Ten years later, her full-time crafting led to writing a regular column in partnership with Tracia Ledford for the respected trade journal *Craftrends & Sew Business*. Less than a year later, Maria also became editor of *The Craft Supply Directory*, a trade journal for professional craft producers. Coincidence and good fortune played no part in her success. Diligence, hard work, and thorough preparation did.

Practical from the beginning, Maria set guidelines for her craft production. Her main product continues to be wooden dolls and other figures dressed in a variety of styles and techniques. Early in her business plan, Maria decided that:

- Raw materials consumed in her products must be available at wholesale costs.
- The production process must lend itself to quick, easy steps.
- She wanted the ability to package, store, transport, and display her products herself.
- The retail price must be reasonable enough to compete, yet profitable enough to produce.
- Designing and producing original items for sale would remain the primary focus of her business. In addition to writing columns and instructions, she finds time to attend fairs and exhibits, to demonstrate craft products, and to design for manufacturers.

Crafts Brief

Business founded: Nerius House Crafts 1986, Nerius House Designs 1992

Legal form of business: Sole proprietorship for both businesses

Home-office? Maria's craft business has literally taken over her residence. Nerius House Crafts and Nerius House Designs take up two bedrooms, the entire living room, and all of the garage.

Her first business produces craft items for direct retail sale to the public. The second business focuses on designing for publication in craft magazines. The businesses are well equipped, with a computer, copier, scanner, and fax machine.

The manner in which Maria acquired the space she needed for her growing business deserves special mention. Her husband felt reluctant to give up his living room to Maria's burgeoning business. To convince him through his engineering background, Maria used the approach he customarily used for his clients—a formal proposal.

"I worked two solid days on a twenty-page document stating why I needed the space, how I would use it, and how much profit I could make. If he would agree to a one-year contract, I promised to give up the space if I did not meet my goals." He relented. She still uses the space, with his blessing, help, and encouragement.

Hours: Success in crafts occurs when the business takes more than forty hours per week to keep up. Not only does Maria work full-time at her career, it takes two more people to keep it going. Her husband, Ken, cuts and prepares all the wood for her designs, while her mother-in-law sews most of the clothing for her wooden doll designs.

Daily routine: Devoting herself full-time to her business, Maria followed her own advice to new crafters by preparing thoroughly. She began with a *written* business plan— nearly always a guarantee of success. Her plan outlined her day. She divides her time into quarters, allowing one segment each for paperwork, new design development, writing and designing for publication, and craft production time.

Maria makes time for the activities most crafters agree bring success. In addition to the above, she teaches, does craft-product demonstrations, frequently attends fairs and exhibits, writes instructions, and spends time networking in the industry.

She begins her day at the computer, writing and dealing with correspondence. Business phone calls receive her attention at this time, too. Maria switches on her answering machine when leaving her office for her workroom. At this time, she dedicates herself exclusively to craft production, usually having many items in different stages of completion.

Best part of craft career: Like most crafters interviewed for this book, Maria admits the freedom, independence, and opportunity for creativity top her reasons for choosing a career in crafts. Working from home means so much to her, Maria intends to continue at any cost. She claims that when the business becomes too large for her home, she'll buy a bigger house rather than work outside her home.

Least favorite: Struggling for credibility and respectability as a serious crafter annoys Maria. Rather than lament the slow pace of the industry to recognize professional crafters, Maria's decided to write a regular column about it, which has smoothed the way for others.

Strengths: Maria's drive and enthusiasm shine after even a brief meeting. Her incredible preparation and organization attest to her success and growth. This talented artisan thoroughly researched her decision to go professional.

"I spent the first year researching everything I could about crafting from home, including local, state, and federal regulations. Next, I searched out information on production techniques, pricing, inventory, display methods, marketing, and advertising. I read every book I could find until my reference librarian recognized my voice on the phone due to my frequent calls requesting information.

"I planned how to produce and design from home, where to store inventory and finished goods. My goal was to get my work published. Though it took seven years to get a design in print, it would not have happened without my five-year Business Plan."

Weaknesses: Occasional lack of confidence and demanding too much from herself thwart Maria at times.

Professional organizations: No surprises here. Maria knows the value of membership in the Society of Craft Designers, Hobby Industry Association, and Association of Crafts and Creative Industries.

Professional journals: *The Crafts Report, Craftrends &* *Sew Business, Gift Supply* magazine, and *The Crafts Supply Directory.*

Goals: As of this writing, Maria has reached one of her major long-range goals. She has gone a long way to gain respect for the role of all craft producers in the United States through her columns and articles.

Advice: "It's possible to earn a good living in crafts. Diversify into production, design, consulting, teaching, and demonstrating. Keep precise, accurate records. Join organizations that center on your goals. Networking within the industry keeps you fresh, on your toes.

"Keep your résumé updated. Freshen your Business Plan. Write up a mission statement. Putting ideas on paper makes them 'real.' Take classes. Attend trade shows and educational seminars.

"Take time to organize. Though it seems like wasted energy, it saves time and frustration. Take yourself seriously even if no one else does. Do your homework and research. Read everything you can find to build confidence and knowledge. Observe others in the industry. Don't be afraid to ask questions. Look at old subjects in new ways, experiment and take risks. Challenge yourself every day."

CHAPTER 10

YOU AS SELLER

RETAILERS SELL PRODUCTS directly to the ultimate consumer. Wholesalers sell to others who in turn sell the product to consumers. Crafters may do either or both.

Selling at Retail

When we think of retailers, we first think of shopkeepers—for centuries, the only retailers. "Professional Crafter" describes a retailer as one who manufactures products in quantity for sale directly to consumers. Today, most professional crafters make their products from home-studios, not shops. Crafters sell their products at retail prices directly to consumers in several ways.

CRAFT MALLS

From push-carts in converted wineries to modern booths in shopping centers, craft malls offer good selling opportunities for artisans. Some require you to sell your wares in person. Others have a system by which you need not be present and someone else sells your items directly to the consumer. Visit malls in your geographical area. What type of customer shops there? Do your products fit in? If you cannot

find a craft mall nearby, you will find them listed throughout the United States in trade publications.

Managers of craft malls advertise in trade journals to
find new crafters and products. Many you will deal with will
be out of state. The largest of these—Coomer's Craft
Malls—continues to open new locations each year in the
Southwest. However, trends show craft malls growing in
popularity from coast to coast. They continue to please
both sellers and buyers along with those who manage them.

CRAFT COOPERATIVES

Consider craft cooperatives if you prefer to spend most of
your time in your studio producing crafts for sale. Individual crafters in a cooperative often take turns selling
merchandise for the entire group. Visit several such cooperatives before committing yourself. Ask important questions such as:

- Must I pay a fee to join this cooperative?
- Do I pay a percentage of my total sales to the cooperative?
- What will it cost me to rent space in the cooperative
  location?
- How much time am I expected to work on-site?
- How much space will I have to display my goods?

Ask to see the cooperative's contract. Study it carefully
before signing.

CRAFT FAIRS, BOUTIQUES, AND BAZAARS

Craft fairs are perhaps the most traditional way to sell craft
items directly to consumers. Do you enjoy meeting the public? Craft shows, boutiques, fairs, and flea markets may be
a good choice for you if you have an outgoing personality
and can express enthusiasm for your products to buyers.

Start with small, local events in your community. Many
experienced artisans who travel across the country to
sell their wares began by selling from a card table at a

community-sponsored fund-raiser. This way, you will learn the system and gather experience before attempting larger fairs.

Home boutiques provide another entry into selling directly to consumers, though you will need time to prepare. Two sisters in Northern California illustrate how simple, yet effective, home craft boutiques can be.

Both sisters work all year making quilts, sweaters, wreaths, floral arrangements, dolls, and home decor crafts. During the first weekend of December, they decorate one of their homes with their collection.

They advertise simply by placing ads in local newspapers and distributing colorful fliers at nearby schools and churches. Shoppers looking for one-of-a-kind hand-crafted items for gift-giving come to buy.

The sisters spend a week before the event arranging an appealing display and pricing each item. In one weekend, they generate enough income to buy craft supplies to make new items for the following year, pay expenses, and add to their bank accounts during the holiday season.

If you decide to sell this way, plan ahead. Collect names and addresses of customers who visit your home show or boutique. Make a sign-up sheet readily available. Each year, you can mail invitations to those who have supported you in the past.

Once you've gathered experience with small fairs, flea markets, and home boutiques, look to larger events. Spend time developing a dynamic display to showcase your products for larger shows where you will compete with seasoned crafters. Attractive displays are critical to lure fair-goers to your booth.

Choose the best display equipment you can afford. Scale upward to regional and state shows as you grow in knowledge and experience. Companies specializing in craft display equipment advertise in trade journals and most especially in *The Crafts Report*. You will find a list of books specializing in how to sell at shows and fairs at the end of this chapter.

You will find *The Crafts Fair Guide: A Review of Arts and Crafts Fairs* a very special quarterly publication offering comprehensive information about craft fairs of all sizes and types. Author Lee Spiegel (Box 5062, Mill Valley, CA 94903) reviews *all* the fairs and exhibits in the United States. Details about heat, air-conditioning, restrooms, booth fees, food, average attendance, and typical customers are thoroughly analyzed by this nationally known craft fair expert.

Many craft trade publications list shows of all sizes around the country each month. Contact names and details about how to apply for exhibit space help you select the best shows to showcase your particular product.

Follow the show listings in *The Crafts Report* and *The Arts 'N Crafts Showguide.* Not only will you learn about local, regional, and national shows of all sizes, articles abound about how to prepare. Learn how to choose a location, create enticing displays, anticipate customer wants, price items, and run your booth profitably.

Don't overlook one of the prime responsibilities assigned to you by each state Franchise Tax Board. States that charge sales taxes require sellers to collect them. You must add the proper amount of tax to each item sold. State Franchise Tax Boards across the country differ in minor details. Check with the office in your county to learn more. Not only will you collect the taxes, you must set the money aside to make annual or quarterly payments to your state Franchise Tax Board.

SELLING BY MAIL ORDER

Mail-order selling continues to grow steadily.[1] Research conducted by Simmons Market Research Bureau shows that the total percentage of American adults shopping by phone or mail was 53 percent in the past decade, compared with an 11 percent population increase.

[1]Source: *Entrepreneur* magazine, February 1996

Yet another source, the Direct Marketing Association, estimates 1995 catalog sales at $62.6 billion. Researcher Maxwell Scroge predicts total mail-order sales at $306 billion for 1996. Though much of this huge market consists of well-known Fortune 500 companies, small individual sellers do well when they understand the process. Don't be surprised at the cost of paper and postage, formidable expenses in mail-order selling.

Exclusive, one-of-a-kind items sell best. Take classes and read thoroughly about this profitable opportunity, for it requires meticulous research and attention to detail.

If working from a home-office appeals to you, consider selling this way. Think about producing kits. Buyers find it easy to craft their own projects when they can use designs generated by professionals like you. Completed items, patterns, and booklets of your designs, for example, can fill your catalog.

Success can lead to a full-time enterprise. Critics occasionally say mail-order selling is a lot of work and prone to failure. I beg to disagree. While a mail-order business certainly takes a lot of work, success is possible with preparation, research, and diligence. I've kept my mail-order craft catalog business going for thirteen years. So can you. Here's how.

Educate yourself about selling by mail order.

A valuable publication about successful mail-order selling is *Direct Marketing News,* 19 West 21st St., New York, NY 10010. This twice-monthly newspaper is free to qualified mail-order sellers. Write on letterhead stationery to request your free subscription. Also consider the books listed at the end of this chapter.

Create your own catalog.

Lillian Vernon and Montgomery Ward catalogs began as one-page fliers. You too can begin with a very small, limited catalog. Consider designing your own and mailing it to a targeted list of buyers. You may compose your own targeted list (called a "house list") or rent a list from a broker.

If you prepare thoroughly, you may find it will cost less than listing your products in an existing catalog. However, writing, pricing, photographing, and mailing your own catalog can be expensive and time-consuming. Research carefully before risking your time and money. However, many successful businesspeople attest to the potential in such a venture. Stuart and Ellen Quay, of Qualin International Silk Importers, profiled in Chapter 1, and Gloria "Mimi" Winer, profiled at the end of this chapter, began their international catalogs from home modestly.

Consider direct mail-order selling from advertising.

Search out the consumer publications read by your target market. I began my mail-order craft business this way. I had little to spend on advertising, but learned through careful research how to select magazines to target my ideal customers. The smaller the subscription base of a magazine, the less they charge for advertising. Highly specialized magazines were what I was looking for.

I wanted to sell needlepoint project booklets to advanced embroiderers. Beginners had many books to choose from, but when I began selling by mail order in the early 1970s, few existed for stitchers with experience.

Writer's Market is a hefty book published by Writer's Digest Books. Each year, it offers a comprehensive listing of magazines throughout the United States in every subject imaginable. Both writers and advertisers can learn demographics and other details about the readers of each publication. Through *Writer's Market,* I found the perfect magazine. Subscribers numbered only 22,000. Thus, a small classified ad would cost me $25. More importantly, *all* the subscribers were serious needlepoint hobbyists—just the market I wanted to reach.

Primarily, I attributed my success to accurately finding the magazine read by my target market. My association with the magazine lasted for eighteen years, ending only when they ceased publication.

Carefully choose the publication in which you want to place your first ads to sell by mail order. This is the real secret to profitability. Make sure the magazine's readers are interested in your type of product.

Select either a one-step or a two-step process. In a one-step sales approach, you sell your item directly to the buyer from an ad. The consumer reads your ad and sends you a check. You send the consumer the ordered product.

If you think you need more ad space than you can afford to explain your product, try the two-step approach. Describe the product briefly. Make it sound inviting. Offer a *free* brochure or catalog promising more details. This will give you an additional opportunity to sell your pieces.

Learn all you can about how to write a persuasive sales letter as part of your direct-mail package. Include an order form, brochure, and catalog. Experienced mail-order sellers differ on how to send an initial mailing to a potential buyer.

Some send a free informational packet to everyone requesting it. Others feel that since expenses for printing, postage, photography, etc., can be costly, one should qualify buyers by sending materials only to those truly interested rather than to everyone seeking free information.

Many years ago, I came to agree with the latter system. Though I pay for producing the catalog sent to potential buyers, I qualify them by asking something of them. Rather than charge for my catalog (which many sellers do), I request a large, self-addressed envelope with three first-class stamps.

Serious buyers seem happy to comply. This small effort and expense eliminates many readers who respond to any free offers whether they plan to buy or not. Though this has proven successful for me, you must experiment to determine the method best suited to you and your product.

Research proved that while I mailed far fewer catalogs when potential buyers had to include a self-addressed, stamped envelope, sales tripled from when I sent free catalogs to all who requested them.

Books such as those by Perry Wilbur or John Kremer describe step-by-step procedures on how to prepare a good direct-mail package. Send for a free copy of the Federal Trade Commission's "Mail Order Rule Book." It will help you abide by the law and satisfy mail-order buyers at the same time.

Consider a co-op catalog with other artisans.

Think about contacting colleagues who have noncompeting products if you feel producing a catalog alone is too much work or too expensive. Invite them to share expenses. You have the same options mentioned above, but more people to do the work, mailings, bookkeeping, and preparation.

Why not start a co-op catalog featuring the work of one artist in each of the following media: fiber, wood, glass, ceramics, toys, jewelry, and metal? Even a half-dozen such craftspeople pooling their resources can create an effective catalog while earning a reasonable profit.

Consider using inserts with other mailings.

Have you noticed that statements from your gas credit card include ads for cameras, luggage, and other items? You need not choose huge companies such as these with which to share expenses. Instead, look for a small, local business interested in defraying mailing costs. Many are happy to allow your inserts to ride along in their statement envelopes for a small fee.

Look for advertising and marketing companies that provide cooperative mailings for up to ten businesses at a time. Once again, you can work with a group of craftspeople. Each pays a small cost to include literature and order forms in a professional looking direct-mail package. Check with local package insert brokers for costs. They can also help you create and mail your documents to your target market.

Trade lists with related craftspeople.

If you make teddy bears, locate doll makers, for example. Offer to trade your house list of past buyers for theirs. Consumers interested in bears also may like dolls. Your only costs will be printing and mailing.

Use "bounce-backs" with every order you fill.

Including literature about your other products every time you fill an order by mail is called a bounce-back. Success in mail order comes from satisfied customers placing repeat sales.

Defray your own expenses by offering to include literature and brochures from colleagues as you fill orders. Suggest they do the same for you. All of you will increase the
size of your in-house mailing lists for little cost, reaching
the consumer directly.

Negotiate with mail-order catalogs.

Consider negotiating with existing mail-order catalog companies. Inquire about their terms. Some will advertise your
product in their catalog for a percentage of the retail price
while you fill customers' orders directly. When established
catalogs see that your item sells well, you can negotiate selling your product to them in quantity in the future.

Become a drop shipper.

When a mail-order catalog company buys from you
directly, it must store your product. It also must fill orders
and package and mail your item. You can reverse the
process by offering to be the drop shipper. The mail-order
catalog notifies you when someone has ordered your item.
They keep a percentage of the cost (usually 40 to 50 percent) and send the balance to you. You mail the product
directly to the customer, using the catalog's return address
label.

Companies benefit if they do not have to store, package, or mail your item. Thus, they may be willing to take
less of a percentage when you offer drop-shipping services.
You benefit in that you can include all your tie-in literature
when you fill the order.

Learn about the needs of the mail-order company with
whom you deal. Read contracts carefully. Do not expect
them to take the time to create, lay out, and write your
sales copy. Make it easy for them to work with you by doing a good job of this yourself.

Selling at Wholesale

Selling at wholesale means you will *not* be selling directly
to the ultimate consumer. You need not collect state sales
taxes. The retailer to whom you sell your products accepts
responsibility for this.

Before considering selling wholesale, make sure you can manufacture your product in sufficient quantity. Retailers who buy to resell expect a reduced price in exchange for buying large amounts of merchandise from manufacturers and distributors, which include you.

Selling at wholesale trade shows is not for beginning crafters. Wait until you are well established in your business. Make sure the quality of your products is consistent. You must have experience setting prices to ensure that the discounts you offer retailers still provide you with adequate profit. Attend smaller then medium-size retail shows before considering renting exhibit space at your first wholesale show.

Remember, retailers do not pay at the time of purchase as consumers do. Your budgeting must allow lag times between shipping your product and receiving payment.

Trade shows are the primary way to sell at wholesale. You will find monthly listings in trade journals. Preparation and quality displays become more important than ever, for your customers are experienced craft businesspeople. They immediately recognize quality and performance. They expect service and readily available information about your products so they can profit as they resell them. Trade shows bring fewer buyers than retail shows, but your reward is volume selling.

Some shows are juried. This means a group of qualified people select the crafters that will participate in a particular show. They screen participants by requesting slides of their work. Thus, merely applying for entrance does not mean automatic acceptance. Expect to pay "booth" or entry fees if accepted. Successful shows often fill so quickly with regulars that newer artisans must be especially diligent in applying and returning completed paperwork.

WHOLESALING TO SHOPS

Approach small shops and boutiques for another way to sell your goods at wholesale. Begin by visiting potential businesses. Observe and browse carefully. Do your items fit in with the existing merchandise? What type of shoppers do you see in the store? Do they show a likely interest in your products? Do you find the store clean, professionally arranged, and appealing?

If you answer "yes" to these questions, do not approach the owner or manager yet. Go home and prepare. Make sure your portfolio showcases your line to every advantage. Select a sampling of your wares, grouped and packaged attractively. Look over the quality of your brochure and business card. They should convey your professional status.

Though many crafters barge into shops unannounced, most managers appreciate hearing from you first. Call ahead to get the name of the contact person in charge of buying. Ask if he or she would like to see your work. Inquire about the best time to visit. Try to avoid catching the person when they feel rushed.

Dress professionally, armed with your materials. *Never* be late for this appointment. Remember, you have come to sell yourself as well as your products. Establishing regular accounts with a few shops in your geographical area is ideal. Treasure such relationships.

SELLING TO OUT-OF-STATE CRAFT SHOPS

Once you have saturated shops within your local area, consider selling outright or by consignment to shops in other states. "But, how do I find them?" you may ask. Craft publications such as *The Crafts Report* feature lists of shop owners across the country seeking specific craft items.

In one recent issue, seventeen shops from coast to coast outlined what they wanted to buy from quality crafters. Shop owners provide their address, phone number, and the name of a contact person. After stating their buying terms, they describe their needs:

- "Pottery, fiber, wood, leather, glass. Must be original designs, hand-crafted by the artist."

- "High-quality crafts in all media except clothing. Please no ethnic or country."
- "Stained glass, fiber, handmade paper, wind chimes, and Christmas ornaments."
- "Interested in purchasing from potters, jewelers, and glass blowers."
- "We need handmade crafts, gifts, jewelry, and furniture for our gallery."
- "All media including one-of-a-kind whimsical, nautical, and sea life."
- "Looking for silver and gold jewelry."
- "Textiles, clothing, weaving."
- "Basketry, pottery, woodcarvings, enameling, and black-smithing."

If selling what you make is your primary source of income, finding buyers may not be as difficult as you may have thought. Remember the four p's to success in marketing your crafts (or any product): *Prepare, produce* quality goods, *price* them fairly, and *position* them appropriately in the marketplace.

BEST OF BOTH WORLDS: SELLING BOTH RETAIL AND WHOLESALE

Every August, in San Francisco, sellers have the opportunity to sell at both retail and wholesale at a large show sponsored by the American Craft Council. During the first two days, this comprehensive show serves the trade only. Buyers from all over the West Coast come to select merchandise to fill their shops.

During the last three days of the show, sellers prepare for consumers. Overnight, they switch price tags on merchandise from wholesale to retail and prepare for a fresh onslaught of eager buyers.

Industry-specific shows sometimes choose to offer both ways of selling as well, but those I have attended do it differently than the American Craft Council. When approaching a vendor with an interest to buy, crafters can identify themselves as wholesale buyers. If you are the buyer, prepare to prove that you either resell products or buy raw materials as a professional crafter to manufacture a finished item. Produce your Seller's Permit number and pertinent identification. Conversely, as a seller, you also may seek out this type of show to sell your wares to both wholesalers and retailers. Search out such shows if you want to benefit from both of these markets.

Resources

Coomer's Craft Malls
(800) 860-9499

To obtain the Federal Trade Commission's free "Mail Order Rule Book," write to:

Federal Trade Commission
Division of Legal & Public Records
Washington, DC 20580

Brabec, Barbara. 1996. *Handmade for Profit—Where and How to Sell What You Make.* New York: Evans.

Gerards, Paul. 1996. *How to Sell What You Make: The Business of Marketing Crafts.* Mechanicsburg, PA: Stackpole Books.

Kremer, John. 1990. *Mail Order Selling Made Easier.* Fairfield, Iowa: Ad-Lib Publications.

Rosen, Wendy. 1994. *Crafting as a Business.* Baltimore: Chilton Books.

Simon, Julian. 1993. *How to Start and Operate a Mail-Order Business.* New York: McGraw-Hill.

Wilbur, Perry. 1992. *Money in Your Mailbox.* New York: Wiley Press.

Gloria (Mimi) Winer
Publisher of "Let's Talk About Doll Making" newsletter and
international mail-order catalog *Books & Patterns for the
Serious Dollmaker*
300 Nancy Drive
Point Pleasant, NJ 08742
Phone: (908) 899-0804   Orders only: (800) 521-5512

DOLL MAKER EXTRAORDINAIRE

Mimi Winer and husband, Jim, have created a second
career—playing with dolls. Through their mail-order catalog, *Books & Patterns for the Serious Dollmaker,* they reach
customers all over the world, enabling them to play with
dolls, too.

Mimi aptly named her catalog. She sells books, fabrics,
patterns, and clothing for dolls. Well-known doll makers
also share their patterns with Mimi's customers. She completes her catalog with a full line of doll-making tools. Says
Mimi: "I have an excellent assortment of books for beginning doll makers and I carry hard-to-find items for experienced crafters who are really 'hooked' on making dolls."

Mimi has written several books providing amazing
detail and patterns for her most famous designs. *Mimi's
Earth Angels* gives readers clear tips and secrets to create
her fabulous cloth dolls. With more than two hundred
pages, this tome is a complete course in doll making.
Mimi's latest book, *New Clays for Dollmaking,* has received
rave reviews.

Mimi designs her own tools and invented many exclusive techniques that she shares in her books. In addition to
their international mail-order catalog of dolls, supplies, and
patterns, the Winers also publish a quarterly newsletter,
"Let's Talk About Doll Making."

Mimi's concern for others is well known. She gives license to others to make and sell the dolls they create with
her patterns. She never hesitates to help, support, or
encourage other crafters. As a doll maker and designer, she

has earned the respect of the craft industry. As a person, she has developed a large, devoted "fan club" whose members enthusiastically praise her generosity, warmth, and nurturing skills.

"Doll makers like items that have more than one use. Knowing this causes me to search for inventory that is flexible enough to use in a variety of ways. I try to buy only merchandise that enables my target customer to sell a finished product."

Mimi treats her customers well. "I use odds and ends of unsold merchandise as surprise thank-you gifts to good customers," she says. When customers order more than $150 worth of merchandise, Mimi tucks in little gifts to thank her customer and increase goodwill. Even when such merchandise is no longer selling well, the effect on the customer is positive and worthwhile. Reorders more than make up for the expense of giving away such items.

Crafts Brief

Business founded: 1983

Mimi reports that her mail-order business nearly started itself with publication of her first doll-making and pattern book. She received so many requests from readers across the country for supplies that a mail-order catalog became the only way to meet the demand. Her first catalog consisted of more than three hundred of the most requested items.

Legal form of business: Corporation

Home-office? Doll-making supplies fill the Winers' basement. Doll enthusiasts everywhere gather at Mimi's studio. They come to study with the famous doll artists who teach there, not the least of whom is Mimi herself.

Hours: Though Mimi's generosity helping others is legendary, she works an unbelievable one hundred hours per week at her business! Jim works in the business, contributing skills as a former systems designer, technical coordinator, and writer. He has a photo studio enabling him to do the photography for his wife's patterns and books. He finds his computer station with a scanner and laser printer invaluable.

Final production of Mimi's books and patterns end up is Jim's responsibility. He operates a booklet binder and collating machine to create the finished product. The Winers maintain a staff of two to six employees depending on demand.

Daily routine: Networking by phone takes much of Mimi's time. New book and pattern development, article writing, and new doll design fill her days. Mimi teaches classes and develops tools for doll makers, too. She adds, "I exercise forty-five minutes a day, five days per week to stay fit so I can keep my business together."

Clearly, Mimi uses her time wisely. Her doll designs have been published in the following magazines: *Doll Reader, Doll Life, Cloth Doll, Contemporary Doll, Doll Crafter, Crafts,* and *Crafts 'n Things.*

Best part of craft career: Mimi echoes the sentiments of many crafters when she says unequivocally, "I always do the work I love!"

Least favorite: Hand ruffling doll costumes.

Strengths: Networking and design skill are Mimi's most valuable assets.

Weaknesses: She shares two common failings with many crafters: She often takes on too much and does not always follow through as much as she would like.

Professional Organizations: The Society of Craft Designers, the American Crafts Council, the International Doll Makers Association, the National Cloth Doll Makers Association, and the National Doll & Toy Collectors Club. Additionally, Mimi founded and was first president of the Society of Professional Dollmakers. To balance her doll connections, she also belongs to the National Association of Executive Females.

Professional journals: "I read them all! I want to keep learning."

Advice: "Learn all you can about your customers," Mimi advises. "I keep detailed profiles of my customers. I am a doll maker myself and know their needs and problems. I study every letter from my customers to widen my market.

"Trade shows are important. I always look for new doll-making merchandise that my customers have requested." She also advises other mail-order sellers to sell exclusive merchandise unavailable or scarce in regular shops. For example, Mimi's book *Mimi's Earth Angels* is unavailable from any other source but her.

Mimi frequently writes articles describing how to use her specialized products. "Make time to educate consumers about your products," she emphasizes. Obviously, Mimi excels in marketing skills too!

CHAPTER 11

YOU AS BUSINESS MANAGER

COMMISSION DESIGNS OFFER important advantages to both craft designer and buyer. Designers feel secure in the knowledge that they have a ready buyer—a sure source of income. Buyers have confidence that the article being made will suit their preferences in style, dimension, and color.

What could be better? No wonder crafters and free-lancers of all types prefer to sell by commission whenever possible. Desirable as it is, design commission can also create problems—primarily for the artisan.

Occasionally, clients change their minds or try to back out of an oral arrangement after you have started work on their project. Jane, a textile artist, shared one of her commission experiences. Most crafters, at one time or another, have faced a similar situation.

Jane received a call from her neighborhood bank. The manager explained that the branch planned to remodel. Jane's large, contemporary hangings, which hung in various locations around town, had received rave reviews. The bank manager wanted to hire Jane to design an 8-by-10-foot hanging for the bank. "I felt elated to have my work displayed in my own neighborhood," Jane admitted. Both artist and manager agreed on a completion date. Jane presented her preliminary drawings of the project to the bank redecorating committee.

Management approved the dimensions, colors, style, and design of the hanging. Jane rushed out to buy supplies so she could begin work immediately on the project, which was estimated to take three months.

After two months of work, Jane moved her piece into the bank. She wanted to complete the project while considering the surroundings and available light. She continued the weaving and construction process on the premises.

Immediately, Jane had a volunteer audience making suggestions as the work progressed. The bank manager asked her to modify the design-in-progress by altering the color scheme and changing the design lines. Jane complied patiently, replacing some materials.

Management suggested more changes; Jane balked. She explained that she would need more time to replace the section in question and begin anew. The manager reminded her of their agreed-upon completion date and total cost of materials. Frustration ensued for all.

Designers working on commission can avoid such problems with a simple contract outlining their terms. I suggest the "$\frac{1}{3}$, $\frac{1}{3}$, $\frac{1}{3}$ commission contract."

Make sure the buyer has seen samples and completed photos of your work and that the final price satisfies both parties. After preliminary discussions with the client, draw up your contract. Here is how the "$\frac{1}{3}$, $\frac{1}{3}$, $\frac{1}{3}$" method works:

THE FIRST ONE-THIRD

State the final price in the first paragraph of the contract. In the next sentence make it clear you will begin the work upon receipt of one-third of the total cost as a down payment. Explain that you will use these funds to buy raw materials.

This protects you in two ways. First, you will not be using your personal funds to buy raw materials for someone else. Second, should the buyer default, disappear, or lose interest in the project, you have not lost your own money. Buyers who sign a written contract must understand that breaching the contract will cost them one-third of the total price.

THE SECOND ONE-THIRD

I call the second paragraph the "review and final approval" section. Invite the buyer to view the project-in-progress once or twice. State a date at which buyers can see the work for the last time before you complete the project. Make it clear that after that date, you can no longer make changes or alterations. After the last review, the second one-third installment becomes due and payable *before* the work continues.

THE LAST ONE-THIRD

Upon completing the work, *never* release it to the buyer without receiving the final one-third payment. Surrendering the completed item before receiving final payment causes you to lose a valuable negotiating position. Pleading for money you have already earned is both unpleasant and damaging to your self-esteem.

Allow me to say a few words in defense of buyers. Though a few deliberately prey on inexperienced crafters, most disagreements occur because buyers do not understand the work process, rather than deliberate efforts to cheat the crafter.

Sandra, a quilter, experienced such a situation. A couple commissioned Sandra to design and produce an elaborate quilt for their parents' twenty-fifth wedding anniversary. Both parties agreed quickly on the design, color, layout, and style of the quilt.

Sandra, one of my college students, drew up a contract featuring the $\frac{1}{3}, \frac{1}{3}, \frac{1}{3}$ system to protect herself. The first third went smoothly. However, during the final review, problems arose.

Though they expressed satisfaction with Sandra's work, her clients had second thoughts about elements in the design. They wanted her to include details not previously discussed and not in the contract. "Just move this section over and add this in," they suggested. They were sincere in their belief that Sandra could accommodate their wish for last-minute changes.

However, Sandra took the time to educate her buyers— both non-quilters. She told them how long it would take to replace portions of the work to make room for other unplanned design elements. She showed them how their idea would disturb the symmetry of the overall design.

She voiced her concern that it might be difficult to match additional materials required with the original purchases. Finally, Sandra gently explained that the alteration would probably affect the promised completion date.

The buyers expressed surprise. They had no idea what their "small suggestion" would mean to a work-in-progress. Because they did not understand the quilting process, they did not realize how much they had asked of Sandra. The couple honored the original contract and design and expressed delight with the finished quilt.

Because Sandra had a *written* contract and conducted herself professionally in educating her customers, she averted hard feelings and misunderstanding. Importantly, she also fostered goodwill for her business by creating satisfied customers.

Expand commission assignments by using promotional methods to find new clients. Contact nearby shops that sell the raw materials you use regularly. Write to them on letterhead stationery enclosing a brochure listing your services. Many shopkeepers and managers keep files of people who work on commission. This way, they can refer customers who want custom-made articles to freelance designers like you. Consider also placing an ad in the "Services Available" classified section of your local newspaper.

Contact local community groups to offer to give programs, exhibits, or demonstrations about what you do.

Show your work at exhibits and fairs. Engage potential clients in conversation. Educate them about the value of handwork. Distribute fliers and brochures describing your services at every opportunity.

Consignment

Think of consignment selling as the opposite of selling by commission. Selling on consignment means you have already manufactured an article and want to display it to prospective buyers. Consignment shops are the ideal place for doing this, but professional preparation is required of the crafter.

Scrutinize local shops and galleries carefully. What items fill the shop? Does your style fit their mood, theme, and price range? Does the staff respect the work of its consignors, protecting it from undue customer handling? Do you find articles for sale tastefully displayed?

Select shops where your goods "feel at home" among the general merchandise. Make a list of establishments you can visit often, preferably unannounced. Visit each shop on your list, introducing yourself to the manager. Request a copy of the consignment contract from each shop you visit. Make sure it contains necessary information and answers to specific questions:

- How much of the selling price goes to the shop owner and how much goes to you? Though percentages vary, you will find 50/50 or 60/40 most common.
- Many consignment shops automatically reduce the selling price of unsold items after sixty or ninety days. Does this meet with your approval?
- How long may the shop owner delay before notifying you that an article has been sold? One of my clients left several pieces of her jewelry at a neighborhood consignment shop for the first time. Unknown to her, they sold immediately. After sixty days, the jeweler called the shop to inquire about the status of her articles. The busy manager

explained he had been waiting for her to return to pick up her check and bring in more merchandise. Unfortunately for my client, the shop had operated on her money, interest-free, and she had lost the opportunity for increased sales. Avoid such an experience by checking in frequently with a shop displaying your merchandise. State in the contract that you expect a call within a specific time limit informing you a sale has been made.

- When will you receive payment for sold pieces? Immediately? Monthly?
- Take care to specify conditions of display should your craft items require special treatment. For example, if you submit a textile, do not allow it to hang in direct sunlight or it will fade while on display. If submitting charcoal artwork, request it be protected from caressing hands.

Crafters feel dismay when reclaiming unsold articles to find they are shopworn and no longer salable. Protect yourself from this by photographing your item *before* leaving it in the store. Keep a snapshot for your files. Give one to the shop owner. This simple precaution establishes the condition of the item when you delivered it to the shop.

Ask the shop owner for proof of insurance protection while your property is on his or her premises.

Another approach to consignment selling is approaching a shop that normally does not take consignment. Ask to display your item in an interesting way to appeal to customers, though it may be unrelated to the shop's business. Examples: crafts in a hospital gift shop, stuffed toys in a beauty shop, hand-knits in a clothing boutique.

Once your pieces saturate nearby consignment stores, expand. Refer to trade journals such as *The Crafts Report*. Remember, shops seeking craft products for consignment sale list their needs here. Refer to Chapter 10 for details.

Once you have selected one or more non-local consignment shops, contact them, introducing yourself with a persuasive cover letter and quality photos of your work. Good relationships with a few consignment shops across the country can keep you in business for years.

Sales Representatives

Sales reps can create markets for you that you might not know about otherwise. Find their ads in craft trade journals, where they describe their lines. Hard-working reps take your items "on the road" for you.

They cover greater distances than you would normally travel. They visit boutiques, shops, and other retail outlets representing you and your work. Reps often learn "what's hot and what's not" (see Chapter 8) and pass this valuable marketing information along to you.

Rarely can a home-based crafter match the selling ability of a seasoned sales rep. Professional salespeople bring a depth of knowledge about markets and customers. They also encourage larger orders as they strive to serve their customers. Working with reps facilitates your cash flow since you pay their commission *after* the customer pays you. Below are questions to ask of someone who might represent you.

- Since reps may represent several artists, do they carry a competing line?
- What percentage of the retail price will the rep charge you? (Average is 15 to 20 percent.)
- Does the rep sell outright or take custom orders on your behalf?
- Before hiring a rep, ask for a generous sampling of present clients. Call them. Inquire about the rep's effectiveness in finding new business and his or her promptness with paperwork. Ask about the condition of unsold merchandise returned to crafters. Is it still salable? Competent reps can expand your market and enlarge your customer base. Choose carefully and nurture successful business relationships.
- What territory does the rep cover? Keep in mind that after repeated sales, you should not try to sell directly to shops originally contacted by the rep. Such shops are still in the rep's territory and you would still be required to pay the rep the usual commission. Details such as this should appear in the written contract.

Craft trade journals such as *Craftrends & Sew Business* and *Craft and Needlework Age* offer an extensive list of manufacturers' representatives arranged by state in their annual directories each December. In addition to perusing craft journals, consider consulting the *Directory of Wholesale Reps for Craft Professionals*.

Resources

Directory of Wholesale Reps for Craft Professionals
Northwoods Trading Co.
13451 Essex Court
Eden Prairie, MN 55347

HIGHTOWERS (a leading rep organization)
1201 Lexington Ave., Suite 280
New York, NY 10028

Gwen Blakely Kinsler
4500 Pride Court
Rolling Meadows, IL 60008
Phone: (708) 776-7941   Fax: (708) 776-0507

FROM HOBBYIST TO NATIONAL CONVENTION ORGANIZER

Finding an unmet need and filling it propelled crocheter Gwen Blakely Kinsler from hobbyist to national and international status in only two short years. Most crafters enter the marketplace "by jumping on the bandwagon." For Gwen, there was no bandwagon. The lack of attention and respect given to her beloved craft—crocheting—disappointed her. "Why isn't crochet exhibited in museums and art galleries as consistently as other needle arts?" she lamented. "Why are there no groups, newsletters, or seminars devoted to crochet?"

Gwen's frustration grew as she attended fiber conventions and seminars hoping they would include crochet skills. Rarely did such groups address crochet in any form. Though she subscribed to various craft publications, few included crochet. Only a handful of magazines expressly devoted to crochet were on newsstands by 1992.

Gwen recognized her mission. Surely there were others like herself yearning for books, patterns, and crochet events. She wanted to meet like-minded enthusiasts like herself. But where were they?

She wrote a letter to the editor of a crafts magazine decrying the lack of recognition given to crochet. She invited others as passionate as herself to write her. The volume of mail overwhelmed her so "a newsletter was the only way I could respond," says Gwen.

Armed with only basic computer skills, Gwen devised her own bandwagon. "Chain Link, A Crochet Newsletter" was born in her home-based studio in January 1992 with 40 subscribers. Within two years the list grew to 650.

Enthusiasm and response to her newsletter grew with such intensity that Gwen reached further. Why not a national convention for crochet similar to those held for knitting, sewing, quilting, and a host of other fiber arts? None existed. Gwen filled the need with many enthusiasts, designers, and teachers helping her.

The First Annual Crochet Conference took place in August 1994 at De Paul University in Chicago. At that time, the Crochet Guild of America was founded with sixty-seven charter members.

Crafts Brief

Hours: Forty hours per week.

Best part of craft career: Gwen admits that doing what she loves and doing it from a home-office is her prime satisfaction.

Least favorite: The constant need to promote one's business and prove professional status.

Strengths: Fascination with crochet and good record-keeping skills.

Weaknesses: Allowed "stepchild" status of crochet to hinder promotion and follow-through, and impatience with those on whom she must depend.

Goals: Develop core organization for Crochet Guild of America.

Organizations: Society of Craft Designers, Association of Crafts and Creative Industries, The National Needlework Association.

Journals: *Craft & Needlework Age, Fiber Arts, Threads, Crochet Fantasy.*

Advice: Get involved in an organization, network, and share your interests with others.

CHAPTER 12

YOU AS ARTIST

Hobbyists usually begin creating to please the self. Experienced professionals often spend their time producing items with the greatest profit potential. Sooner or later, both groups face a common dilemma.

Should the potter make endless coffee mugs depicting the Golden Gate Bridge, for example, because customers always snatch them up at craft fairs? How many can one manufacture before the definition of "hand-crafted" becomes "handmade by assembly line"?

There are more questions to face as success grows. Am I prostituting my craft by overproducing a particular item just because it pays the bills? Will buyers hesitate if they see too many identical products? Might they conclude that the uniqueness of the item is compromised?

On the other hand, the artist within us frequently demands self-expression. If we use all our energy to work and never "play," frustration follows. "I work so hard, it seems I never have time to make what I want anymore," successful artisans lament. "I start feeling burned out when I feel like a production machine."

It takes discipline to keep working on a product that bores you. Must we personally like everything we create for sale? Does quality suffer when we push ourselves to work with colors or textures that we no longer find pleasing? When do we get to have fun?

These are weighty questions. While I do not presume to have all the answers, I have a few suggestions that may help you face this dilemma.

First, why must it be one way or the other? Craftspeople often conclude they must either mass produce sure-to-sell pieces or earn less if they take time out explore their medium. "How can I preserve my integrity as an artisan and maintain enthusiasm?" they wonder. Why not compromise and make room for both profit and nurturing the artist within? Faced with this conflict myself, I turned to my calendar for help.

Determine how many hours per month you work at your craft. Set aside a portion of total craft time to produce the items that pay the bills, say 75 or 80 percent, for example.

Reserve the remaining craft time to nurture your creativity. Many argue, "How can I justify setting aside so much time that does not bring in dollars?"

My answer? Look at the benefits you will reap by allocating time for research and experimentation. If you think of it as "wasting time," guilt and frustration may follow. To avoid feeling guilty or self-indulgent, I view creative craft time with the following in mind:

- It provides an opportunity to explore new design concepts.
- It provides a chance to experiment with new materials—to familiarize yourself with the latest products in your field.
- Time spent developing techniques for artistic growth is not unproductive simply because it does not directly generate income. It generates style, skill, expertise, proficiency, and facility. In short, it feeds your art.
- Time spent broadening one's skill results in improved quality for future sales.
- Playing with raw materials provides the opportunity for serendipity—a booster shot for your career.
- End guilt by telling yourself that you assigned this time to develop and nourish your artistic integrity. Think of it as maintenance time for your most valued machine—yourself.

Craftspeople may encounter another problem. How many of us find that after creating "special pieces," it is too painful to part with them? Again, compromise. If the artist knows that not everything created from the heart will be sold for dollars, the inner self will feel satisfied. When we guarantee that, occasionally, we will make an item for ourselves, we feel better. We find it easier to sell most items if we know we can keep a few favorites.

Crafting for profit does not mean you must ignore your own creative needs. Both aspects can live in harmony if each receives respect and its own scheduled time. Moderation in the creative process provides balance. Thus, we can avoid feeling too commercial, frivolous, self-indulgent, or worse, and ultimately fend off burnout.

Nourish Your Creativity

Do you believe creativity is learned or innate? Is one simply born with or without it? I believe strongly that not only can we learn it; we must study and develop our design ability. Creativity does not begin on paper, from a book or raw materials. It begins in the right side of the brain, which houses our creative self. Here is how I see the process.

First, the body relaxes so the mind can begin to visualize. The mind projects its ideas on a mental screen and begins the process of organizing images.

Next, you begin to make choices. Drop some ideas in favor of others. For example, ask yourself, "What do I want my hands to make?" You may reject choices such as pottery, chocolate cakes, and floral arrangements if you are fascinated by stained glass.

Continue to narrow your choices. "What will satisfy the creative urge?" the mind asks. One more wall hanging, a window, a sculpture?

The body may remain very still while the brain races along. Creating a new project requires artists to select from available design elements. Once the brain chooses a project, it continues questioning. Do I want a contemporary or traditional design? Have I ever seen anything like it before? Can I capture the colors I see in my garden flowers? In a rainbow? In the bricks and stones of a building? Do I want a romantic mood full of curves and diagonal lines or a classic design that emphasizes vertical, horizontal, and geometric shapes?

What style will I express? Victorian, casual, elegant, country? In short, the next phase of creativity is refining one's choices based on preferences and personal interpretation.

Finally, call upon your body. Hands need to feel textures and other materials you might use. Await just the right "feel" envisioned by the mind. Eyes examine color and proportion.

Artists begin to gather the materials that bring reality to what began as an abstraction. Many artists say the raw materials in hand can suggest the direction of the design.

When artists love their medium, when they are fascinated with its raw materials and possess a passion for the finished product—only then can materials lead one to create. The artist feels compelled to stretch the possible uses of available materials.

We may notice two colors that accidentally came to lie beside each other. Perhaps, we never considered combining them, but there they are, right before our eyes!

Creative minds, always prowling for new impressions, record the textures, lines, and colors the eyes see. Our brains grab ideas from everywhere and file them for future use.

Hands and mind eventually begin to work together. The mind, with its idea in place, commands the hands to begin. We begin to choose, cut, sand, solder.

The selection process continues as hands check with the real control—the creativity center in the brain. "Is this what I had in mind when I saw that garden, or was it this?" "Does this feel right or should I try something else?" As you add finishing touches, you begin to feel a sense of completion as you realize you have made something come into being that had not existed before.

Observe everything around you. Your mind will translate your experiences and impressions into your own art form. If you listen to your inner self, without fear of failure, creativity will come through. Not only that, with each creation, the artist within improves and matures. Next time, you will have even more to draw from with additional self-confidence thanks to your recently completed project.

Design Idea Binders

Before ending this chapter, a word about "designer's block." Magazine editors or customers may request a design idea—and you draw a blank. Other times, you may begin a project only to bog down in the middle, unable to continue. What can you do? Plan for such eventualities, for they are sure to come. Design Idea Binders are my solution.

Supply yourself with design ideas by continually feeding your Design Idea Binder. Start with a large three-ring binder. Fill it with plastic page protectors. Each time you peruse craft and other magazines, remain open to good design ideas. Don't limit yourself to pages featuring craft projects. And remember, copying others' work is not the goal.

Look for ideas that can serve as a springboard to stimulate and inspire original work. Tear sheets from magazines offer a plethora of ideas. For example, look for ads that combine colors in an unusual way. What are models wearing? Look not only at their clothing, but jewelry and accessories, too. Home decor magazines offer a wealth of ideas.

I once made a coat inspired by the floor tiles in a Middle Eastern mosque. The ad appeared in a travel magazine encouraging international vacations. As unlikely as it sounds, I also designed and knit a sweater motivated by a penknife advertisement! Shades of charcoal gray and maroon on a cream background inspired me. Colors from flowers in your garden can find themselves on your next jewelry project or quilt.

Looking through several of my Design Idea Binders, I found the following items:

- A scrap of beautiful wallpaper
- Greeting cards
- Yarn and fabric swatches
- A paper bag from a stationery store covered with butterflies
- Gift wrap
- A dozen postcards
- Tear sheets from garden and seed catalogs
- Photos of Tiffany glass
- Pictures of gardens and floral arrangements
- Tearsheets from an aquarium magazine filled with breath-taking fish and underwater flora and fauna
- Computer graphics and clip art

Collect and file such treasures in your binder as you find them. If an unexpected request for a new design leaves you momentarily at a loss, skim through your Design Idea Binder for a starting place.

Resources

Rico, Gabriele Lusser. 1983. *Writing the Natural Way.* Los Angeles: Tarcher Publications.

Sandra (Sandy) R. Wilson
A Ceramic Happening
1728 Silverwood Drive
San Jose, CA 95124
Phone: (408) 265-3519

FROM HOBBYIST TO DEDICATED DECORATIVE PAINTER

Sandy Wilson indulged her painting hobby for fourteen years. She knew herself to be a perfectionist and wanted to acquire all the artistic expertise she could muster before going professional.

Opening a ceramics business was Sandy's way of entering the professional crafting world. Sandy's husband, Chuck, had a full-time outside job but he devoted himself to her shop at every opportunity.

Both Wilsons spent eleven years developing the business. At that time, store employees began managing the store occasionally, granting the Wilsons their first respite during evenings and some weekends.

California's 1989 earthquake precipitated the Wilsons' decision to close the store and take their business home. Today, Sandy continues her crafting with more emphasis on decorative painting, less on ceramics.

"Creating original one-of-a-kinds takes most of my time," says Sandy. "I also design for magazines, which requires painstaking instruction writing." As time allows, Sandy also teaches and judges crafts. Recently, she added giving craft-product demonstrations to her busy schedule.

Crafts Brief

Business founded: 1979 by Charles and Sandra Wilson

Legal form of business: Partnership

Home-office? The Wilsons converted their garage to use as a classroom for students retained from her shop. Kilns and supplies line the walls. Sandy paints and designs in a separate studio converted from a spare bedroom.

Like many of her contemporaries, Sandy values her computer and copier. She describes her home as allocating more space to the business than to living quarters and looks forward to purchasing a larger house.

Hours: Flexible, but averages forty hours per week.

Daily routine: Sandy begins her day with correspondence, bookkeeping, and phone calls, followed by designing, painting, and embellishing ongoing projects. Though Sandy is the creative artist, Chuck often works with her on special designs. The Wilsons derive their income from sales to boutiques and gift shops followed by revenue from teaching classes and workshops.

Best part of craft career: Sandy says she enjoys the flexibility of her career the most.

Least favorite: Deadline pressures and inadequate payment for her creations at times discourage Sandy. Like many crafters, she finds consumers do not realize the time it takes to produce one-of-a-kind pieces.

Strengths: Creativity and artistic talent rank high with Sandy.

Weaknesses: Procrastination and lack of organization plague her.

Professional organizations: Sandy finds national organizations such as Hobby Industry of America and Society of Craft Designers invaluable to her career.

Professional journals: *Craftrends & Sew Business, Craft & Needlework Age,* and *Gifts & Accessories* magazine top Sandy's list.

Goals: Sandy looks forward to receiving recognition in her field from her peers and to having her family and friends recognize that full-time crafting is indeed a "real business."

Advice: Again, Sandy's advice dovetails that of many interview subjects. She strongly recommends crafters take both business and craft classes regularly and join professional associations. She feels it's important to maintain a deep love for one's work and to continually nurture one's creativity.

CHAPTER 13

YOU AS LEGAL ADVISER

*W*HEN STARTING YOUR own business, you find that there are many foms to fill out and permits to obtain. In every aspect from choosing a business name, to tax deductions, to insurance, you must now become your own legal adviser.

Fictitious Name Forms

A fictitious name is any other name for your business besides your full, legal name, first and last. Without filing a fictitious name form, you can be Mary Smith's Ceramics Studio. You *cannot* be Mary's Studio or Smith's studio. Unless you use *both* your first and last name in the official title of your business, you must file a fictitious name form with the County Clerk's Office in your county. Expect to pay a filing fee when you submit your application.

Check if the name you want is available, not in use by someone else in the same county. You may have the same name as a business in another county, but your name must be the only one in the county in which you live. To keep your business' name in force, you must refile every five years (this time period varies from state to state).

After filing, you must publish basic information about your business in a countywide newspaper in consecutive issues. County clerks call this an "Affidavit of Publication."

The public has a right to know who owns area businesses and where to find business owners.

Avoid choosing vague names that can cost name recognition. "Connie's Ceramics Corner" or "Pat's Florals" identify the nature of the business better than "Connie's Corner" or "Pat's Place," for example.

Business License

Cities charge a fee for permitting residents to generate an income within city limits. While a few cities across the country do not require home-based workers to file and pay for a city business license, most do. Call your city hall for information, since rates vary. Business licenses must be renewed every year.

Home-based business owners living outside of city limits generally do not have to purchase city business licenses. However, many local and county taxing agencies want to generate tax revenue from *all* home-based businesses. They see the proliferation of home-based businesses as a way to increase their coffers. Many now require you to pay for a county business license even if you live outside city limits. Check with local government offices to determine who must have a business license in your locale.

Home Occupation Use Permits

Each city sets the amount and conditions of this arbitrary fee, which is in addition to business license fees and zoning variances. Shopkeepers performing the same services or offering the same products do not have to pay this tax.

Many cities surprise new home-based business owners with an application for the Home Occupation Use Permit when they apply for a business license. The form outlines ten conditions of approval for the permit. Conditions are usually already covered by the city's business license statutes or zoning variances, yet home-based workers must still pay for the permit. These permits cost anywhere from $25 to $200.

Many experts agree that this tax offers a disincentive to the very workers who help decrease congested freeways and increase the tax base of their cities. Others call it double taxation. Call your city hall to learn about local regulations.

Zoning Variances

Most homes and housing developments within city limits have been zoned for residential use, while business districts are zoned for commercial use. When you conduct a business from your home, many cities require you to apply for a variance to alter the zoning. Expect to pay a one-time fee. Research carefully, as in some areas you will find that while it is easy to obtain a zoning variance, specific neighborhood associations and condominium regulations forbid home businesses. Call your city planning commission to learn the zoning status of your home and the cost of obtaining a variance.

Cities prefer that home businesses remain invisible so neighborhoods look and feel "residential." This means they want no smells, loud noises, or other visible signs that you conduct a business from your home. (Buzz-saw sounds and large truck deliveries are examples.) Your neighbors want assurance that your customers will not deprive them of parking spaces. Many cities will not permit you to have a sign in front of your home advertising your business. As your business' legal adviser, it's up to you to check with the city planning commission to learn about local regulations.

Home-Office Deduction

The IRS allows home-based workers to deduct a percentage of their rent or mortgage payments along with utilities. This is a valuable deduction, for it lowers the annual gross income on which you pay taxes. Remember, the most important aspect of this deduction is that the room or space you write off *must* be used *exclusively* for business. Remove all non-business furniture and personal items.

You may not simply clear off your family dining room table and expect a tax deduction. You may not use a home-office as a spare guest room or to store personal family possessions. Specific answers about home-office situations are best answered by the IRS or a qualified certified public accountant. Plan to follow IRS guidelines. Ask for Form 587 (Business Use of Your Home), from any IRS office.

If you *do* meet the criteria for deducting a portion of your home as a work space, determine the total square footage of the entire dwelling. You can obtain this information on mortgage papers, from your local planning commission, or from your property manager if you rent.

Next, determine the square footage of the space you use for your business. Measure the room carefully. Determine the percentage of the total square footage used for your work space—this is the amount you may deduct from your gross business income every year.

For example, my office and studio take up 22 percent of the total square footage of my home. I use the room exclusively for teaching, writing, designing, and storing student materials. Clients who consult with me meet me in my office regularly.

You will see nothing of a personal nature in my studio/ office. The room contains:

- A desk
- A large table and six chairs for students and clients
- A computer and three printers
- A fax machine
- A copy machine
- A blackboard
- A bulletin board displaying my business license, Seller's Permit, etc.
- Several large bookcases for books, magazines, and patterns

- A file cabinet
- A sewing machine used to demonstrate techniques

Next, take a look at your utility costs. Add together all your utility bills, except the telephone, for the year. Take the same percentage from this total as you did for the floor space. Keep utility receipts to verify these amounts in case you are audited.

Costs incurred while using a personal phone line to conduct a home business are not deductible. If you have only one phone, you can only deduct long-distance calls as a business expense—and they must be itemized and identified. If you install a second phone line for business use you can deduct 100 percent of the costs for installation, monthly charges, and an answering machine.

IRS Form 587 details what to do if you have more than one place of business, if you make home repairs or improvements associated with your business, or if you rent rather than own a home. You should not have any problems if your home is the *primary* location of your business, you spend most of your working hours there, and you use the space *exclusively* for business. In general, artists and craftspeople qualify to deduct for business use of their homes, but more specific questions should be answered by tax professionals.

Seller's Permits

If you want to purchase supplies at wholesale cost to sell at retail prices, you will need a Seller's Permit. This permit is available from any State Board of Equalization office. Chapter 10 gives detailed information about Seller's Permits and the differences between selling at wholesale and selling at retail.

Insurance

Operating a home-based business *may* alter your insurance needs. Make sure your homeowner's or renter's policy protects your business goods and equipment. Check to see if you have adequate liability to protect customers while they are in your home-office. Ask your agent about an umbrella policy as well.

Banking

You must have a separate bank account for your business. The IRS will not accept a business operating from a personal checking account. They call that practice "commingling of funds." If the IRS audits you, they may disallow legitimate deductions if you paid using checks from a personal account. Such a procedure forces you to pay penalties and interest if you cannot separate *business* deductions from *personal* ones. If you want all the deductions to which you are entitled, open a separate checking account. It need not be an expensive business account. A second personal account where you now bank will do. Avoid "cute" checks. Ask for plain bank-issue paper stock instead. Vendors and sales reps will take you more seriously.

Calling your second account your "business account" makes it so. Place the name of your business in the upper left-hand corner. Remember, monthly banking fees are deductible.

Along the same lines, do not use a personal bank credit card to make deductible business purchases. Secure a second card to use for business items only. While annual fees and interest rates are no longer deductible on personal credit cards, they *are* deductible for business expenses and purchases.

Resources

Brabec, Barbara. 1994. *Homemade Money*. Virginia: Betterway.

Muriel Spencer
715 Walnut Drive
Rio Dell, CA 95562
Phone: (707) 764-3721   Fax: (707) 764-2311

WATER COLORIST, CRAFT DESIGNER

Animals provide much of Muriel Spencer's creative inspiration. Cats, dogs, horses, rats, guinea pigs, ducks, chickens, goats, fish, lizards, and pheasants live in or nearby the Spencers' home. Portraits of animals Muriel paints continue to be popular with her customers. As a crafter, her stuffed animal patterns continue as the mainstay of her business.

Though she designs for many craft publications, manufacturers also seek Muriel's unique animal designs. Three dozen of her stuffed animal patterns comprise Spencer's Zoo, an important adjunct to her business.

Crafts Brief

Business founded: 1982

Legal form of business: Sole proprietorship

Home-office? Though Muriel began her business in one large room in her home, she admits her work overflows into a spare bedroom and even her kitchen. She describes her sewing machine and computer as being of greatest value to her but adds, "My copy machine and opaque projector run a close second."

Hours: Muriel credits self-discipline and taking her work seriously for her success. Today, we find her crafting three days per week, allowing nothing to interrupt her current creative project. She sets aside one full day for research and correspondence, working from forty to sixty hours weekly.

Daily routine: This busy artist begins her day with a walk among the redwoods each day. By 9 a.m., she begins crafting or painting, ending her day at 5:30. Like many of us, Muriel admits to eating as she works. Her husband does not help in the business, but does help with household and shopping chores.

Best part of craft career: She defines her work as "fun." She says, "I don't do the same thing repeatedly. Each new design is a part of me to share with others."

Least favorite: Muriel admits that ignoring housework in favor of working causes frustrating clutter.

Strengths: "I don't give up easily," says Muriel. "Each new day excites me as much as the last."

Weaknesses: Many artists and crafters agree with Muriel that the temptation to push oneself too far, too fast, causes stress. She also lists procrastinating about bookkeeping and paperwork as a continual battle.

Professional organizations: Muriel credits the Society of Craft Designers as her most important networking opportunity. She also belongs to the Representational Art League, the Fortuna Art Council, and the National Society of Decorative Painters.

Professional journals: *Craftrends & Sew Business* and *Craft & Needlework Age* inform her about the craft industry.

Goals: "I have reached my primary goal of working at what I love earning enough to attend national seminars frequently. Recently, I completed another goal when I qualified as a Professional Craft Demonstrator by the Hobby Industry of America. I plan to demonstrate craft products in shops and to concentrate on mass marketing my fiber art."

Advice: "I believe in maintaining both long- and short-term goals. Also, I advise enlisting the help of children still at home to include them in the business. Reward them with praise and special activities, taking care to place them above career demands. Learn to say 'no' when you need to. When you work at home, you must set limits with friends." Finally, Muriel advises, "Always keep growing. Persistence is the key to success."

CHAPTER 14

YOU AS FINANCIAL PLANNER

CREATIVITY MAY BE your most valuable asset when "crafting for dollars," but the IRS prefers you to stick to standard, business practices. Remember what you learned in Chapter 1 about proving a profit motive to the IRS? Begin with good bookkeeping. It proves that you are a professional and keeps your business running smoothly and profitably. Document deductible expenses and all income in your business ledger. Choose expensive systems or simple bookkeeping notebooks, sophisticated computer spreadsheets or bookkeeping "share ware" (free or lower-priced software you can download from the Internet). The style of your bookkeeping does not concern the IRS as much as the simple fact that records are kept.

Organize invoices and receipts to affirm expenses and income. Canceled checks alone do not satisfy IRS requirements. Request receipts and/or invoices for every business expense. Here is a simple system for beginners.

Use envelopes as bookmarks in an inexpensive double-entry notebook like EKONOMIC brand ($6 to $10 from stationery shops). Each time you buy anything for your business, enter the amount in the book and note the entry line where it appears. Write the page number and entry line from your notebook on the invoice itself. Place the invoice in an envelope bearing the same page number.

Each time you complete a page in your notebook, file the envelope containing the invoices that correspond to the notebook entries on that page. Start a new page with a new envelope. By the end of the year, you will have what the IRS calls "a paper trail." Should you ever face an audit with questions about a particular entry, find the envelope containing the receipts and invoices for that page. Thus prepared, you can substantiate expenses immediately.

What Is Deductible?

While it costs money to make money, all business expenses are deductible. Below, you will find a list of deductions common to crafters who are just starting out. Add to this list as your business grows:

- Office equipment and supplies
- Postage and freight charges
- Marketing and advertising expenses
- Licenses
- Taxes
- Insurance
- Improvements to your home-office or studio
- Photography costs
- Automobile mileage set by the IRS. Keep a notebook in your car. Note every trip to the post office, bank, wholesalers, and all other business-related errands.
- Visual aids, including materials to make samples, display items, and teaching aids. Deduct anything you use to market, advertise, and demonstrate your craft.
- Continuing education, including courses, workshops, and books you need to stay on top of your business. When traveling away from home to attend national seminars, document expenses *carefully.*
- Dues and subscriptions to professional groups, magazines, and journals
- Wages paid to anyone who works for you part- or full-time
- Fees paid to consultants, attorneys, tax preparers, or graphic artists

- Costs associated with installing a second phone line for business use, plus cost of an answering machine. (Remember, you may *not* deduct telephone costs if you do not install a business line.)

Me? A Bookkeeper?

Crafters just beginning their businesses often express distaste for bookkeeping. Considering how the brain operates, this is understandable. (See Chapter 1.) No matter how much you may prefer crafting to bookkeeping tasks, your position as a business owner demands that you make time for this critical activity. There is only one alternative—pay someone else to keep your books if you don't want to do it yourself.

Computers make the task easier. Quicken users take note: This excellent program is a single-entry system similar to the register in your checkbook. Businesses rely on double-entry formats. Instead, consider QuickBooks, also produced by Intuit Co. Though you must make time for the learning curve, this double-entry system will:

- Record income and expenses
- Show profit and loss information in seconds
- Pay your bills, write checks and invoices
- Balance your checkbook register against bank statements
- Produce graphs and charts to show profit, loss, and accounts past due

Merchant Credit-Card Status for Craftspeople

Obtaining merchant credit-card status from a bank can be arduous for home-based crafters. New and seasoned craft professionals expect it will be easy. They express surprise when they find it's not at all like applying for a business license or a Seller's Permit. Everyone agrees that giving customers the option to pay by credit card increases sales. Nonetheless, it seems few craftspeople can acquire Master-Card or Visa merchant accounts.

During the college classes I teach to prepare hobbyists to become professionals, I tell students that perhaps one in fifty of them *may* succeed in acquiring merchant credit-card accounts.

Recently, I invited our banker and the merchant sales representative for the San Francisco Bay Area to visit my class. Students asked them if I was unduly pessimistic stating so few would gain credit-card status from a bank. My guests replied that probably *none* of them would qualify! They share the banks' perspective below:

1. Banks prefer storefronts to home-based businesses.
2. They prefer clients with whom they have a long-term banking relationship.
3. Usually, you must be in business for at least one year before becoming eligible for a merchant credit card.
4. Credit managers want proven business and personal stability.
5. A craft business must be in compliance with local and state business regulations (licenses, Seller's Permits, zoning variances, etc.).
6. Collateral such as certificates of deposit or savings accounts are not considered by card-issuing banks in deciding whether to grant merchant status.
7. If you take the home-office deduction, a bank officer may come to your home to verify it.
8. If you want to apply for merchant credit status, prepare to provide your banker with many documents, such as:
   a. credit references from vendors and distributors.
   b. bank references from other banks.
   c. résumé.
   d. feasibility studies showing how you expect sales to increase if you offer your customers credit-card privileges.
   e. your average annual sales. You *must* document your figures with careful records and bookkeeping.
   f. copies of your fictitious name form, if applicable.

g. copies detailing the legal structure of your business, including:
   1.) partnership agreements.
   2.) articles of incorporation.
h. income tax returns as far back as three years.
i. copies of your business license and Seller's Permit.
j. brochures, catalogs, or advertising to prove you are in business.

Bankers need this information to protect their financial position. Disgruntled customers may charge back orders to the bank for up to seven years. Disputes and nonpayments by merchants who close their business become the bank's responsibility.

If you are granted merchant credit-card status, you may choose from several different credit-card authorization formats. The two used most often by small businesses are terminal systems and toll-free telephone numbers. Another method growing in popularity makes use of a program on your personal computer that reports directly to the bank via modem.

Terminal systems plug into a phone line to verify each customer's credit-card account at the point of sale. Touch-tone systems work differently. First, fill out an authorized sales slip for your customer. Then, pass it through your imprinting machine which bears a plate with your merchant number to identify your business. Next, dial the toll-free number your bank provides. A computerized voice asks you specific questions. You respond by pressing numbers on your touch-tone telephone. After providing all the information required, the voice will tell you whether the bank wishes to authorize the sale for that particular customer. If so, they provide an authorization number. Write this at the top of the sales slip.

Deposit sales slips to your business account with your regular banking transactions. At the end of the month, you will receive a monthly statement reflecting the sales posted to your account resulting from credit-card sales.

Remember that the bank will charge you a percentage of each sale. Amounts vary from 2 to 8 percent. If you must pay a higher percentage than you would like, you may negotiate after you establish a good record.

Keep your business account running smoothly. Never permit overdrafts on your business checking account. The amount of your credit-card sales and the way you handle the authorization process will be a factor in reducing the percentage you must pay later.

If, in spite of your best efforts, no bank will grant you merchant status, consider working with an Independent Sales Organization (ISO). These groups can secure merchant credit for you for a series of fees.

ISOs act as brokers, easing some of the frustration home-business owners inevitably feel when they are denied merchant credit. This may cost you more than a bank would charge, since ISO companies set fees for each service they provide. For example, you must pay for monthly bank statements, initiation fees, a fee for each check processed, and equipment rental. To assist your search for a reliable ISO, I have included the address for the National Association of Credit Card Merchants in the resources section at the end of this chapter.

Setting Prices

No perfect formula exists for setting prices for products and services, but here are some guidelines. Before deciding on a pricing system, look over your finances. Make sure you pay wholesale prices for everything you buy for resale. Are you paying the lowest possible prices for office equipment and supplies? Check out merchandise at discount stores, chain office supply stores, and mail-order houses.

Check to see if the vendors and wholesalers with whom you deal offer "2 percent 10 net 30." Translated, this means if you pay in ten days what you would have paid in thirty, you can take an additional 2 percent off your entire order.

Now, let's make sure we all define the following terms the same way.

Labor does *not* mean what you will accept to craft an object. It is equivalent to the value you place on the time it takes for you or someone else to make your item. Even if you don't plan to hire employees, what would you do if you became ill or needed to pay someone to help if you received a big order?

Build labor cost into your prices, but consider these questions: Do you want to work for less than minimum wage? Could you find workers who would work for you at minimum wage? Estimate labor costs to be higher than minimum wage.

Raw materials are the supplies required to manufacture your product. Wood, fabric, metal, and glass seem obvious. But don't overlook the small items such as glue, nails, pins, and paint.

Overhead refers to the nonproductive, incidental expenses not directly accountable to a particular part of the work or product. Examples: rent, utilities, postage, insurance, wear and tear on your equipment, travel, repairs, and maintenance.

Profit is the amount of money that remains after you pay expenses generated by making the product.

Crafters often use this standard formula to estimate price for a single item: Add up the figures for labor, raw materials, overhead, and profit. Double the amount to determine the wholesale cost. Triple it to arrive at the retail cost. Keep in mind, however, that the final deciding factor in price setting should be what your market will bear.

Residents of large cities may be willing to pay more for an object than citizens in small, rural towns. People will pay more for an item when they recognize an element of increased value—cotton over blends, for example, or glass over plastic. In short, it makes no difference *how* you arrive at your asking price if it is too high or too low for your market.

Here are nine different methods to help you set a price for one craft unit. Choose the one best suited to you, your product, and your market. You can combine elements from two or more methods.

1. Direct Material Costs
    The information in this sample worksheet is provided by the Small Business Administration (SBA). This method works when costs for materials and labor remain consistent. Take, for example, sewing work shirts. Let's assume you can make fifteen simple shirts per week and that raw materials total $76.25. Assume you want to earn $100 per week for your labor.
      Your direct material costs are $76.25 per week. Add the profit you want to make ($100) to the direct material costs ($76.25) and divide that by the number of shirts you make per week (15). The resulting cost per shirt is $11.75. The SBA calculated $59 per week for overhead. Divide the overhead ($59) by the number of shirts (15) and the result is $3.93 per shirt. This brings the total cost of each shirt to $15.68. Add to this $10 profit per shirt and the total is $25.68, or $26 rounded up, per shirt.

2. Direct Labor Costs
    This method focuses on labor. It works for crafts that are labor intensive but require very few or no raw materials. Take beaded earrings as an example. Seed beads and earring findings are inexpensive, but what if it takes three hours to make a pair of Bedouin earrings? You could charge $8 per hour and add $4 to the total for supplies for each pair. You would charge $28 per pair using this method.

3. Hourly Rate
    Setting a price this way works best when performing a service. Suppose you offer to re-string necklaces for your customers. You need no raw materials other than stringing cord. Time yourself to determine an hourly rate.

4. Markup Pricing
    This system works for pricing products rather than services. Let's say you make gift baskets. If the empty basket retails for $10 and you pay $6.50 for each one, the difference between $10 and $6.50 is $3.50, or 35 percent. You can add 35 percent to any size basket you plan to resell. Check the typical markup price of items in your industry.

Once you know the profit margin for the basket alone, you can use the same system to calculate the price to charge for each item placed inside.

5. Break-Even Point

Try this method when making similar or identical items. The break-even point comes when income equals expenses. Take Christmas tree ornaments as an example. Suppose you want to make a hundred ornaments to sell at a local craft show. Add up the cost of all raw materials you will use. You would need a hundred Styrofoam balls, plus ribbons, sequins, pins, glitter, beads, and glue.

Let's say the total comes to $300, including freight charges to ship the items to your studio. Selling each ornament for $12, you will break even after you sell twenty-five. Selling the remaining seventy-five would be all profit, including labor for all one hundred ornaments.

6. Percentage of Actual Costs

Building contractors often use this simple system. They add up the actual costs: labor, raw materials, and overhead. To this they add 15 percent for profit. Crafters who make objects requiring costly materials can make this system work to their advantage.

7. Profit System When Selling at Retail and Wholesale

I offer a true example of a hard-learned lesson in my craft business. Like many teaching crafters, I decided to self-publish instructional pattern booklets. Desktop publishing capabilities enabled me to produce them from my home-office. I calculated labor at $2 to produce a single sixteen-page copy. Raw materials totaled $1.50 for paper, plastic slide cover, and a color photo. Overhead came to $.50 Total cost to produce each booklet—$4.

Several other teachers in my network charged $6 to $8, but 1 charged $5, feeling satisfied with my first self-publishing effort in 1980. Searching diligently, I found a specialty magazine offering an ad rate I could afford. Readers ordered one or two booklets at a time. Smug satisfaction set in. The first two titles sold well, so I promptly added four more. What could go wrong?

I found out the first time a shop asked to buy multiple copies. The owner wanted to use my booklet designs for group classes. She wrote that she expected the usual quantity discount of 50 percent off the retail price. After all, she planned to resell them to her student-customers, didn't she?

Selling copies at 50 percent off would bring in only $2.50 per book—less than the cost to produce each one. Feeling like the novice I was, I realized that the more I sold, the more I would lose.

I had neglected to build in an element of profit in my pricing system. Recalculating my pricing structure, I came up with this: $2 labor plus $1.50 raw materials plus $.50 overhead plus $2 profit. The total of $6 became the new retail price.

Still, I owed the shop owner information about quantity buying. Bookshops nearby explained they usually paid $6 for every book they sold at $10, but, of course, they bought in large quantity. My solution? Method 8 below.

8. The Discount System

My "instant" discount schedule for quantity buyers read as follows: For 3 to 7 copies: 10 percent off; for 8 to 12: 15 percent; for 13 to 18: 20 percent; for 18 to 24: 25 percent; for 25 to 50: 30 percent; for 51 to 99: 35 percent; for more than 100: 40 percent.

Adjust these figures and percentages to suit your needs and product. I offer mine as a guideline. This schedule became a mainstay of my booklet mail-order business for many years. This way, when selling both at retail and wholesale, you will still earn a fair profit for each unit you sell. Though you make less than when you sell a single unit, you will make up the difference by selling in volume.

9. By the "Each"

Grocers use this term to sell, for example, a single can of soda rather than the whole six-pack. Why not crafters? You may find it easier and more practical to charge by each element consumed in producing your product or service.

Quilters in our area charge by the spool of quilting thread. Thus, when a client wants a quilt-top hand-quilted, the price depends on the amount of thread consumed. Large quilts with sparse hand quilting may cost the same as small wall hangings bearing profuse, close quilting. The concept is simple. It takes the same amount of time to make the same number of stitches, be they widely spaced or close together.

Knitters may adapt the concept by charging by skein of yarn. You will find it simple to calculate price no matter what size item the customer wants. Build in additional pricing elements based on the degree of difficulty of the knitting technique and you will find it easy to set a fair price. Consult the example below.

	Simple Patterns	Intermediate Patterns	Advanced Patterns
4-ounce skeins	$12	$13	$14

For a woman's sweater requiring seven skeins, you would charge $84, $91, or $98, depending on the difficulty of the knitting technique. Not enough? Adjust the price per skein for the market in your area.

Other crafters can use the same system for doing custom work. Consider charging: by the board foot, by the yard, by the page, by the inch, by the pound, by the head, or by the project.

Taxes

Realize you must pay taxes on your earnings. As a self-employed person, nothing is withheld from money you earn. You may need to pay your federal taxes in quarterly installments. Estimated taxes can be made on the current or past year's taxes. Make an appointment with your CPA to learn which system applies to you.

Ask also about paying self-employment taxes to replace Social Security taxes withheld by employers. The amount varies slightly from year to year. Since tax rates depend on the legal form of your business, whether or not you have an outside job, and whether you file a single or joint return, seek competent advice from a tax expert.

Many, but not all, states also levy state taxes based on your net income. Some cities and counties also impose an inventory tax based on inventory, equipment, and other business assets. Feeling overwhelmed? I can only think of one bright star concerning business-related expenses. All are deductible!

Get all the support and information regarding taxes— a most important issue. Start with the IRS. Visit your regional office or call them at (800) 829-3676. Request Publication 910, which lists free publications helpful to any business.

When it arrives, read it thoroughly. Call or write to order each additional publication you find of interest. Make sure your list includes the following:

334, Tax Guide for Small Businesses
463, Travel, Entertainment and Gift Expenses
505, Tax Withholding & Estimated Tax
533, Self-Employment Tax
535, Business Expenses
587, Business Use of Your Home
911, Tax Information for Direct Sellers
917, Business Use of a Car

Paying Yourself

Earning money working for yourself is why you work, isn't it? However, when people previously employed become self-employed, two extremes sometimes occur.

First, the ever-diligent worker plows every dollar earned back into growing the business. Perhaps necessary to get started, this practice should not last forever. Crafting for dollars means you must enjoy the benefits of earning money. Crafters tempted to reinvest every dollar earned risk the danger of losing their motivation.

On the other hand, I've met crafters starting their business who literally drain its income by writing paychecks for themselves that are out of proportion with their profits. Insufficient funds remain on hand to run the business properly. Both extremes can be avoided with a *written* but flexible budget.

Since most crafters start their business while employed elsewhere, they can afford to reinvest profits back into the business for a while. Once established, though, start to set a specific amount to pay yourself. Self-employed people call this "owner's draw."

When entering the amount you plan to pay yourself, take care not to list the amount as "salary," or it will appear to bookkeepers and auditors that you have employees. "Draw" is the word to list in your records.

How much should you pay yourself? Start with a percentage of your profit rather than a fixed amount of money. This way, you'll earn more when business is good, less when it slows. Think of it as being paid on commission.

Part-time crafters working less than ten hours per week could start by taking a draw of, say, 20 percent of profits, *not* of total income. Full-time crafters working forty hours or more might consider taking a draw of 50 percent of profits.

As your business grows and shows steady profit, adjust the percentage based upon the number of hours you work. If you follow sound business practices, working more means you should earn more, just as if you were working overtime for a company.

Follow good bookkeeping practices when paying yourself. Do not write a check for weekly groceries with a business check. Instead, write a check from your business account and deposit it into your personal account. List the check as a draw in your business ledger. Pay for your groceries with a personal check.

A word about borrowing money from your personal account to buoy business expenses: Resist the temptation to simply make a purchase for the business with a personal check. Instead, make a "loan" to your business. Write a personal check and deposit it into your business account. Then make your business purchase with a business check.

Later, when business improves, you can pay yourself back and keep your paper trail intact, making it easier for your accountant to balance your books. When you deposit personal funds into your business account, list the amount as "transfer of funds" in your business ledger.

Pay yourself back the same way. Write a business check and deposit it into your personal account. List this as "transfer of funds, repayment of business loan" in your business' account ledger.

Resources

For a copy of *How and Where to Get a MasterCard/Visa Merchant Account for Your Home-Based Business* ($19.95), write to:

The World Trading Co.
9505 East Vista
Hillsboro, MO 63050

For a list of approved ISOs, write to:

National Association of Credit Card Merchants
217 N. Seacrest Blvd.
Boynton Beach, FL 33425

Betty Auth
Auth-antic Designs
14719 Earlswood Drive
Houston, TX
Phone: (713) 879-0430   Fax: (713) 879-4310

From Store Manager to Doll Designer

Betty Auth credits her position as a craft shop manager to her practical education in crafts. "I organized and taught classes, conducted demonstrations, created store displays, and ordered merchandise for the store," Betty explains.

Dolls became Betty's passion: "Dolls are fun, allowing me to combine many craft techniques with my commercial art experience." Betty defines her niche in the marketplace when she states, "I show the average person how to make *easy* dolls."

An important decision gave focus to Betty's business. "I knew mass production was not for me. I don't want to make one item repeatedly. Patterns take more time to develop, but once done, you have repeat sales for a long time."

Attending the National Cloth Doll Maker's Convention gave Betty the validation she needed. Armed with a professionally prepared portfolio, she also displayed a dozen of her best creations. Preparation paid off. She sold several of her dolls from a booth sponsored by *Cloth Doll* magazine.

Betty chose the Houston Quilt Market as her next choice for exposure and to establish herself as a professional. Working as a volunteer in the doll-making booth, she broadened her knowledge while connecting with editors of doll publications.

Organizing her business required more effort for Betty than most. She did it while she and her family relocated from Texas to Louisiana, then after two years, back to Texas. She kept her notes together maintaining a business to do list amidst moving chores. She explains her system further: "I divided tasks into those which I needed to complete once I could get into a studio and those I could do anywhere." Like many crafters, Betty performs more than one task at a time.

She has diversified her craft business—a frequent decision made by successful crafters. In addition to designing, Betty produces her own kits, works on product development with manufacturers, performs craft demonstrations in shops, exhibits at fairs, and teaches classes and workshops.

Crafts Brief
Business founded: 1990

Legal form of business: Sole proprietorship

Home-office? Yes. Works from a detached studio, ten feet behind her home.

Hours: Works alone eight to ten hours per day.

Best part of craft career: The freedom to create, working with materials she loves.

Least favorite: "I love my finished projects, but writing detailed, precise instructions frustrates me at times."

Strengths: Unlimited imagination, curiosity, and natural artistic ability.

Weaknesses: Unlimited imagination, curiosity, and procrastination!

Daily Routine: Betty lists the important equipment in her studio: her computer, telephone, sewing machines, drafting and work table, file cabinets, sewing and painting supplies, and, in her own words, "Just about every craft book or magazine in print." Most home-based crafters both deride and cherish their isolation. Betty says her telephone provides human contact for "reality checks" as she works alone.

Professional organizations: Betty joined the Society of Craft Designers in 1992 after reading about other successful craft designers who are members.

Craft journals: "In addition to doll magazines, I read all the craft and needlework magazines from Victorian to country. I study those devoted to decorating, collecting, sewing, quilting, and antiques. I always read related trade journals to keep up with trends." Betty advises: "Read the ads as well as the articles."

Goals: "I want to write a book and expand my knowledge in the field."

Advice: "Explore everything until you find what will hold your interest over time. Next, read, read—study everything you can related to your interests. Take courses, hone your skills—then, dream big dreams."

CHAPTER 15

YOU AS LEGAL WATCHDOG

As a craft professional, the time will surely come when you wish to protect your ideas, original designs, text, names, logos, and instructions. By protect, I mean you may wish to prevent others from benefitting from what you create through your own hard work and research. The United States government offers its citizens many different avenues to protect what they refer to as "Intellectual Property."

Trademarks

A trademark is any name, symbol, figure, letter, word, or mark used by a manufacturer or merchant to distinguish a product from those manufactured or sold by others. If you want exclusive use of your name and/or logo, you must register it with the Patent and Trademark Office (PTO) in Washington, D.C. Service marks provide similar identification except they distinguish a service rather than a product.

Crafters interested in obtaining a trademark would be wise to study the most recent literature available free from the PTO. The Trademark Revision Act of November 1989 made substantial changes to former regulations.

Trademarks protect only a business name or logo. They do not protect ideas or products from being copied—patents or copyrights do.

You must pay a fee to register your trademark. You may hire a private search company or an attorney to determine if your trademark is available to you or if it is registered to someone else. Learning that your idea for a name/logo is open means you can proceed with registration. While the search is under way, however, you may choose to begin manufacturing your product. Signify this by placing the notice ™ in superscript to the right of your logo. When you receive your trademark, change the notice to ®, indicating the trademark is registered.

Many businesspeople pay attorneys to conduct searches. If you are thorough, why not do it yourself? Consider visiting the U.S. Depository Library (there is one in each state) to save attorney's fees and do your own research. Consult telephone directories under "trademark search services" or the local bar association for lists of attorneys specializing in trademark law if you want help.

Once it is granted, trademark protection lasts ten years. If you decide to renew to keep the trademark in force, you must pay an additional fee. You also have the option to secure a trademark within your state. For details, write to the Secretary of State's office in your state's capital.

Patents

Patents permit you to exclude others from making, selling, or profiting from your work for a given period of time. The PTO oversees registration, applications, and approval of patents. Few crafters require patent protection. However, if you devise a truly unique item or process, you will find the PTO offers abundant free literature.

Choose either a design or utilitarian patent. Stated simply, a design patent covers how the item looks (its design).

Utilitarian patents cover how an object works. Each protects your idea for fourteen or seventeen years, respectively.

Your item cannot simply be a variation of something protected by an existing patent. It must be a useful industrial or technical process, a machine, a manufactured item, or a composition of ideas.

Obtaining patents can be difficult, expensive, and time-consuming. Though a few brave souls manage the process on their own, most consult patent attorneys. Briefly, here are the steps involved:

1. Document proof of origin. Patent experts offer help.
2. Perform a search for prior known art.
3. Submit application forms and fees.
4. Await patent office review.

Licensing

Few craftspeople require trademarks or patents, but many want to acquire license from another source to enhance their original product with unique designs. Licensing describes a process where the owner of a copyright, trademark, or patent gives or sells permission to another to use, in part or whole, a protected work.

Textile painters, for example, cannot paint a Mickey Mouse or Snoopy character on a line of shirts for sale. Disney and Charles Schultz own their creations. They are not in the public domain for others to use. "But I've seen shirts featuring such cartoon characters," you say. "How do those artists do that?" Licensing is the answer.

Artists who freely design and sell such garments legally acquire license to do so from the copyright owners. Take Snoopy for example. Bed linen manufacturers have sold children's sheets for years depicting characters from the Schultz strip, "Peanuts."

To do this, the manufacturer contacts the owner of the copyright, in our example, Charles Schultz. Mr. Schultz may choose to grant license to the manufacturer for a fee agreeable to both parties. When you see cartoon, movie, or TV characters on commercial products, take into account that someone acquired *written* permission to use them.

Trademarks, advertisements, logos, and other intellectual property not in the public domain cannot be used by anyone without permission. Likenesses of living people such as movie and TV stars belong to these specific individuals. You cannot use event logos such as the five interlocked rings owned by the Olympic Games, either.

You may not take graphs or charts sold for cross-stitch and employ them in a different craft medium like knitting or rug hooking, for example. Using someone else's design as a foundation for your own does not constitute original design.

At times, copyright and trademark owners grant license to another without charging a fee. In such cases, they usually request acknowledgment of the original source placed prominently on your item or literature.

Licensing is a strong trend in the craft industry. People enjoy buying hand-crafted items bearing familiar and popular figures, trademarks, and names they love. If you want to enhance your craft design with the work of another, ask permission to avoid legal problems.

Trade Dress

This term describes the way a product is packaged, not the item itself. An example: toothpaste packaged in a pump rather than a tube. Shapes, colors, and styles becoming the trade dress of certain glue sticks in the craft glue gun industry is another example. Innovative ways to prepare or package a product for sale may require trade dress protection. Though not applicable to many crafters, look to the PTO for more information.

Copyright

Copyright protection is the proprietary right most often needed by crafters. It is also one many artisans unknowingly violate as well. Many excellent books cover the topic in detail. See the list at the end of this chapter.

Copyright laws perplex many people. Allow me to try to shed some light on copyright issues as they affect crafters. Let's go to the direct source: Copyright Law of the United States of America, Title 17, Section 102. "Copyright protection subsists in accordance with this title, in original works of authorship fixed in any tangible medium of expression . . . in the following categories: (1) Literary works . . . (5) Pictorial and graphic works. In no case does copyright protection for an original work of authorship extend to an idea, procedure, process, system, method of operation, principle or discovery . . ."

Copyright protection provides designers with a monopoly to benefit from their *original* ideas. The copyright owner *alone* has the right to make copies, reproduce or distribute the work, or prepare derivative works. Others must secure *written* permission before using all or part of another's copyrighted work.

How long does copyright protection last? *The Copyright Handbook* states, "Copyright work created after January 1, 1978, subsists from its creation and endures for a term consisting of the life of the author plus fifty years."

Crafters often want to know when a work enters public domain. They must determine when a copyright has expired, enabling them to use or copy a design freely. Without renewal, "Any copyright existing before January 1, 1978, shall endure for twenty-eight years from the date of registration," states the law.

Problems arise when determining copyright status *before* the 1978 law took effect. Works published at least twenty-eight but less than seventy-five years ago received protection for twenty-eight years *unless* the owner filed a renewal. Very few designers and magazines renewed copy-rights during this period. But if they did, they received an additional forty-seven-year renewal term.

Let's say you found an unusual sketch in a maga-zine published in 1963. Without renewal, it entered pub-lic domain in 1991, meaning anyone could use it at that time.

Check with the Library of Congress to learn whether a copyright renewal for a specific design is in effect. You can research yourself or, for $20 an hour, the Copyright Office will to do it for you. If you cannot determine whether or not a renewal exists, subtract seventy-five years from the current year to be absolutely safe. Anything copyrighted before that date has entered public domain.

How do traditional quilt patterns, for example the "Texas Star," "Dresden Plate," and others fit in? The designs themselves are public domain. Anyone can design a quilt based on these patterns that have been used for decades.

If you design an original quilt based upon "Dresden Plate," for example, you can copyright the quilt's design. You are not copyrighting "Dresden Plate," but rather how you used color, fabric, scale, overall measurements, and borders. Copyright protection also extends to your instruc-tions and template drawings for the quilt.

Exclusivity is not required with copyrights as with patents and trademarks. Thus, an artist may express her interpretation of a dolphin in oils on the East Coast while a West Coast crafter designs a nearly identical one and paints it on a shirt. Both may receive a copyright. Docu-ment original designs with sketches, drawings, and samples. Better still, take a series of photos to show the evolution of the project-in-progress.

You cannot copyright a design simply because you have conceived it in your mind. But the moment you put draw-ings, graphs, instructions, etc., on paper—"a tangible medium," according to copyright law—copyright protec-tion begins. Even without registration, you have common-law copyright protection.

Placing the copyright symbol on your project instructions, however, is not the same as registering the copyright with the Library of Congress. Since 1978, a work is copyrighted from the moment you put it on paper. Using the copyright symbol © without registration announces your intention to claim the work as yours, preventing it from becoming public domain.

Common-law copyright does serve a purpose, however. It protects your design while it goes through the process of being published in a magazine, for example. Upon publication, the publisher copyrights the entire contents of the magazine as a compilation, including your contribution. Unless you sell your rights, the rights to your article return to you after publication.

Registering a copyright costs $20. Why not save money? Merely seal the originals in an envelope, mail them to yourself, and file the unopened contents in the event of future infringement lawsuits. Many people believe this "clever" idea protects them while saving the registration fee. Lawyers and judges tell us, however, that sealed envelopes, too easily tampered with, have no legal position in court if there is trouble. **To protect your work, pay the fee and register the copyright.**

Registration is a prerequisite to infringement suits. You cannot defend a copyright without registering it first. If someone copies your new booklet of angel woodcuts and you never registered it formally, you must delay proceedings while you register. You must pay extra fees to expedite registration. You will find limits on the amount you can collect even if you prove the design is yours.

Copyrighted designs do not become yours if you make a certain percentage of changes. Though many crafters believe this to be true, it is not. The copyright law states that modifying someone else's design is "preparing a derivative work." Changing colors, fabric, and other details is not creating an original work.

If you alter an existing design, remember, the craft world has an extensive network. Members report violations

to one another regularly. If the owner of an original copyrighted design sees your imitation and takes legal action
against you, you must defend the similarities in court. If a
judge finds that a design uses a "substantial part of a copyrighted design," the copier is in violation of copyright laws.
Fines soar to $25,000 and can include large legal fees.

"Fair use" means you may use the work of another
without written permission within certain parameters. Take
care here. Limitations and conditions exist to protect
copyright holders. Here are examples of allowable "fair
use" situations:

- Book reviewers can reproduce certain specified portions of
  a work for review purposes.
- Teachers may make copies of patterns for educational use
  in *nonprofit* settings. Thus, a painting instructor may make
  copies from a current magazine explaining a brush technique for each student in her high school class. The same
  teacher may not use the same reprint to teach the project
  in a local shop or seminar. Why not? These are for-profit
  settings (Section 107, copyright law).
- You may not make copies of directions for a woodworking
  project from a magazine and distribute them to members
  of your church. When groups or individuals photocopy the
  work of others and distribute them, even for nonprofit purposes, they deprive the legal owner of profiting from his
  or her design.
- Purchasers of commercial patterns expect to re-create designs according to copyrighted instructions. This is "fair
  use." You can make a dress from a sewing pattern to keep
  yourself and one to give as a gift. However, if you attempt to
  profit from the design, mass produce the dress for sale in
  nearby shops, you would surely hear from the pattern company in time. They have the right to seek an injunction to
  stop further production and force you to turn over profits
  that are legally theirs.

Resources

Choose the appropriate copyright form. The Copyright
Office (address below) will send them at no cost along with
instructions on how to fill them out.

- **Form TX** covers literary works. This includes patterns, instructions, template drawings, articles, and books.
- **Form VA** (Visual Arts) protects creations such as statues, wall hangings, framed pictures, etc. The Copyright Office requires photos of your designs.
- **Form GR** (Group Registration) is best to copyright a line of similar items. Greeting cards, a series of etchings, a line of T-shirts are examples. Form GR permits you to register similar works with one copyright for a single fee.

The handbook from the Library of Congress, *Copyright Law of the U.S.*, is the definitive source of copyright information. Write to:

The Library of Congress
U.S. Copyright Office
Washington, D.C. 20559

For patent information, application forms, and free literature contact:

The U.S. Department of Commerce
Patent and Trademark Office
Washington, D.C. 20031
(Make sure to request the free booklet "Basic Facts About Trademarks.")

BOOKS

Blue, Martha. 1988. *Making It Legal.* Flagstaff: Northland Publishing.

DuBoff, Leonard. 1993. *Law in Plain English for Professional Arts & Craftspeople.* Colorado: Interweave Press.

Fishman, Stephen. 1992. *The Copyright Handbook: How to Protect and Use Written Words.* Berkeley: Nolo Press.

Pressman, David. 1995. *Patent It Yourself.* Berkeley: Nolo Press.

CHAPTER 16

YOU AS MARKETING AGENT

BUYERS WHO ARE most likely to show an interest in your product or service make up your target market. Since the product that appeals to everyone does not yet exist, the challenge of marketing lies in identifying the people who are most likely to want your product.

Targeting your market correctly reduces the time and money you spend on advertising. Rather than paying to reach everyone—even the least likely buyers—target marketing enables you to focus your efforts on those who have shown an interest in your product and can afford it.

Advertising works most efficiently if you send the right message to the right people, choosing the appropriate media. To accomplish this, learn all you can about your target buyers *before* attempting to reach them. Marketing is *not* synonymous with selling. Think of marketing as an active process by which a business develops strategy to sell. Whether your business is product, service, or both, it depends on market positioning. Your position in the market is established by the way customers perceive your business and product and how they compare to the competition.

Consider the three marketing myths below. New businesspeople often believe them.

- This product is so good, it will sell itself! (It can't.)
- Everyone will want this. (Some will. Some won't.)
- People will stand in line to buy this. (Not without marketing.)

Before you advertise, study these basic marketing goals:

1. Establish a memorable element about yourself, product, or service that will set you apart in the busy marketplace.
2. Define your marketing niche by selecting the specialty area you wish to serve. National toy companies, for example, can manufacture a complete line of dolls to fulfill every little girl's dream. Individual doll makers must specialize. Choose between comical or beautiful, porcelain or cloth faces, large or small, whimsical or glamorous. You can't make a doll to fill every need. What style suits your skill? What element makes your dolls distinctive and unique? Most important, what do you do best?
3. Select the publication read by your target market. Here's my favorite tip: Read the current edition of *Writer's Market.* Updated each year, this book reviews every magazine published in America, its focus, and its readership. Write to those of greatest interest. Request a media kit prepared by the magazine for its advertisers. You will learn even more about the magazine's target market and typical reader.
4. Remember, to succeed you must sell what people want to buy, not merely what you wish to sell. You can take fullest advantage of selling opportunities if you can develop the mind-set of your consumers. Learn what they want and why they want it.
5. Ask yourself if your business is product-driven or market-driven. Product-driven companies assume sales are assured by having the best product or service in a particular category. Owners of such companies rely on in-house experts to identify and select the best features, quality materials, and best production techniques. When confronted with market changes, product-driven companies simply add more features, increase quality, or introduce another model, believing this to be the only solution.

   Market-driven companies place more importance on what customers want. When business lags, they quickly

determine how the market has changed. They make
changes based on marketing information and rush to satisfy demand as opposed to remaining focused on their
own product exclusively. How will you react to future marketing changes? Will you simply alter your product or
study the marketplace?

Below you will find an outline you can use to begin your
Marketing Plan. What? Another plan? Successful businesspeople either draft a separate Marketing Plan or include it
in their Business Plan. You can pay a marketing consultant
to write your plan or do it yourself. Begin by answering the
following questions:

I.   Describe your business. (List specifics.)
       A. What image do you want to project?
       B. How will you convey your business image?
       C. How do you wish customers to perceive your
           business?
II.   What do you want to sell?
III.   Does a strong trend or demand currently exist
       for your product/service?
IV.   Does your product relate to the needs and wants
       of the external marketplace?
V.   Is your product a fad or is it something that
       will endure?
       A. If it is a fad, can you move fast enough to be
           profitable?
       B. If it is durable, how long has it been in de-
           mand? Is interest waning?
VI.   Why do you think your product/service will sell?
VII.   Can you explain the principal benefits of your
       product? How can you prove they are real?
VIII. What do you know about the demand of your
       product/service?
IX.   Learn about your potential customers. Who
       are they?
       A. Gender: Is it important?

B. Age: What age group would have greater interest in your product? Children, young adults, middle-aged adults, seniors?

C. Education: Does your product require users to have special skills?

D. Marital status: Does this matter?

E. Job: In what field is your target customer most likely to work? Is he or she a professional, a tradesperson, an administrator?

F. Health status: Healthy, average, or ailing? Markets for those with physical limitations have grown recently. Can your product reach them?

G. Income: Must your customers be affluent to afford your product? What of those with modest incomes?

H. Do you understand the "yuppie" market? Here are the basics:
    1. They were born between 1945 and 1965.
    2. They number more than 79 million.
    3. They entered middle age in the '90s.
    4. They have more discernible income and buying power than other groups.
    5. Do you know their current buying habits?

I. Where will you find your customers?

J. What magazines and newspapers do they read?

K. Do organizations exist for their special interests? Do they attend regular meetings and seminars?

L. Do those interested in your product subscribe to trade journals? Which ones?

M. Do newsletters and journals exist to inform your target customers about available products? Make it your business to find and read these yourself.

X. How will you reach your target customer?

A. Trade journals

    B. Consumer publications

    C. Direct mail

    D. Telephone directory

    E. Television/radio

    F. Promotional programs

XI. What about the competition?

    A. Where are they located?

    B. How is your product/service better?

    C. What do they offer customers that you do not?

    D. Where do they advertise?

    E. How have they positioned themselves in the marketplace?

    F. Where else can consumers buy your product? Mail order? Retail? Wholesale? Out of region, area, or country?

    G. If no competition exists—why not? (This may suggest your product line idea is not sound.)

    H. How much does your competition charge?

    I. What kind of customers do they have?

    J. Which vendors, distributors, wholesalers serve them?

XII. Examine the external marketplace.

    A. Is the market for your product/service likely to expand or diminish?

    B. Do you have a reliable source for raw materials?

    C. Is your product/service tied to other similar products or services for which the market could expand or collapse very quickly?

    D. Does your entry into the marketplace depend more on price or quality?

Marketing never ends. It is a continual process of evaluating what works and what doesn't. Mail-order businesses continually test their markets. For example, they may send out brochures with two different messages to see which gathers the most response. They may advertise identically throughout the year to see which months generate the most sales. The ultimate way to learn what consumers want is to ask them. Hordes of telemarketers badger consumers to gain firsthand information. Questionnaires and requests for information appear on the warranty cards for all kinds of products. Everyone seems interested in consumer opinion.

Benefits

All products and services must promise (and deliver) a benefit to the buyer. Even a subtle message encourages customers to buy. Consider the following, and ask yourself, what benefit does my product offer?

Convenience sells fast food.
Sex appeal sells cosmetics.
Ego and status sell luxury items.
Financial security sells life insurance and investments.
Health concerns sell vitamins and exercise equipment.
Personal fulfillment sells recreational and hobby items.

Your Marketing Plan

Yes, you really do need a Marketing Plan. A formal Marketing Plan should:

- Be written
- Be updated annually
- Always consider the external marketplace
- Have defined objectives
- Define strategies
- Provide a timetable for implementation
- Be easy to understand
- Be clear and precise
- Include goals that are practical and realistic
- Be flexible and adaptable to change
- Be as complete as possible

A practical marketing theory divides every product and service into three camps. All products or services are the fastest, the cheapest, or the best. Let's take pizza, one of America's favorite foods, to explore this simple but accurate idea. Study the pizza ads in your telephone directory and on TV.

Domino's has long based its advertising on fast deliveries. Remember those promises offering free pizzas if they were not delivered within thirty minutes?

Elegant Italian restaurants boast the best, most authentic, and widest variety of pizza. They don't promise speed or the lowest prices.

Several food manufacturers brag about the convenience of having frozen pizzas waiting for you in your freezer. They emphasize low prices and instant gratification.

How clever of 7-Up, "the uncola," to use negative positioning to avoid competing with its two prime competitors, Coke and Pepsi. What stationery cares enough to send the very best? What brand of peanut butter do choosy mothers choose? You know the answers—thanks to years of market positioning of these products.

Now, it's up to you. What special niche can you create for your product? Do you want your customers to perceive your business as the fastest, the cheapest, or the best? Your answers will enrich your Marketing Plan.

Marketing Resources

When developing a Marketing Plan, research is vital, but not knowing where to start can make the task seem more daunting. *Finding Facts Fast* by Alden Todd tops my list of favorite resources. Begin with this thorough little book when doing research for any purpose.

Here are some other helpful resources:

Title: *Standard Rate and Data Service*
Where to find it: public library.
What it is: a quarterly listing of TV and radio stations, newspapers, magazines, and trade and business publications

organized alphabetically and by category. Also lists owner's name, address, dates of publication, advertising rates, size, deadlines, and cost of advertising space and display ads.

Title: *The Reader's Guide to Periodic Literature*
Where to find it: public library.
What it is: a listing of published articles by topic.

Title: *The Cumulative Book Index*
Where to find it: public library.
What it is: a listing of books published by subject.

Title: *The Industrial Index*
Where to find it: public library.
What it is: a listing by subject matter of articles published in trade journals. Such journals have limited readership, but because they are so specialized, you will find they contain valuable information.

Title: *The Encyclopedia of Associations*
Where to find it: public library.
What it is: a listing of clubs, societies, and business and trade organizations with a common interest, updated biennially.

Title: *Thomas' Register of American Manufacturers*
Where to find it: public library or bookstore.
What it is: a large set of books listing products and manufacturers including trademarked names. You may purchase your own books or refer to the recently published version on CD-ROM.

Title: *Guide to American Directories*
Where to find it: public library.
What it is: lists of directories in specific industries.

Title: *Ayers Directory of Newspapers and Periodicals*
Where to find it: public library or bookstore.
What it is: a geographical listing of magazines and newspapers printed in the United States. Frequently used by mail-order firms.

Trade Associations

Nearly every trade has an association to educate and serve its members. So does crafts. Crafters who take their profession seriously know the value of belonging to such groups. Here are two of the best.

THE SOCIETY OF CRAFT DESIGNERS (SCD)

From the SCD brochure, here are some clearly stated benefits for all crafters.

- Educational seminars held every June in a major American city
- An informative newsletter with practical tips on improving your business
- A referral service used by manufacturers and publishers seeking qualified designers in specific areas of expertise
- Scholarship opportunities to aid those interested in converting a specific craft hobby into a profitable career
- A register of craft designers
- A listing of manufacturers interested in supporting individual craft designers with complimentary products and endorsement fee programs
- An excellent reference library covering important areas such as copyright law, contracts, taxes, insurance, health hazards, photography, portfolio preparation, and instruction writing
- Networking opportunities for designers

SCD maintains a referral system within the crafts industry to bring designers to the attention of manufacturers, publishers, and editors.

SCD mentors volunteer their time to assist and support new craft designers. Volunteers field questions, provide information, advise, and provide important contacts.

Designer's Showcase is yet another important opportunity SCD provides for crafters. During each Summer

Seminar, designers set up displays to showcase their work. In addition to the designers who attend the seminar, manufacturers, magazine editors, and publishers scrutinize it closely.

Portfolios and contact information from each designer are readily available to those seeking to purchase designs, hire designers, or request commission pieces for publication. One cannot underestimate the importance of such exposure.

Especially helpful to all designers is information offered by manufacturers. Every Summer Seminar features opportunities to see and learn about new products. Hands-on demonstrations put unfamiliar products in the hands of designers who might not otherwise try them.

Lectures by magazine editors describing designs they need and look for always prove invaluable to members. Why complete a project only to find it has no market value? Why not design and complete a project with its profitability clear in your mind? Working on an assignment to satisfy the specific needs of a publisher or manufacturer may not guarantee a sale, but it will go a long way toward encouraging profit.

In 1994, SCD instituted a new course called the Certified Craft Designer Program. Interested persons may study and prepare for an exam by mail. Final exams administered by SCD take place at each national seminar. The designation "CCD" announces to the craft world that you have succeeded in meeting high professional standards in your chosen field.

Whether you need tax information, help preparing a professional portfolio, or advice on how to write instructions to sell your designs, SCD helps you achieve your career goals.

The membership fee is $100 annually. Write to: The Society of Craft Designers, 6175 Barfield Road, Suite 220, Atlanta, GA 30328. Phone (404) 252-2454 for additional information.

HOBBY INDUSTRY ASSOCIATION

"If crafts and hobbies are your business . . . Hobby Industry Association (HIA) is the association with the tools and connections you need!" So states the HIA brochure. Slogans such as this often prove themselves to be overstated, but in the case of HIA, they most certainly are not.

Crafts may be a hobby for millions of consumers, but for those of us who choose it as a business, HIA has much to offer. Permit me to introduce this valuable association by answering three basic questions: What, exactly, *is* HIA? What does it do? What can membership do for you?

What Is HIA?

The Hobby Industry Association is the largest craft organization in the *world*. Yes, after HIA's successful European craft show in March 1995, "world" is the operative word. HIA is an organization of thirty-six hundred companies that support the craft industry. The list includes:

- Manufacturers
- Wholesalers
- Manufacturer representatives
- Trade and consumer publishers
- Independent and chain store retailers
- Professional craft producers
- Service suppliers

Freelance teachers and designers are part of the strong subgroup of service suppliers, which now boasts its own national newsletter.

What Does HIA Do?

This well-organized, efficient organization serves professionals in every aspect of the craft business. HIA educates, informs, supports, and points its members toward success. Professional training programs continue as HIA's prime service. Here is a list of programs HIA offers.

Certified Professional Demonstrator Training Program This training system trains craft experts in every specialty to give polished product demonstrations. Whether in small shops, a TV studio, or during a national convention, you can learn how to get paid to showcase products you use. After receiving your certification, your name will appear in the HIA Registry as a Professional Demonstrator. Manufacturers have confidence that HIA-trained demonstrators will show their product effectively. They will hire you directly as they prepare to promote a specific product. Many demonstrators establish permanent business relationships with specific manufacturers, representing them often throughout the year. Why not consider developing an ongoing liaison with the supplier of your favorite products?

Certified Teacher Training Program One of HIA's newest training programs, this course teaches you how to teach craft classes from your home-studio, neighborhood shops, or at regional and national conventions and seminars. Again, once certified, your name will appear in the HIA Registry providing credibility, reassuring those who hire you of your qualifications.

Product Workshops This wonderful program encourages manufacturers to offer hundreds of hands-on workshops to its membership. From brief "make and takes" to in-depth classes, members learn how to use the very latest craft products to their advantage. Manufacturers and their staffs—experts in the products they've developed—show you how to use them.

Continuing Education HIA sponsors continuing business classes to help retailers become more knowledgeable. Many crafters in business for the first time often slip up here. They often think technical knowledge is all they need to succeed, often overlooking basic business skills. HIA's prime goal is to help every craft professional become more profitable.

Market Research Every two years, HIA publishes its "Nationwide Consumer Study." This extensive, detailed survey provides an up-to-the-minute comprehensive overview of the craft world. The current size and makeup of our billion-dollar industry is always of intense interest. Review the latest data for 1995 in Chapter 1.

Membership Benefits for You

Attending the convention means you can see the very latest in craft supplies. You will also have hands-on opportunities to sample and receive new products and see how they work. Here's more:

- Learn to anticipate trends in style, color, selection, and design.
- Choose the training program which appeals to you and help increase your income.
- If you are already in business, HIA's annual survey will help you make decisions about how and where to advertise.
- If you sell or manufacture craft items or literature, you will be in touch with what consumers want and what they are currently buying.
- Teachers can plan classes around consumers' preferences and promote topics and techniques in a timely manner.
- Designers! Here's one of my favorites: During each convention you can attend panel discussions. Listen to editors of premier craft magazines tell you "what's hot and what's not."

The Best Part: The Annual Trade Show

Should you take me up on my suggestion that you attend HIA's annual trade show each January, a word of warning. Learning that more than twenty-two hundred booths fill the convention hall can overwhelm a first-timer. Not to worry, HIA thinks of everything.

Located in the lobby, you will find computer kiosks. Take courage and approach one of these. With the push of a button you can select one or more categories that you find of prime interest. In minutes, you receive a printout listing the locations of booths that fit with the category you selected.

Manufacturers, sales representatives, and company staff members are generous with information and product samples. To summarize in one sentence: HIA is so sure you will find their annual show worthwhile, they invite all craft professionals to attend even if they are not HIA members! For membership and other information, write to: Hobby Industry Association of America, 319 East 54th St., Elmwood Park, NJ 07407.

Networking

Expanding your personal network of business contacts is critical to your success. Though you may prefer to work in solitude, you cannot succeed in business alone. Yes, crafters keep busy, but doesn't everyone? Artisans sometimes avoid social contacts, saying that it takes too much time and effort. Fresh business contacts, however, become valuable sources of new information, ideas, and additional contacts.

Many artisans recognize the importance of developing a craft network, but you should not overlook other opportunities. Connect with non-crafters and other small-business owners to refresh yourself and your ideas. Becoming visible in your community bolsters confidence, increases market potential, and provides continuing stimulation. Here's how:

1. Visit your Chamber of Commerce and obtain a list of local organizations.
2. Check off at least five that sound interesting. Attend a meeting or two of each group.
3. Select one or two favorites and join! Participate! Always attend events with a pocketful of your business cards. Promote yourself, but be attentive to others. Ask questions. Share your expertise by giving short talks or demonstrations or displaying your work. Above all, *listen.*
4. After a while, begin the process again. Choose another organization and become involved with its activities and members.

Does this sound as if you're creating your own little world? You are. It's called networking.

Your Professional Statement: Your Portfolio

"Portfolio" is *not* synonymous with "scrapbook." Show your professional acumen. Purchase a proper zippered portfolio in a stationery or art supply shop. Portfolios should contain plastic pages to position documents, photographs, tear sheets, and published clips of your work. They are available in very few dark, conservative colors in up to six sizes.

Avoid a photo-album or scrapbook look. Allow plenty of space around individual documents to avoid overcrowding. Do *not* cut up photographs to make a collage. Do *not* add batting, lace, and a ruffle to a scholastic binder and call this a portfolio. This still shouts "scrapbook" Below, you will find a list of items that should appear in your portfolio and a description of each item.

Your business card Professional portfolios provide a window on the inside cover to place your business card. Take care that your business card projects a professional image as opposed to "cute" cards not taken seriously by those who peruse your portfolio.

Your card should only include your business' name, your name (if different), your address, and your telephone/fax numbers. You may include your logo, but place other information elsewhere.

Your brochure Tri-fold brochures are simple and effective. Take an 8½-by-11-inch sheet of paper. Fold it in thirds. Now you have six small panels in which to organize your information. Your name, business name, address, phone number, fax number and e-mail address should appear on the cover. Inside, describe your style, products, and services. You may extend information to the back panels. If you wish, you may reserve the center back panel for the name and address of recipients to whom you can mail the brochure without an envelope. Select heavier stock than 20-pound bond paper for brochures.

A short biography Limit your "bio" sheet to one page. Ideally, you should use your letterhead stationery to create a well-written statement about yourself. Mention when you began crafting, followed by details about when and where you became a professional. End with your recent achievements. Take time to write this document. Professional writers rewrite many times to choose the perfect words. Your bio should provide readers with a brief description about you.

Your résumé Your résumé should follow traditional guidelines. Students in my small-business classes who are learn-

ing how to start a craft business often ask, "I am just starting my business. I don't have much to list in a résumé.
What can I do?"

I tell them to list their education, past work records, and
crafting and professional experience they've had so far.
Readers of your résumé also consider as background information other positions you've held. For example, the first
time I used a résumé to apply for a position as a knitting
instructor, I had not taught that subject before. However,
my résumé listed my other teaching experiences in
church, for 4-H, and craft classes other than knitting. I got
the job.

A professional "head shot"   Choose a professional photog-
rapher to take a head shot of you. Polaroids and fuzzy
snapshots do not project the image you want. The pho-
tographer you choose will take a series of pictures presenting you as a business professional. Head shots feature only
your head, face, and shoulders. You will have plenty of
opportunity later to include snapshots of your work.

Your Mission Statement   I like to see one-page Mission Statements written on a sheet of business letterhead. Mission
Statements explain, in your own words, what you do, how
you do it, and why you care about it. Let your passion for
your work shine through.

Tear sheets of published articles and/or designs   Tear sheets
of published articles and/or designs form important contributions to your professional portfolio. Those entering
the field lament that they are as yet unpublished. Don't
despair—this may come in time.

I suggest to those just beginning their career to consider
writing a letter to the editor of a magazine or newspaper.
You also might write articles for newsletters of local craft
groups or fraternal organizations. Though you will not receive payment for these, copies of such writings can get you
started on the road to professional credibility.

Each time established crafters write for publication, they
receive one or more complimentary issues of the magazine
or newspaper in which the work appeared. Trim ragged
edges. Cut away ads or text other than your own. Place in
a plastic page cover. Remember to cut out the name, date,
and issue of the publication and place it above your article.

Magazine covers featuring your work Having your work featured on a magazine cover is most desirable, though not all professionals reach this level. However, if you do, remove the staples from the magazine's binding and include the entire front and back cover in your portfolio. Discard any pages other than those featuring your article inside. Place the magazine covers with your article tucked inside prominently on a separate portfolio page.

Occasionally, a magazine will feature many craft items on the cover of their publication, yours among them. Do not circle your project with a felt-tipped pen. Do not draw an arrow from your item to the page margin adding, "This is mine."

To maintain a professional image, use a paste-on arrow leading from the item to the margin. You may buy copyright-free clip-art books for less than $4 that contain borders, logos, and arrows. Photocopy these and cut them out. Paste them on the magazine cover to point out your contribution.

I usually use a computer-generated arrow featuring heavy bold lines as a border. Before cutting it out and pasting it on the magazine cover, I write a short sentence describing my item on the arrow itself, between its thick borders.

Clips of articles written about you by others Clips of articles written about you are always impressive. Again, include not only the article itself, but the publication's name, date, and issue number. You may find it difficult to "blow your own horn" and write about yourself and your work. Take every possible opportunity to have a professional writer write about you. Though they rarely pay you, the ensuing publicity adds credibility to your professional status. Why settle for a small classified ad if someone else can consume a magazine page or more describing your contribution to the craft world?

I enjoy writing profile or interview articles about others. Generally, I invite their participation after observing them at workshops, exhibits, or other professional events. Read *The Craft of Interviewing* by John Brady or *Conducting Interviews* by Michael Schumacher if you would like to interview others and write about them.

You should create and maintain a personal portfolio. Include articles you've written about others and articles that others have written about you.

Quality snapshots of completed craft projects Quality snapshots of completed projects form the heart of your portfolio. Show them in a variety of styles, both inside and out of doors. Separate those no longer available from those you hope to sell or see featured in a publication. A simple heading such as "Available Designs" will suggest to prospective buyers, editors, and consignment shop owners what they may purchase.

A series of quality snapshots showing some of your work-in-progress A series of quality snapshots showing a project-in-progress always catches the viewer's eye. You can include several photos showing a collection of raw materials for a project, a shot of a partially assembled project, and a finished piece.

Quality snapshot of your work on display at shows and exhibits Snapshots of your work on display during shows and exhibits also provide credibility. Take care not to overcrowd them. Provide a label showing where your work was displayed, along with the name, location, and date of the show.

Photographs of awards, ribbons, and recognitions Treasure your awards, ribbons, and recognitions. Including the actual ribbon creates too much bulk. Instead, take a close-up photo of the project with the ribbon attached. Again, add a label to provide details. Include the name of the event, location, and date.

Copies of class schedules and descriptions If you teach, include copies of class schedules describing your classes. Always make sure that the name of the school, shop, or event appears at the top of the sheet. Include the date and location of your classes.

A collection of quality photographs of completed projects and related items shown in realistic settings Group together photographs of completed items that you hope to sell. For example, photos of quilts on beds or hanging on the wall, or models wearing your hand-sewn, knitted, or crocheted fashions. A header labeled "Available Designs" should separate these from completed projects no longer available.

A photograph or two of your studio or work space This is optional.

Not sure how to arrange your portfolio? Choose one of the styles listed below.

ARRANGE YOUR MATERIAL CHRONOLOGICALLY

Show your earliest work in the front tand add new designs to the back as you create them. Or, reverse the organization, adding new designs to the front with older work behind.

ARRANGE YOUR MATERIAL BY STYLE

If you work in different styles, you can group all your Victorian pieces, for example, in one section with contemporary items in another. Use headers or page dividers to separate the sections so viewers can skip what may not interest them, going right to their prime interest. There may be time to browse through the entire portfolio later.

ARRANGE YOUR MATERIAL BY TECHNIQUE OR CRAFT

If you work in multimedia, group your materials in sections. For example, ceramics in one section, jewelry items in another, woodwork in a third.

Remember, you are creating an image—a vital marketing tool. Your portfolio should contain quality photos supported by well-written, well-arranged documents. You are selling not only your design ability, but yourself and your creativity as well.

Resources

Edwards, Paul and Sarah. 1991. *Getting Business to Come to You*. Los Angeles: Jeremy Tarcher.

Levinson, Jay Conrad. 1984. *Guerrilla Marketing*. Boston: Houghton Mifflin.

Smith, Brian R. 1984. *Successful Marketing for Small Business*. Lexington, MA: Lewis Publishing Co.

Kathy Lamancusa
Visual Design Concepts
7750 Gatewood Circle
P.O. Box 2717
North Canton, OH 44720
Phone: (216) 494-7224   Fax: (216) 494-2918

A FAMILY CRAFT BUSINESS

Kathy and Joe Lamancusa have created the ideal craft career. As a happily married couple, they successfully combined their professional skills and included their two sons in their business. Describing their relationship, Kathy says, "Though Joe and I work together, we don't get in each other's way. We understand each other's business. We keep our marriage alive by remembering to respect the person with whom we work, sleep, and play all day. Our business works because Joe, a left-brain, practical person, handles all business matters. As the artistic, right-brain person, I manage the creative aspects."

Kathy shared the challenges of working at home while raising small children. Joe and Jim, now 14 and 16, follow in their parents' footsteps. They write their own column, "Just Kidding," for *Crafts 'n Things* magazine. Astonishingly, they have each written a book published by McGraw-Hill. As if this were not enough, they review craft products designed for children for *Craft & Needlework Age*.

The talented youngsters have been interviewed many times on the Business Radio Network in Colorado and the Kids Radio Network in Pennsylvania. This fall, they will appear on the Discovery Channel's "Easy Does It!" Joe Jr.'s

book, *Kid Cash: Creative Money-Making Ideas,* received a recommendation from the *Wall Street Journal.* Kathy's mother
and sisters contribute to the business when needed. Joe's
sister, a regular employee, also adds her valuable skills.

Visual Design Concepts develops new products, packaging, and effective communication for clients. They
develop corporate strategies, create advertising and marketing plans, and facilitate management education.

Kathy has written twenty-five instructional craft booklets
and co-authored ten others. She has produced fifteen
instructional videos sold worldwide. She has sold more than
80,000 instructional booklets.

She writes regularly for trade magazines such as *Craftrends & Sew Business, Craft & Needlework Age,* and *Giftware
News.* She writes a regular column for *Pack-O-Fun* magazine
and publishes her designs in many consumer publications.

As florists, the Lamancusas have produced fifteen
instructional floral design and wedding how-to videos
as part of their product line. They also develop educational programs for national and international craft
manufacturers.

Crafts Brief

Business founded: 1987 by Joseph and Kathy Lamancusa

Legal form of business: Sole proprietorship

Home-office? Yes. The Lamancusas converted their basement into a design and workroom. They added lots of shelving and storage boxes since they prefer a well-organized
workplace. Next, they added 500 square feet to the back
of their home, which provided them with two floors for
a home-office. They have two business phone lines plus a
fax line.

They affirm the importance of their computer for all
aspects of the business by maintaining three computer work
stations. Additionally, they list their laser printer and scanner as very important equipment.

Hours: Both Joe and Kathy work full-time at their business.

Daily routine: A typical workday finds both Joe and Kathy on the phone developing good relationships with their clients. They frequently contact publications to arrange publication of stories, articles, and designs. Together with their team, the Lamancusas also produce designs and craft instructions, primarily for the floral industry.

Kathy explains that though she and her husband are the driving force, the company functions efficiently due to the cooperation and teamwork of all its members. "Since our business includes our sons, we have a true family affair," says Kathy. "The positive experiences the craft industry offers will help them throughout their lives, no matter what they decide to do."

Best part of craft career: "I like the versatility of our business," Kathy states. "I never do the same thing two days in a row or even two hours in a row. I like the flexibility of spending time with my family when they need me. I plan my work schedule around them."

Least favorite: Kathy admits that at times, work overwhelms her. A successful business like hers produces endless chores. She acknowledges the challenge of ending a working day to avoid overworking and burnout.

Strengths: "We are an exploding creativity team," says Kathy. The Lamancusas agree that their primary strength is recognizing new opportunities plus the drive to pursue them vigorously.

Weaknesses: Kathy admits that limiting her work schedule to forty hours per week challenges her continually. Second, she acknowledges she does not enjoy dealing with the financial side of the business.

Professional organizations: Kathy states, "I believe professional crafters should be active members of trade organizations in their field of interest." She follows her own advice and belongs to the Society of Craft Designers, Hobby Industry Association, Association for Crafts and Creative Industries, Society of American Florists, American Floral Services, and National Speakers Association.

Kathy continues to enrich herself. She has earned the designation CPD (Certified Professional Demonstrator) from HIA, CCD (Certified Craft Designer) from the Society of Craft Designers, and RMC (Redbook Master Consultant) for Redbook Floral Services. Currently, she serves on the board of directors of the Ohio Speakers Forum and North Canton Chamber of Commerce.

Professional journals: *Craft & Needlework Age* and *Craftrends & Sew Business.* Kathy emphasizes the importance of reading consumer publications too. Her favorites? *Crafts, Crafts 'n Things, Country Handcrafts, Quick & Easy Crafts, Wearable Crafts, Bride's, Better Homes & Gardens,* and *All American Crafts.*

Goals: To continue to work with manufacturers from crossover industries on a national and international basis. The Lamancusas hope to publish larger books, develop Kathy's professional speaking career regarding crafts, and increase their radio and TV exposure.

Advice: "Anyone beginning a craft career should think of building it like a building—brick by brick. Once secure, add more. Don't add new responsibilities until you have a strong ground with previous ventures. Build relationships as you expand into other crafts areas. Crafts are a fulfilling career."

CHAPTER 17

YOU AS ADVERTISING AGENT

GOOD ADVERTISING INFORMS consumers about your product and induces them to buy. Radio, TV, and print advertising are the principal media in which to announce product information, but more modest means are available to you as well. Advertising costs money and, at best, produces uncertain results. No wonder businesspeople of all kinds feel apprehensive when considering how and when to advertise. There are no guarantees your advertising will work, so why pay to advertise at all? Here are a few reasons.

Advertising can:

- Encourage and build sales
- Remind customers about the benefits of your product
- Establish and maintain your market niche

Advertising cannot:

- Create a sharp increase in sales
- Solve cash-flow problems
- Make up for low-quality merchandise or indifferent service

Classified Ads

In classified advertising, you pay by the word. Perhaps the most pervasive way to advertise, it is also the least complex. Consider the three important elements if you decide to advertise this way: persuasive writing, repetition, and media selection.

Professional writers strive to achieve tight writing. This means eliminating extra words that weaken a written message. Never is this more important than in classified ads, since the amount you must pay is based on the number of words you use.

Crafters just starting out often lack the confidence to compose their own ads. Too often, they turn to others who may not have objectivity.

Recently, a telephone company representative called me to encourage me to renew my ad in our local directory. She suggested I would increase sales if I increased the size of my ad and included more information. Her goal was to increase revenues for the phone company.

Sources exist to help you write strong, tight ads on your own. *Thirty Days to More Powerful Writing* by Jonathan Price offers excellent tips on writing ads and strengthening your overall writing skills. Save money in the long run by reading books about writing as writers do. Titles published by Writer's Digest Books will help you learn to write effective ad copy.

Study the two ads below. Which do you find easier to read and understand and more persuasive?

"Everyone longs to make their own beaded jewelry. Why not you? There are thousands of beautiful, exciting beads on the market today. Wouldn't it be nice to learn how to make use of them in making your own, beautiful earrings, bracelets, and necklaces? We are proud of our new publication. Send your check in the amount of $9.95 for our new booklet about making your own jewelry, *Beaded Treasures.*" (seventy words)

"Make beautiful beaded jewelry for yourself, family, and friends. Design tips from our pros make it quick & easy. Get started today. Order *Beaded Treasures,* our latest book, just $9.95 ppd." (twenty-five words)

Display Ads

Advertisers pay by the inch for display ads. Study the back pages in your telephone directory. Most feature a page illustrating the different sized boxes in which you can place your display ad.

If you think your product might benefit from an ad that includes sketches, line drawings, or other graphics, display ads will do the trick. Place your information within the space you choose and pay by the total number of inches the space consumes. Newspapers, magazines, and phone directories all feature display ads. Write to request their press kits. Here, you will find ad rates, readership information, and details about publishing frequency.

Trade Directories

Trade journals exist to serve a specific trade. You will find three publications that serve the craft industry and that also publish annual trade directories. Professional crafters receive free subscriptions, but prepare yourself to prove your professional status. The leading craft trade journals are *Craft & Needlework Age, Craftrends & Sew Business,* and *The Craft Supply Directory.* (Addresses are provided in the additional resources section at the end of this book.)

Each trade directory listed above publishes an annual listing of manufacturers including names, addresses, phone and fax numbers, and, most important, the name of the contact person to whom you should direct inquiries. Search for a specific craft product you need to manufacture your item. The directories provide all the American companies that sell a particular product at wholesale or retail.

Co-op Advertising

Cooperative advertising offers many benefits. Working with either an ad agent or an organized group of crafters, co-op advertising pools the resources of several crafters. Rather than bear the cost and time of reaching out to consumers on your own, consider joining forces with others. A co-op ad envelope may contain individual flyers or a large catalog describing the work of each member of the group. Expenses for printing, preparing the ad package, and postage are shared equally by the participants.

Contact interested crafters and divide the tasks yourselves, or contact an agency with experience in this field.

Radio and TV

Don't discount these opportunities too quickly. Though it costs thousands of dollars to advertise on a national news broadcast, consider small, local-information TV and radio stations instead. They are more open to supporting local businesses and charge more modest rates.

In California, you can create a thirty-second ad for $250 to $500. The ad appears on local channels many times per day for a given period. Check the prices in your geographical area for more information.

Advertising experts agree that to achieve success, repetition is critical. Do not make the beginner's mistake of placing an ad in a single issue of a magazine or newspaper. Readers must become familiar with you and your product. Repetition also conveys reliability and credibility.

Promotional Opportunities

Paying to get the word out defines advertising. But getting the word out for little or no cost defines promotional activity. How can you promote your business? Consider the following:

- Visit your local Chamber of Commerce office. Ask if you can leave brochures, business cards, or fliers on display tables.
- Join non-craft-specific organizations in your community to increase your visibility.
- Consider your car. Add logos and other basic information advertising your business. Don't forget license plates and their holders to add brief messages.
- Give demonstrations at local craft events. Invite questions and distribute flyers. Create interest in your craft.
- Practice what you preach. Jewelers, textile artists, and others—wear your products.
- Place flyers on windshields. (Always check with local agencies for permission.)
- Premiums keep your product in the minds of consumers. Though you must invest a small amount, personalized pens, balloons, caps, and more make it easy for consumers to find you. Write to the companies below for free catalogs of premium items.

Sales Guides, Inc.
10510 North Port Washington Road
Mequon, WI 53092-5500
(800) 352-9899

Sales Promotion Today by Nelson Marketing
210 Commerce St.
Box 320
Oshkosh, WI 54902-00320
(800) 722-5203

Parkway Business Promotions
315 Fifth Ave.
New Brighton, MN 55112
(800) 562-1735

Best Impressions Co.
348 North 30th Road
Box 800
La Salle, IL 61301
(800) 635-2378

- Offer selected customers free samples. Mrs. Fields started her business this way. Recently, I attended a craft show and observed many participants wearing a small, silk boutonniere. A clever silk painter gave one to everyone visiting her booth. Soon, everyone was clamoring to know where these were available. The booth vendor kept busy writing orders for two days.
- Write short articles about your craft without pay. Share a little of your expertise in print. Describe a particular process, for example, or how you use a specific product. In the reference box at the end of the article, request that readers write to you for more information.
- Contact publishers of newsletters aimed at specific but narrow markets. They often welcome submissions from nonprofessional writers. You will find a comprehensive list in the *Encyclopedia of Associations,* available at a public library. Many freelance writers began promising careers this way.
- Find a newsworthy slant about yourself or your product to interest local newspapers or radio stations. Bear in mind that the piece must be informational and not merely blatant advertising. Short, humorous articles are especially successful.

Volunteer to Give Demonstrations

Visit your Chamber of Commerce. Ask for a list of groups and associations in your community. Look for the name of each program chairperson or president of organizations of interest. Don't be too hasty to discount non-craft groups. Often, they know the least about crafts but are the most eager to learn.

Prepare to send a direct-mail package to each person on your list. Include a cover letter, preferably written on letterhead stationery, a business card, and a brochure describing your business.

Introduce yourself in your cover letter. Explain your interest in presenting lively, educational programs about your field to members of your community. In your letter, make your demonstration sound like an interesting learning opportunity, not an advertisement.

Offer a variety of programs ranging from very short "quickies" to an afternoon's presentation. Invite the officers of the organization to contact you to schedule a preliminary meeting. You may include a calendar of your availability as well. Sharing yourself, your craft, and your business this way establishes you as a professional in your community who is eager to open new windows of opportunity.

Resources

Smith, Cynthia S. 1989. *Step by Step Advertising.* New York: Lyle Stewart.

Whitmyer, Claude, Salli Raspberry, and Michael Phillips. 1989. *Running a One Person Business.* Berkeley: Ten Speed Press.

Patsy Moreland
13409 Southeast Clatsop St.
Portland, OR 97236
Phone: (503) 760-1452   Fax: (503) 698-8126

FROM SHOP OWNER TO TEXTILE ARTIST

Patsy Krause Moreland entered the craft world in 1971. Working for the Oregon Visitors and Greeters Association, she heard tourists wishing they could buy handmade crafts from local artisans. This helped her decide to open a consignment shop in Portland to sell the crafts of others to tourists.

In 1976, she took on two partners. One was an excellent seamstress with bookkeeping experience. Over time, the business focused increasingly on quilts and decorative painting.

Patsy and her partners were instrumental in forming a group of independent fabric businesses that eventually included thirty stores. Patsy's two partners left the business in 1982. After soul-searching, Patsy and her husband maintained the business for two more years on their own. Then, Patsy's husband fell ill so she closed her shop to care for him.

After her husband's death, Patsy joined the Society of Craft Designers to learn about becoming a textile designer. Patsy describes her work today succinctly: "I am a professional craft designer working with textiles. Whether the project surface is three dimensional or flat, I manipulate fabric by cutting, piecing, quilting, beading, painting, fusing, stitching, and using image transfer to bring my ideas to completion. Crafts should be easy and fun so people become excited about their creativity."

Patsy gives craft demonstrations, produces manufacturers' trade-show models, and teaches classes. Agreeing with many crafters, Patsy explains how she chose her career: "I love being my own boss in a business I can take with me anywhere."

Crafts Brief

Business founded: 1971

Legal form of business: Sole proprietor

Home-office? Yes. Patsy converted the daylight basement in her home into a working studio. Most important equipment to her: camera, computer, fax, and sewing machine.

Hours: About thirty hours per week.

Best part of craft career: "Doing what I love and the freedom to design!"

Strengths: Ability to market herself and the knowledge to be a successful designer.

Weaknesses: Procrastination challenges Patsy.

Professional organizations: Like others in this book, Patsy chooses to belong to SCD for its education and networking opportunities.

Professional journals: "Quilter's Newsletter," *Threads,* and *Craftrends & Sew Business.*

Advice: "Find a niche and fill it. Make a marketing plan and always present a professional image. Maintain business ethics and don't be afraid to hire others when needed to help you complete projects in a timely manner. Treasure your business relationships."

CHAPTER 18

YOU AND YOUR COMPUTER

"*PURCHASING A COMPUTER* for my craft business is definitely not on my list of priorities. Are computers appropriate for creative people like me? Business and computer magazines promise that computerizing a business would help *any* enterprise, but do they mean crafters?" If these are questions you've been asking, you are not alone.

How will you know when the time has come to computerize your craft business? What tasks can you expect a computer to perform? Will a computer improve your business? How? Every small-business owner, including crafters, asks these questions. Let's take them one at a time. You will know when you need a computer in your craft studio when:

- You need help with the business but not enough to hire an employee.
- Paperwork takes too much of your craft production time.
- Your documents need a more professional look.
- You need to organize information.
- Bookkeeping chores overwhelm you.

Computers perform four primary functions: word processing, data management, accounting and bookkeeping tasks, and desktop publishing.

Think of a computer as a willing slave, on duty in your studio-office night and day. Contrary to popular belief, computers do not eliminate paper. They do, however, lessen time spent shuffling paper, which provides more time for craft production.

Word Processing

Word processing simplifies correspondence tasks. Letters are not the only writing tasks that become faster and easier with a computer. Do you write instructions so others can reproduce your craft designs? Record your creative process as you work, directly into the computer. Modifications and revision take a fraction of the time they do on a typewriter. Did you find an omission early in the document? A computer allows you to find the spot, and insert the missing information, eliminating the need to retype.

Have you considered writing articles about your craft projects? In addition to a word processing program, you can add other writing aids. Grammar checkers, dictionaries, and spellers will help you polish your article and produce professional looking documents. Selling project instructions can generate extra income for you. (See Chapter 22 for details.)

Teachers of craft classes can create lesson plans on their computers. You can revise lessons and lectures about specific techniques as needed. For example, have you written a speech about how you use color in your craft process? When your local craft group invites you to speak about your craft business, a word processor enables you to retrieve the original speech and modify its contents. You may then rename the speech, preserving the original outline for future use while creating a new speech from the old.

Word processing programs help you write better letters and allow you to save each in a separate file. Use the computer's filing system like a file drawer of manila folders. Next time you write to a vendor or wholesaler, for example, you can review your correspondence with them long after you've put the letter in the mail. While in the general file of the "ABC Company," you can copy the name, address, and other repeated information. Paste it into a new document file to begin your new letter in seconds. All your correspondence to the same company will accumulate in the file, providing a permanent record of your relationship.

Software drawing and graphics programs enable you to write your own advertising copy and press releases. You can make eye-catching fliers, hang tags, and insert cards to include with your craft products.

Get off on the right foot once you purchase a computer for your craft studio. Start with a directory system to organize your data. Think of your computer's hard disk as a file cabinet. Subdirectories do the job of manila folders. They help you find and retrieve stored information, making it much easier to manage your business as it grows. Here is the directory list I use on my personal computer. Add to it to suit your own needs.

After powering up the computer, open your word processing program. Your hand is now on the proper door of your filing cabinet. I use the Windows version of Word-Perfect—its main directory greets me.

Under the WordPerfect parent directory—identified by my business name—I created subdirectories. Remember, these are your file folders.

Letters   Copies of letters I have written with the last name of each person appended with "ltr." Example: Smith.ltr.

Lesson Plans   Each class has its own name, appended "lpl," which stands for "lesson plan." Examples: color.lpl, textile.lpl.

Patterns   Along with instructions, patterns are filed by name, appended "pat." Examples: sweater.pat, doll.pat.

Bibliographies   Book lists for each class level I teach, appended "bib." Examples: design.bib, applique.bib.

Lists   Lists of all kinds, appended "lst." Examples: wholesal.lst (a listing of all my wholesale sources); mailing.lst (those to whom I send regular mailings); resource.lst (people, groups, associations); workshop.lst (all topics I offer).

Articles Alphabetical listing of all articles I have written appended "art." Example: teaching.art.

You can store information both on your hard drive and disks. Organizing files efficiently requires you to back up your work as you end each day. This provides critical insurance that should your computer fail, your work remains on floppy disks. Assign a separate disk for each subdirectory listing. Save your work on its appropriate floppy.

Data Management

Data management may sound vague so here are a few examples of the type of data you can organize and store on a computer for your craft business. You can:

- Create a mailing list of your customers, vendors, and craft shows.
- Maintain a list of all the craft books in your library. Take it with you when you shop. Eliminate inadvertently buying the same book twice.
- Keep a list of all the products along with company names and addresses you use to create your product.
- Replace your Rolodex file of business contacts' addresses and phone numbers with a computerized card file. A computerized list will avoid the hassle of lost business cards that may cost you valuable contact information. Computer card files not only contain names and addresses, but provide extra space to add comments and notes to create a history about a specific business contact.

Accounting and Bookkeeping Chores

Creative artisans usually do not relish bookkeeping chores. Make them painless and fast with a computer spreadsheet program. A good one will:

- Keep an accurate record of your income from all sources
- Show all your expenses at a glance
- Provide a cash-flow statement so you will know the status of your business
- Record all the information you need at the end of the year to prepare your income tax return
- Automatically separate out-of-state customers from those who must pay sales tax in your state
- Maintain an invoicing system to keep track of what clients owe

We chose QuickBooks rather than Quicken, the personal finance version distributed by the same company. Make sure to distinguish between these two because their differences relate to business. Quicken is an excellent single-entry bookkeeping system. It does a good job helping you maintain personal accounts. However, QuickBooks is a full accounting program, double-entry style, essential to a business. Enter deductions and expenses all year and you will find that, in minutes, you'll have a printout to take to your tax preparer to begin your federal income tax returns each year.

In seconds, QuickBooks produces a graph or pie chart providing a visual picture of what you've earned and what is owed to you. You can compare weekly, monthly, or yearly records with those of previous time frames. You can also request a bar graph to see the percentage of profit generated by each of your business activities.

Desktop Publishing

When you add desktop publishing capabilities to your word processor, an entire new world opens to you. You can create your own:

- Brochures
- Letterhead stationery

- Résumés
- Flyers
- Newsletters
- Teaching handouts
- Instructional booklets

Check out the graphics capabilities of the computer program you may be considering. Specialized design programs are one of the most delightful options for creative people. There are programs that will draw, make grids, and show how your color choices will look on a finished project. Paint programs allow you to create any shape and color it to demonstrate how a new design will look.

Clip-art collections are another welcome addition if your computer has graphics capabilities. Choose from literally thousands of images for your documents.

Specialized programs exist for specific arts and crafts. For example, fiber artists may choose programs that will design a knitted sweater, lay out a quilt, or create a cross-stitch chart. Seamstresses can draft a pattern on a computer. Embroiderers can draw a design and assign colors and stitches to each area. Architects may choose Computer Aided Design (CAD) programs to design objects from a two-story house to a sailboat. Woodworkers and landscapers also can lay out original designs with CAD programs.

If you choose a laser printer for your computer, the finished copy bears such a professional look, it is difficult to distinguish it from expensive typesetting. Creating your own professional documents saves time and money. You no longer need to pay someone else to do what you and your computer can do together.

Decide whether an IBM-compatible or a Macintosh system will serve your needs. Take time to make thoughtful decisions *before* making software selections. Take computer courses for beginners and again after you gain proficiency, for the industry changes constantly. Subscribe to computer business magazines to remain informed about the latest technological developments.

Designing by Computer

Writing about the myriad of computer design software on the market can be risky. New programs appear, while old favorites are updated, upgraded, and become faster. Color and drawing capabilities are astounding. Industry-specific programs for crafts keep growing.

Designing in any medium can be done on a computer. Recently, several programs have moved from two-dimensional formats to 3-D capability. For example, if you want to design a house, you can start with two-dimensional drawings. Switch to 3-D formatting and you can simulate a walk-through of each room.

My quilting design program, Electric Quilt, takes a quilter from start to finish. Begin by creating an individual block, any dimension or style. Apply different color combinations until satisfied with the final result. The program actually allows you to place "printed fabrics" in certain areas so you will know exactly how the quilt will look. Adding borders and finishing touches becomes easy by computer. But wait, there's more! This program actually prints out template shapes for any block more accurately than you could ever draw them.

You can even buy inexpensive programs that calculate the math required by your craft project and work in conjunction with spreadsheet programs such as Lotus. Tedious pencil-and-paper graphs become quick and painless by computer.

The Internet: What's in It for Crafters?

I'm a computer user not a "techie." This means I can't tell you how the Internet works, or even why. Details like how my car's engine works don't interest me. When I turn on the ignition, I just want my vehicle to take me where I want to go. So it is with the Internet.

Once you go online, you will be able to find answers to nearly every question imaginable. Information on any subject from the all the world's resources are but a click of the mouse away. "The world" is not used flippantly here. Indeed, information from the entire world, online, reaches you in seconds.

"Crafts" was the first word I typed when doing a search on the Net for the first time. If you do likewise, decide whether you prefer to learn about them, chat with others, or request business information. Not only can you learn and read about crafts; you can communicate with other artisans in your field. Even IRS business forms and publications come to you, via cyberspace, ready to print.

Electronic mail (e-mail) provides instant communication! In minutes, you can post a letter or place a phone call without paying for postage or long-distance toll calls. Anyone who has an e-mail address (those mysterious little codes) can send or receive messages from anyone in the world.

"News groups" are where the fun begins. Groups of people addicted to a particular topic gossip via the Internet. They ask and answer each other's questions. They complain about problems and find solace from others who respond instantly. They share successes and provide sources for hard-to-find items. They recommend books on specific topics, encouraging further research. Other addicts invite you to reply on whether you solved your problem with their help. Via news groups, you can also subscribe to specialized subgroups that provide a sort of daily newspaper of events and information.

There are large, national networks dealing with craft marketing such as CraftNet and CraftWeb. To search for information, you enlist the aid of search engines with names like WebCrawler and Yahoo. Sound intriguing?

Here's the bottom line: the World Wide Web's profit potential. The Web is like a gigantic bulletin board—or rather a series of bulletin boards connected to one another on the Internet—to advertise anything and everything. People can buy items on the Internet, but most prefer to sell. By designing a home page on the Web, crafters can maintain a sort of large display ad describing their products and services that is accessible to everyone in the world (at least those who surf the Internet).

When you learn to navigate the World Wide Web, you will see some words highlighted in different colors denoting hypertext links. Clicking on any of the highlighted words takes you to a home page or Web site containing information regarding the highlighted word. It's like driving in your car, following road signs to get where you want to go.

Hyper-text links remind me of a huge book containing information on all subjects. Just mention the topic you want and voilà! your computer selects the right book. Pages open to the right place. Indeed, computers enhance your creativity, they don't replace it!

Marlene Watson
Marlene's Design Studio
1278 Via Del Carmel
Santa Maria, CA 93455
Phone and fax: (805) 937-6415

TELEVISION CRAFT STAR

Marlene Watson began her craft career as a shop owner on Catalina Island, California. Careful planning enabled her to build a home-based craft studio in 1979, large enough to include a classroom that seats fifteen students!

Though Marlene teaches for local colleges and high schools, she spends most of her time as a freelance designer and writer of pattern booklets. Marlene's face is familiar to TV craft show viewers. She frequently demonstrates her techniques and design ideas on "Aleene's Creative Living," which is shown on many PBS stations.

Crafts Brief

Business founded: 1970

Legal form of business: Sole proprietorship

Home-office? Marlene's studio measures 700 square feet. In addition to her classroom, she has two sewing machines and a large inventory of paints and undecorated clothing. Important equipment: computer, two printers, scanner, copy machine.

Hours: Marlene is a hard worker, devoting fifty to sixty hours weekly to her business. She needs help regularly and loves to include her family in her business. Her husband, married daughter, and four grandchildren pitch in, with additional support from a certified public accountant.

Without a doubt, designing for TV produces most of Marlene's income, followed closely by teaching and retail sales of supplies and her booklets and patterns. Marlene has had more than 20 craft books published by major companies and has self-published two of her own plus ten wearables patterns.

Best part of craft career: Without hesitation, Marlene replies that she cherishes making a living doing what she loves most.

Least favorite: Receiving phone calls before 5 A.M. from Eastern time zones.

Strengths: Teaching and designing top Marlene's list.

Weaknesses: Marlene must discipline herself to attend to bookkeeping and marketing tasks, her least favorite tasks.

Professional organizations: Like nearly all interview subjects, Marlene lists SCD as the most valuable to her for networking and contacts with manufacturers and magazine editors.

Professional journals: *Craftrends & Sew Business* and *Craft & Needlework Age* keep Marlene in touch with new products and national trends.

Advice: "If you want a craft career—not just a hobby—you must acquire a business mind-set. Record keeping is extremely important. You must be willing to establish a practical work schedule and stick to it, but remember—have fun!"

CHAPTER 19

YOU AS PERSONNEL MANAGER

SUCCESS CAN CREATE a new problem for a home-based business. Sooner or later, work expands to the point where we can no longer do everything alone. Hiring consultants is a modest way for home-based crafters to find the help they need. Consider turning over bookkeeping chores to a tax expert or certified public accountant. Or, hire a part-time secretary to deal with your correspondence and paperwork.

Increasing numbers of home businesses have spawned a new batch of available services. You can hire experts to prepare marketing literature, design brochures, or do your photography. Computer consultants can help you learn programs or trouble-shoot. College students can perform mail-order chores such as packaging, wrapping, and mailing. Consider hiring a housekeeper or gardener to help you with household tasks. While many crafters believe this luxury is only for the affluent, think again. When housekeepers charge less per hour than you earn working at your craft, paying them to do your chores makes good sense. Even young children can contribute to a home-based business. Under supervision, they can collate, fold and stuff envelopes, and perform simple crafting tasks.

Eventually, it may become obvious that your business needs another pair of hands. You can always hire part- or

221

full-time employees, but most crafters turn to family members, and spouses in particular, for help.

Couples in Business

Thinking of taking on your spouse as a business partner? At home or at a work site, problems arise when couples deal with each other in business in the same way they maintain their personal relationship. Business decisions require concise communication that is not fraught with emotion. Married partners must learn how to handle two different budgets, personal and business, and how to separate business from personal issues. They must also focus on the concept that if one person "loses" at the other's expense in a marriage, the relationship loses. But if one person loses at the other's expense in business, the business loses!

Couples who work together part- or full-time agree on the reasons they choose to do so. They list:

- Personal satisfaction
- Taking control of their lives and work
- Togetherness
- Flexibility of schedule and location
- Enjoying the increasingly respected status that accompanies owning one's own business

Working together, couples and other relatives may find themselves working with a person with whom they clash, or, conversely, someone who is too much like themselves. They must learn to strike a balance in skills and temperament. Sharing social experiences with your spouse or relative does not guarantee you will work together well. Issues of control, equity, and commitment have to be addressed in business differently than the way they are dealt with in personal relationships.

Working couples soon realize the advantage of shared agendas. No longer must you try to make the other understand business problems and demands. Working together, you now share this common concern. Rather than allow the business to sprawl unchecked across both of your lives, take control. Plan the business together. Here's how: Start with a notebook in which you will make five lists. They will lead to a Business Plan and a division of labor agreement.

1. **List all the tasks required to run the business.** Do you remember what you learned about action boards in Chapter 3? Use the system again to make a complete list of business tasks. Don't attempt to rank the tasks or assign them at this time. Do not overlook any chore as too trivial. Often, trivialities set off disagreements, which lead to hurt feelings later. Work at this list until every task required by your business is included.

2. **List the business strengths and weaknesses of each person involved in the business.** If family members will participate in the business, include them now. (Ideas on how to determine strengths/weaknesses are featured later in this chapter.) Keep in mind the skills each person brings to the business. Consider also the chores each person prefers to avoid. For example, an extrovert may feel comfortable dealing with confrontations, while an introvert dislikes them. Creative artisans may avoid marketing tasks, while a pragmatic person welcomes them.

3. **Division of labor contract—the only way to determine who is boss.** No good relationship can survive if one person wields all the power and the other has none. Prepare to share power so both parties have the ultimate say in an issue where compromise seems elusive. Examine each other's strengths and weaknesses to allocate each job to the person for whom it is best suited. The heart of your business partnership is the division of labor list. Divide a page in your notebook in half, vertically. Write each person's name at the top of each column. Return to the list of business tasks. Choose a chore you like and for which you will take responsibility. Next, have the other person select from the list. Continue working down the list, taking turns choosing tasks. Copy each task on alternate sides of the page under the name of the person taking responsibility for it.

   When tasks remain that neither of you like, compromise. Who can perform it best? For whom is it most convenient? Determine if there are any chores that both refuse to do. Can you pay someone else to do these?

4. **Consider a new list: I call it, "The Last Word List."** Now you can solve the big questions for couples working together—Who is in charge? Who is the boss? Who has the power? This list records who will have the last say concerning specific issues. Continue making every effort to reach mutual agreement. But, in case of a stalemate, this list becomes a safeguard.

   Another reason for this list is the frequent dilemma faced by founders vs. joiners in a business. Founders may find it difficult to relinquish control of a business they created. They can be reluctant to give the other responsibility. Joiners may soon feel relegated to menial tasks or limited to gofer duties.

   By all means, consider the preferences and talents of each person as you reach a decision about who has the last word on specific issues. This way, each of you will have equal power, diminishing the enemy of all home-based working couples—the struggle for control.

5. **The stress list.** While we cannot eliminate all life's stressors, why not banish those you can? Continue your free-flowing idea system, listing everything you can think of, large and small, that each person finds stressful. If partners know what causes the other stress, the person feeling less to no stress over an issue or situation will know when to step in and relieve the other. The stressed partner, on the other hand, can feel secure knowing his or her partner will come through when the going gets tough.

   When we completed our fifth list, my husband and I began to feel like real business partners. For example, when we both noted how uncomfortable it was to work in our office when the afternoon sun poured in, our path was clear. We installed an air conditioner.

Here's a summary of the lists:

1. All tasks involved in the business
2. Each partner's strengths and weaknesses
3. Division of labor—who does what
4. Tasks for which each partner will have the ultimate say
5. Stress list

Notice that we have limited the discussion so far to the business. However, partners who are spouses generally share a home and the accompanying household tasks. Shared work means shared lives. You can apply what you've learned to distribute household responsibilities as well. Consider the stress list and strength and weakness list you compiled for your business as you assign and accept household tasks.

Managing Personality Differences

When we began working together, my husband and I felt like the only couple in the world with so little in common. The differences between us seemed so vast that we seriously wondered if we could stay married, let alone work together. Similar reactions between couples in business together became apparent in workshops held by my husband and I, "Couples in Business." But we learned that many couples sharing both a personal and business relationship could work together while sustaining wide personality differences.

Spouses, siblings, parents working with adult children, and even good friends need to learn about each other to work together efficiently. This is critical if you want to protect the personal relationship and maintain a productive working partnership.

What can we do about personality differences? Do we grin and bear them? Do we try to convert our spouses/partners to become more like ourselves? Do we expend energy convincing them that *they* are the weird ones? The inefficient ones? The inexperienced ones? The ones who must change?

In all honesty, I must admit we tried all of the above, as have many of our students. Trying to convert the other comes naturally as people blend personal and business relationships. Fortunately, there are better ways to benefit from the differences between ourselves and those very strange people we married and with whom we now *choose* to work.

Psychoanalyst Carl Jung, an early associate of Freud's, created a way to identify personality types. His system explains personalities across cultures. Jung said that when we know ourselves, we can better deal with others who don't see the world as we do. His system assigns four basic personality traits to each person. Each of these traits is one of a pair.

After studying Jung's theories, we recognized that his system provides the answer to the main problem of couples working together. Each person wants to proceed his or her own way and have the other follow. We used Jung's ideas to write a business contract that avoids conflict over authority issues. We call it our division of labor contract. *Please Understand Me,* by Marilyn Bates and David Keirsey, explains the theory in detail. Included in their book is a short test based upon the Myers-Briggs Type Indicator. Knowing your personality types helps you divide business tasks so they place the least stress on the personal relationship. Here's a brief synopsis:

Dividing all of us is the difference between introverts and extroverts. Many assume introverts are simply quiet, unassertive people who prefer solitude over companionship. Not so. Introverts reach within themselves for motivation. Usually creative personalities, their ideas come from within and they require solitude to work and renew themselves. According to Jung, this personality type produces most of our craftsmen, artists, writers, teachers, musicians, and philosophers.

Extroverts need stimulation from others. They seek companionship and relate to others well. Introverts often marry extroverts because they bring them out of themselves. Extroverts choose introverts because they find them deep and interesting. They often marry and misunderstand each other and proceed to try to convert the other to be more like themselves. Introverts and extroverts can get along better if each develops more of the other side. If this difference exists between you and your partner, let it work for you.

For example, in a division of labor agreement, extroverts could have the last say in matters that come naturally to them, while the introvert's preferences for writing, designing, and developing ideas can flourish.

Jung describes the next pair of personality differences as based on how a person decides issues—using intuition or sensation. The sensual person wants to know, "How does it work?" The intuitive person wants to know, "Why does it work?" Sensualists think intuitives are dreamy and vague because they seem impractical and rely too much on their intuition. The curiosity of intuitives, on the other hand, demands they find information in depth, including details that seem trivial to sensualists.

Ideas that inspire intuitives frustrate sensual types. For example, the intuitive may refuse credit to a customer because he or she "feels" the person is unreliable. The sensual type wants to dismiss hunches from the business altogether. He prefers to check a credit record or talk to a customer's bank to decide a customer's credit eligibility. Intuitives value their feelings and their gut reactions. They feel more comfortable speculating, taking risks, and experimenting with ideas and materials. They like bold thinking and easily grasp abstract ideas. This is a common dilemma in a marriage between an artist and a corporate employee, for example.

To work together, intuitives must see the value of being practical and sensualists must learn there is more to life than what you can prove. Make cohesive decisions together by combining your different styles. This is what being a couple is about.

Jung calls those who make choices impersonally "thinkers" and those who act on personal feelings "feelers." Thinkers relate to what they already know. Usually, they prefer to work on one project at a time until they are finished. They like detail and see themselves as being thorough, objective, logical, and rational. Feelers give more importance to emotional response. They often will work on many projects at once. They choose what to work on next based on how they feel. Jung points out that these two different styles of decision making are more complementary than the first two sets of personality traits.

Judgers and perceivers form the last pair of personality types, according to Jung. Ask yourself, "Do I prefer closure and settling issues or do I prefer to keep options open and fluid?" Those who prefer closure over open options are usually judgers. They like deadlines and adhere to them. Judgers have a work ethic that requires work to come before all else. One must work before rest or play. Members of this group are society's most diligent workers. Perceivers—intuitive or sensual, thinking or feeling, introverted or extroverted—want the work process to be enjoyable. Perceivers tend to procrastinate. They are more process oriented; judgers are more results oriented. If a couple differs here, irritation and frustration may result. One may push toward making a final decision "now," while the other prefers to wait for more information.

Worldwide Personality Types
(as researched by Carl Jung)

Extroverts	75 percent	Introverts	25 percent
Sensualists	75 percent	Intuitives	25 percent
Thinkers	50 percent	Feelers	50 percent
Judgers	50 percent	Perceivers	50 percent

Independent Contractors or Employees? Know the Difference!

"Under today's conditions, many employers find it more efficient to contract work to independents to minimize their staffs than to continue supporting a permanent payroll," writes Herman Holtz, author of *The Complete Guide to Being an Independent Contractor.*

Small-business owners often choose to hire independent contractors rather than employees since independents need not receive pension and medical plans, worker's compensation, and other benefits. Business owners can hire independents as needed rather than keep workers on their payroll during slack times.

Problems arise when a business hires employees and classifies them as independent contractors to avoid the extra bookkeeping and benefit provisions. When you hire someone to help, make sure you understand the differences between employees and independent contractors.

IRS auditors list several considerations to determine employer-employee status. The following factors appear in IRS Publication 937, Employment Taxes. You've hired an employee, not an independent contractor if you do the following:

1. Control how the worker performs the work
2. Dictate methods workers must follow
3. Prevent workers from delegating work to anyone else
4. Prevent workers from hiring assistants
5. Engage the worker's services on a regular basis
6. Set work hours
7. Require that work be done on the premises
8. Establish the order or sequence of work
9. Pay by the hour, week, or month rather than by the job
10. Pay certain expenses such as travel, use of a car, etc.
11. Furnish tools or other materials

If the IRS decides that you hired an employee, not an independent contractor, you may have to pay back taxes and benefits to the worker. To avoid this, make sure you treat the person you hire as an independent. Here are some guidelines:

1. Contractors do not follow precise instructions.
2. They do not receive training.
3. Contractors can hire others to do the work.
4. They set their own work hours.
5. Contractors usually work for several businesses, not one exclusively.
6. Contractors receive pay by the job, not for time spent hourly, weekly, etc.

7. They pay their own work-related expenses.
8. Contractors receive a check without deductions or withholding.

Remember, these definitions work both ways: when you hire someone to help you and when someone else hires and pays you to work for them. Study the IRS publications or see a business or tax consultant if you have further questions.

Mentor-Apprentice Relationships

Reading about the European crafts guilds in the seventeenth and eighteenth centuries, I learned how the system passed on high skill levels from one generation to the next. We find actual documentation of the process used by eighteenth-century British knitting guilds.[1]

Men served an apprenticeship under a master knitter for six years. Apprentices received bed and board from the "master" while learning basic skills of commercial knitting. After the apprentice completed the fundamentals, he entered the second phase of his service. He began to help the master produce goods. (Yes, in early times, master knitters were usually men, not women.) In effect, the master had an assistant who worked under his direction without pay. In exchange, the apprentice received a professional education in the trade of his choice as well as bed and board. He exchanged his labor for what we would call "defrayed tuition costs" today.

When the apprentice's skills reached a certain level, the mentor continued to further his helper's future. He helped him prepare his "masterpieces," which were intended to prove his skills. Craft guilds consisted of the master craftsmen in a local community who voted as a group to decide the qualifications of a new apprentice. If they found his

[1] *Mary Thomas' Knitting Book,* 1938. Now available from Dover publications for $3.95.

work suitable, the apprentice would leave the home of his mentor and set up his own shop. Money did not change hands. The relationship was clearly an exchange of experience and education for assistance and labor.

When today's crafters need help yet cannot afford to pay a regular employee, they should consider an apprentice. For those wanting "hands-on" experience, why not trade labor for assistance and practical learning opportunity? It's important for both parties to believe in the mentor-apprentice system with a trusting heart. If one feels overly concerned with being taken advantage of, the relationship may become primarily a defensive one rather than one of open sharing and exchange.

Let the guidelines below help you arrive at your own agreements when considering taking on an apprentice. Complete Figures 1 and 2 to define your expectations. Strive for a relationship where everyone wins.

Figure 1
For Mentors Only

Describe your needs for assistance. Provide specific details:

Days: Preferred hours: Frequency:

Describe the skills you require in an apprentice:

Do you prefer references from past employers? Yes ___ No___

What skills and experience do you have to offer your apprentice?

What educational and learning situations will you provide?

Figure 2
For Apprentices Only

Days: Preferred hours: Frequency:

Skills you have to offer your mentor in exchange for experience:

Skills and experience you seek in exchange for your labor:

Personal references available to mentors? Yes ____ No ____

State why you want to apprentice in this field:

State your long-term goals in detail:

GUIDELINES AND SUGGESTIONS FOR MENTORS AND APPRENTICES

Be honest about your needs. The more you can express what you want out of the relationship, the better your chance of fulfilling each other's needs. Avoid feeling taken advantage of by scheduling regular evaluations. Meet every month, for example. Allow each person to state clearly how the relationship is working. If each person feels they receive as much as or more than they give, there are no losers. Here are some ideas for determining how to exchange services for labor:

- Use a measure of time. Trade an hour for an hour or a day for a day.
- At times, the above proves inequitable. Experienced experts place a higher value on their time than that of a novice. If this is the case, use dollars as a means of exchange. Let's take the example of a silversmith who charges $50 per hour for services and wants secretarial help. If the secretary charges $25 an hour, she may agree to work for two hours in exchange for every hour of design instruction she receives from the silversmith.
- You may prefer less structure. If your apprentice works alongside you as you produce a product, you can offer tips, instructions, and explanations as you work. Take your apprentice to shows, classes, or conferences.
- Personally, I've had four of nine apprentices prefer to take work home. While in my studio, I devoted one hour of intensive counseling and advice for every two hours the apprentice took to work on a project-in-progress. Any arrangement to which both parties agree works with regular evaluations.

WHERE TO LOOK FOR APPRENTICES

- Send notices to arts-and-crafts instructors in high schools, colleges, and craft shops. State your need for enthusiastic apprentices willing to work and learn.
- Attend meetings of arts-and-crafts groups. Explain your search.

- Place newspaper ads in the personals and help-wanted sections.
- Place fliers under windshields on parked cars belonging to people attending or participating in craft shows.
- Place ads in trade publications serving the artisans and students of crafts in your community.
- Write brief press releases and send them to local newspapers. Include photos of a few interesting pieces of work. Invite interested parties to call or write.
- Place posters in shops in your community that sell crafts and art supplies.

WHERE TO FIND MENTORS

- Watch the newspaper for advertising by arts and craftspeople in your community. Contact them in a professional manner. Point out the benefits of having you as a helper. State clearly what you want to learn from them. Explain other areas in which you can help, such as office work, for example.
- Visit craft shows and exhibits in your community. Note those artisans whose work you admire and follow up with a call or letter.
- Take fliers describing your skills, what you have to offer, and what you want to learn more about. Distribute them to busy artisans manning booths at shows and fairs. The busier they look, the easier for you to convince them that the next time they work a craft fair, you could help.
- Visit arts-and-crafts groups as crafters do. Prepare a well-organized short talk on why you want a mentor. Explain your needs and what you have to offer.
- Place ads in trade publications read by craftspeople. Start your ad with a title such as, "Do you need help with your arts-and-crafts business? Why hire an employee? I will trade labor for experience!" Explain more in the ad.
- Sign up for college arts-and-crafts courses. Offer your services to busy teachers who also work at their craft.

If you can see the advantages of learning a craft from an expert . . . if you can appreciate the help of an eager learner and support their education . . . if you can see the beauty of exchanging experiences in our beloved field without reducing everything to cash . . . then consider a mentor-apprentice relationship. Do your best as a mentor. Share the gift of creativity from your heart with another person entering your field. They will carry your influence with them forever.

Resources

Barnett, Frank and Sharan. 1988. *Working Together.* Berkeley: Ten Speed Press.

Bates, Marilyn, and David Keirsey. 1978. *Please Understand Me: Character and Temperament Types.* Del Mar: Prometheus Nemesis Books.

Goldstein, Jerome. 1984. *How to Start a Family Business and Make It Work.* New York: Evans Co.

Holtz, Herman. 1995. *The Complete Guide to Being an Independent Contractor.* Sunland, CA: Upstart.

Nelton, Sharon. 1986. *In Love and in Business.* New York: Wiley.

Beth Brown-Reinsel
Knitting Traditions
P.O. Box 421
Delta, PA 17314
Phone: (717) 456-7950

MASTER KNITTER

Beth Brown-Reinsel's name is one recognized by most serious knitters. You will find Beth, generously giving of herself, at nearly all national crochet and knitting seminars and conventions.

Beth began her career as a production spinner and dyer. Next, she opened her own shop, attracting her customers with excellent instruction in the spinning and knitting processes.

Having gathered valuable experience as a teacher, Beth reached out and began teaching for her local community college. Soon after, she applied for a teaching position with the Knitting Guild of America's national convention.

Freelancing as a knitwear designer came next. Beth found herself drawn to the traditions and history of ethnic garments. Hearing of her research skills and avid interest in the subject, the Knitting Guild called. They invited her to draw up a national correspondence course on ethnic knitting.

Beth's course met with great success. "Writing my course led me to write my book, *Knitting Ganseys,* published by Interweave Press," Beth says. "I spent three years writing my book. It was laborious, tedious, and stressful, and exhilarating, inspiring, and fulfilling. I loved writing it, in spite of the difficulties I encountered."

The success of her book along with years of hard work and research sent Beth directly on the road to success. Today, she is one of America's most respected knitting experts, designers, writers, and teachers.

Crafts Brief

Business founded: 1989

Legal form of business: Sole proprietorship

Home-office? Beth works from her customized home-studio built by her husband and son.

Hours: Though Beth planned to work at her craft part-time, she found herself working sixty- to eighty-hour weeks. "There is always so much to do when you own your own business. I no longer spend much energy on projects that don't contribute income." With a part-time outside job, Beth has reduced her weekly schedule to three or four eight-hour days.

Best part of craft career: Beth declares she loves being responsible only to herself, having the latitude to create and write as she pleases. She loves teaching, traveling, and meeting new people.

Least favorite: Living with a variable income bothers Beth at times, as does having to leave her family with her frequent traveling. "Constant interruptions," also appear on Beth's least favorite aspects of crafting from home.

Strengths: "Attention to detail and the ability to write clearly."

Weaknesses: She finds it difficult to say "no," thus she sometimes works beyond her limits, finding it difficult to end a long day.

Professional organizations: Beth belongs to the Knitting Guild of America, the Hartford Knitting Guild, the Professional Knitwear Designer's Guild, the Knitting Guild of Canada, and the British Knit and Crochet Guild.

Professional journals: As a serious knitter, Beth subscribes to, *Knitter's Spin-Off, Piecework,* and *Cast-On* magazines. She continually searches for new techniques, trends, and information about historic garments.

Advice: "Keep focused on what you are doing, but keep an eye open for new possibilities," Beth advises. "Be flexible and adjust to continuing opportunities. Don't expect to become rich, but you'll reap satisfaction from following your heart."

CHAPTER 20

YOU AS CONSULTANT

READ INFORMATION ANXIETY by Richard Saul Wurman if you want to know why people demand to know more about everything. The words on the cover of his book explain why consulting is booming in every business arena in the country, including crafting. "Information anxiety is produced by the ever-widening gap between what we understand and what we think we should understand. It is the black hole between data and knowledge, and it happens when information doesn't tell us what we want or need to know," writes Wurman.

From my experience as a craft-business instructor and consultant, I assure you, people are more concerned than ever about gathering information. The trouble is, there is more to know than ever. Our fast-paced, technologically complex world has so much to offer and demands that we pay attention. But it is too difficult for a single individual to know everything. Specialized consultants have become a solution to the problem.

Consultants help others by offering professional, expert advice. Attorneys, marketing experts, financial planners, computer trouble-shooters, and many others all wear the consultant's hat. When called upon to give information, provide resources, answer questions, or share the benefits of your experience, you become a consultant. Think of it as renting out your brain for an hourly fee.

Who uses consultants? People who need help for a specified period of time or who need specialized expertise. Looking for fresh ideas and approaches, clients seek help from consultants to acquire unbiased judgment, and to diagnose and objectively evaluate specific problems.

Successful consultants determine the needs of the client, then work to develop appropriate strategies. Since an individual consultant cannot be everything to everyone, you must define the exact services you can deliver. More than anything else, you must be client-oriented. This includes keeping promises and giving clients what they need and want.

If you think becoming a consultant does not pertain to crafts, think again. Several years ago, I received a call from Planned Parenthood of America. What has this to with crafts or consulting? Simple. The local chapter was considering establishing an annual craft show as a fund-raiser. They wanted to include local crafters and also invite well-known artisans from all over the country to participate. Since no one on their board was a professional in the crafts field, they hired me as a consultant to help them decide whether such an endeavor was practical for our community. They needed guidance to begin.

Suffice it to say, this annual event was successful for five years, yielding more income for the local chapter than anticipated. I acted first as a consultant, later as a paid resource. In the end, I also received payment as a judge for the first annual event.

If you decide to add to your income this way, here are several guidelines to consider:

1. Begin by drawing up a contract. Outline what you will do for a client and what the client can expect from you.
2. Set up a realistic fee schedule. Find out what other consultants charge in your community and field. Generally, consultants charge by the hour or the job.
3. Do not offer guarantees that your advice will result in specific profits or results.

4. Do your homework. When a potential client contacts you, learn all you can about them and their needs early on.
5. Ask specific questions. Before you can help a client, you must know exactly what they need.
6. If the client decides to make an appointment to use your consulting services, prepare thoroughly. Research all you can about their specific needs or focus before the first meeting.

Once you've decided to do some part-time consulting, answer the phone as if every caller were a potential client. Many will be. Have a pencil in hand and write down their name as they introduce themselves. Let's say you receive a call from someone who has heard of your success as a professional crafter, demonstrator, and teacher. The caller wants to know if you will offer guidance on how they can do likewise. Here are some points to remember:

- Make notes about their prime concerns and questions. After listening carefully for a time, ask what their *principal* concern is at this time. Focus on this as you do research in preparation for your first meeting.
- State your hourly fee and set a mutually convenient time when you can meet, preferably in *your* territory, not theirs.
- Suggest they prepare for the visit with a *written* list of questions, but don't be surprised when they arrive unprepared.
- Prepare for the client by researching the issues of greatest concern to them. Try to provide copies of pertinent articles, IRS regulations, and other contacts you may have. Type up a suggested reading list. Include all other practical resources you can find. Give them tangible, written material to take away with them.
- Limit your time with the client to business matters only. Avoid discussing the weather, household pets, and making small talk. Remember, clients are "renting" your brain and paying by the hour.
- Ask the clients to read their questions to you. Suggest they take notes on your response next to the written question. Once home, they will have your answers beside their

written questions. Otherwise, valuable data is too quickly forgotten.

- Be a good listener. Clients need to crystallize their own ideas, priorities, and goals as they bounce them off you.
- If charging by the hour, alert the client when time is up. Ask if they prefer to continue or if they have processed enough information for the moment. Let them decide. Make it clear that charges continue to accrue if you extend their appointed time.
- I disconnect all phones during consultations so the client will not feel interrupted. Clients have the right to your undivided attention.
- Wind up the last five minutes of the hour by summarizing important points covered and repeating where the client may find additional information.

What Will You Offer Your Clients?

1. Be prepared to offer a few contact names of past satisfied clients to prove your credibility.
2. Provide a thoughtful reading list enabling the client to do research on their own.
3. Refer the client to others in your network who can add to the information you have provided. These may be other consultants, teachers, classes, or simply other experienced crafters.
4. Prepare photocopies (respecting copyrights, of course) of pertinent articles addressing the client's prime concerns.
5. Prepare a list of national agencies, associations, and organizations that may provide additional information.
6. List upcoming local events, meetings, fairs, and exhibits where the client can continue to learn.
7. Prepare a list of manufacturers, distributors, and sales representatives that may be of interest.
8. Offer recent copies of craft journals you have finished reading. (I save my journals for just this purpose.)
9. Offer a written outline of ideas and suggestions for your client to follow.

10. Answer all questions thoroughly and honestly. Admit when you need more information yourself. Offer to get back to the client when you have found the answer to their question.

Setting Your Fees

Earnest curiosity and intense questioning plus requests for free information are problems all professionals face after demonstrating expertise in a particular field. As long as you will listen, some people will proceed to pump you dry for information. Jeffrey Lant, author and consultant, says, "Don't *give* someone a piece of your mind. Sell it to them."

I read that consultants should charge $10 to $15 less per hour than psychologists do in the same geographical area. Humorous as it sounds, I've found this works well. Remember, you are selling more than an hour of your time. Included are your resources, contacts, research, experience, and expertise. Set your fee too low and your credibility may come into question. Set it too high and wise clients who shop around will go elsewhere.

Consultants working with individuals, as opposed to corporations or government agencies, usually charge on a cash-and-carry basis. That is, they do not offer credit, instead collecting the full fee at the end of the consulting period. Unless the relationship will be ongoing, this policy saves headaches later. However, should you hire an accountant, a computer consultant, an attorney, or similar more formal consultant, monthly statements may be appropriate.

A consultant may be simply an adviser, taking no responsibility for implementing the advice and information he or she provides. Today, however, many consultants do offer specific implementation services. Frequently, clients assume that receiving your advice means you will also implement it. Make it clear if this is not the case. For example, if you suggest to a client that they draw up a business plan, you may assume *they* will do the work. Clients, on the other hand, may assume *you* will draw up the plan. Early in the discussion, say something like, "Yes, I can draw up the business plan for you, but I must charge my regular hourly rate."

Setting Limits

Consultants and other professionals who are perceived as having valuable information frequently complain about receiving an onslaught of calls and requests for free information. Though most of us want to be kind and answer occasional questions at no charge, many eager learners don't know when to stop. They assume you will be a willing and eternal resource for them. Nip this impression in the bud.

After you have answered a few questions and you realize the caller has a list of more to come, you may need to say something like, "I can hear you have many more questions and need further information. I must get back to my own work but will be happy to see you in my office if you care to schedule an appointment. My hourly consulting fee is—"

You should make it a policy to watch the clock when speaking to potential clients who seem to be reading from an endless list. After ten minutes, for example, indicate that you will have to bill for any further information you provide. Callers may choose to become clients or end the conversation when they realize you are not a free information service.

My friend and colleague, Barbara Brabec, who wrote the forward for this book, is one of the country's foremost authorities on home businesses. For years, people called her from all over the country expecting her to answer all their questions and provide them with information.

Barbara, the consummate businessperson, set a policy that callers could reach her for ten-minute phone consultations only during certain hours—for a modest fee.

This policy eliminated unreasonable callers who had no respect for her time, while at the same time it provided her with a little extra income from those who truly valued her expertise.

Resources

Lant, Jeffrey. 1981. *The Consultant's Kit*. Cambridge: JLA Publications.

———. 1986. *Tricks of the Trade*. Cambridge: JLA Publications.

Wurman, Richard Saul. 1989. *Information Anxiety*. New York: Doubleday.

Special Contribution from Cindy Groom Harry, Craft Consultant

Cindy Groom Harry, vice president of design and public relations for Craft Marketing Connections, Inc., lives in Iowa. Cindy is well known and highly respected in all the major craft organizations and associations across the United States.

She consistently shares her valuable information, support, and ideas with designers, manufacturers, and editors. Frequently serving on educational craft committees, Cindy also heads up conferences and meetings, always ready to contribute her valuable input.

Recently, I asked Cindy two questions. Here are her answers:

Q: How do you define craft consultants?

A: "Craft consultants are experts knowledgeable about an area or areas of the consumer craft industry. They earn their living providing information and advice to clients who pay for their expertise.

"There are many types of craft consultants, ranging from those knowledgeable in product development, project design, instruction writing, and education to sales, marketing, import/export, and fulfillment. But the one thing they all have in common is the responsibility they have to their clients. They must make sure the information they provide is accurate and will point each client in the right direction for their particular company—a profitable direction.

"The best recommendation I can make to a company interested in hiring a consultant is to check credentials and ask for references. Unfortunately, there are many "wanna-be" consultants who don't have the knowledge or experience necessary to guide a company properly. Mistakes can be costly both in time and dollars."

Q: How do you define your company?

A: "Craft Marketing Connections, Inc.'s area of expertise is marketing consultation. Companies from other industries wanting to cross over to the craft industry hire us to help them develop marketing plans to generate an increase in sales. We also serve companies already in the industry who have new products, programs, or line extensions.

"We're proud to have CMC staff members with extensive experience in marketing, design, sales, and fulfillment. CMC non-craft clients include Black & Decker, Inc., The Dial Corp., Hunt Manufacturing, and Forester/Diamond, Inc."

Allow me to provide an example of Cindy's marketing skills. I first met her at a national seminar for the Society of Craft Designers, an organization mentioned frequently in this book. Exhibiting great enthusiasm, Cindy showed me a set of cutting tools manufactured by Black & Decker, Inc., a company not tied to the crafts industry. In simple language, she explained how the tools could make the work of craft designers easier.

Using materials known to challenge crafters' cutting patience, Cindy deftly cut out intricate shapes. Quickly, a group gathered around, fascinated with how easy Cindy made the process appear. Gracious to the end, she invited each member to try the tools.

From that moment, many of my colleagues joined me in adding these tools to our studios. Without Cindy, we would never have been exposed to Black & Decker's excellent products. Black & Decker, on the other hand, would never have been able to reach out to a market like ours without Cindy's experience and energy.

For more information, write to: Cindy Groom Harry, Craft Marketing Connections, Inc., 2363 40th St., Ireton, IA 51027.

CHAPTER 21

YOU AS TEACHER

Whoever would be a teacher of men, let him begin by teaching himself before teaching others.

—*Kahlil Gibran*

WE ALL KNOW wonderfully talented, skilled crafters who do not fare well as teachers. Successful teachers must begin with good communication skills. Expertise alone is not enough. It is one thing to be a proficient technician and quite another to communicate it clearly, sequentially, and in a manner that is beneficial to students.

You must be an expert in your subject before you can teach it to someone else. Though we all learn as we teach, the classroom is not the place for a teacher to *learn* a technique. We must be skilled, informed, and enthusiastic before becoming teachers.

Teaching Credentials and Qualifications

If you have a teaching credential, state it in your advertising and on your résumé and stationery. Teaching experience and/or credentials add credibility to your teaching status.

If you want accreditation and are not a college graduate or have no specific teacher training, look to your state community college system or university for help, as rules vary from one state to another. Look for courses to help inexperienced teachers who may know their field well but need basic teaching education. Consider adult psychology courses at local community colleges. You will find them helpful in managing groups of students. Teaching from a home-studio or nearby shop does not require teaching experience or credentials, but those who have them may have a better chance at success than those who do not.

Individual craft groups, guilds, and associations often offer teacher certification programs. Contact a specific group for specialized programs, or national craft groups such as HIA or SCD and industry-specific associations for more information.

Trained teachers find it easier to inspire students to return to class. Good teachers instill an appreciation for the subject and help students feel confident about their new skills. Craft teachers, particularly, must generate enough enthusiasm that students dispense that most valuable form of advertising: word-of-mouth.

Your Own Home-Teaching Studio

Teaching from a home-studio provides dependable income for your craft business. You may also consider renting a commercial site with established foot traffic or teaching from a shop, community college, parks and recreation department, or other community center. Teaching from a home-based studio provides many advantages. Some examples: You have fewer expenses than when teaching for a craft store, school, or other agency. Fewer federal, state, or local regulations apply to you when you hold classes in your home-studio. You can teach weekdays, evenings, or weekends, setting your own pace.

Teaching as a business requires careful marketing. This is as critical to the success of your studio as it is to your crafting business in general. Here are questions to consider:

- Who are your potential students?
- What are their ages and gender?
- Will it be easy for them to find your classes?
- Where do they live?
- How will they learn about your classes and services?
- Can they afford classes?
- Will they buy supplies from you?
- Check out the competition. What do they offer? What do they charge?
- What are the competition's strengths and weaknesses?

If you live in an affluent area, teaching classes in silk embroidery or flower arranging is appropriate. However, if you live near an economically distressed area, classes in quilt making or woodworking may be more practical. Learn about your market *before* you start.

Deducting Teaching Expenses

Begin your classes with proper bookkeeping. In addition to regular business expenses discussed earlier in this book, you may have additional deductions, such as:

- All equipment, furnishings, and office supplies you need to set up your classes.
- Travel expenses when you leave town to teach, including meals, gasoline, parking, tolls, convention expenses, airfare, shuttles, and taxis.
- Visual aids and materials to make samples.
- Photography and developing costs.
- Dues to craft and teaching organizations.
- Continuing education expenses such as classes, workshops, conventions, and correspondence courses.

The method you choose to document your teaching business must show income and expenses your classes generate should you ever be audited.

Setting Fees

Everyone wants a hard-and-fast fee system that automatically ensures a profit. Unfortunately, no rule exists that is suitable for everyone everywhere. Teachers must set their own fees, considering several factors. You are the ultimate decision maker.

Consider teaching ceramics from home as an example. Students pay you directly when attending your classes. You can arrive at the proper amount to charge with a little research. Find out which classes are popular and well attended in your area. How much do they cost? Visit local shops. Ask if they give classes and what they charge. Call your local community college, adult school, or city-sponsored recreational classes. Check out their fees. Last, determine the minimum amount per hour that would satisfy you. Learn whether ceramics is of major interest in your community by observing displays, contests, and classes nearby. Let us say that a shop you visited charges $20 per student for four classes of one hour each. Let's further assume the adult school or community college offers classes for $15 for ten weeks of two-hour classes, with twenty students per class. When you call the city recreation program, you learn that the fee is $25 for six two-hour private classes. Call a few private craft teachers who advertise in the phone directory. Ask what they charge for individual lessons.

Now, sit down and do a little figuring to arrive at a sensible fee for you and your students that will fit in with your community. The highest amount is the student paying $20 for four lessons of one hour each, or $5 per hour. The lowest is $15 for ten classes of two hours each, or $.75 per hour. The median is $25 for six two-hour lessons, or $2.50 per hour. The highest hourly payment from each student is for private, individualized instruction. The lowest is for large classes where individualized instruction is minimal. Now you have an idea of what the traffic will bear. Figure this information into setting your tuition fees for two-hour classes.

Learn what craft instructors earn at local community college or city programs. Assume an art teacher with a college degree earns $20 per hour. If you do not have a degree, perhaps $20 is too high, but minimum wage is too low. Try averaging. How about $15 per hour as your minimum? You can set the tuition high to attract a few students at a time and stress the individualized attention they will receive. Or set your fees lower, which means you must hold larger classes to reach the same base pay. How about a series of two-hour classes once a week for five weeks? With four students paying $35 each you would earn a total of $135 per class, or $14 per hour. The students would be paying $3.50 per hour of instruction, which is in line with the fees charged in the community. You also could charge each student $20 and require at least seven to a class to earn about the same amount: $140, or $14 per class.

Workshops

Manual skills such as crafts, art, photography, florals, and woodworking lend themselves to a single-workshop format. In a one-day workshop, you can demonstrate brush strokes on a canvas, how to run a sewing machine, or how to make a picture frame. Workshop teachers demonstrate new skills to small groups, then each student tries the new skill. Enhance your class with visual aids, slides and movies, charts, drawings, graphs, and handouts showing step-by-step examples of the craft.

After the teacher feels each student has understood the new skill, students must practice it to reinforce the learning experience. Good teachers move about among students observing, offering encouragement, tips, and suggestions for improvement to each participant.

Offer one- or two-day workshops in which you can thoroughly and intensively cover a specific topic. You can also offer your services to members of community organizations interested in learning new skills, such as groups for retirees, church groups, and other community organizations.

After gaining local teaching experience, determine from trade journals the location of national or regional seminars that offer workshops. Contact such organizations. Send a résumé and a list of the workshops you have taught accompanied by brief descriptions.

Before you leave home to teach, make certain you have a good contract. Draw up a contract similar to the one in Figure 3, or use the sponsoring group's contract forms if they include the essentials. Strive for a clear understanding about dates, locations, hours, minimum/maximum number of students, required materials, meals and transportation, and, of course, your daily fee. Learn from such opportunities after they are over. Jot notes on copies of contracts, listing the number of students in attendance, mileage, and other details to help you prepare future workshops.

Teaching Methods and Lesson Plans

Every session of every class must follow an organized format. Teachers call these lesson plans. Maintain your students' attention and interest by offering variety during each session. Have a well-organized lesson plan and you'll rarely run out of time before covering all the material you've promised.

Teaching crafts involves more than demonstrating hands-on techniques. Whether I teach a single two-hour session or a semester comprised of many weeks, each class includes the following five elements to keep my students' interest piqued:

Figure 3
Contract Form

This contract confirms the understanding between teacher/speaker, Sylvia Landman, and _____.
I understand I am being hired as an independent contractor and am solely responsible for payment of taxes from my earnings.

Date of program:

Hours of program:

Location of program:

Subject of program/workshop:

Required materials for each participant:

Kit cost of materials provided to each participant by teacher:

Contents of kit:

Maximum number of participants attending _____ .
Minimum number _____.

Deadline for group to cancel without penalty: 10 days before presentation.

Penalty if canceling in less then 10 days: cost of materials and copy costs of printed literature.

Travel by car: $.30 IRS allowance per mile (1996).

By air: airline ticket plus ground travel to and from airports.

Meals and lodging provided by group from:

Fee per diem: $____ for full-day program; $____ for partial day or evening.

Fees for expenses and program are due and payable at the conclusion of the presentation.

Nonsmoking home-stays are acceptable.

Sylvia Campbell-Landman, teacher   Group Representative

_____   _____

1. **Lecture Period:** Use this time to present new information to the entire class. Prepare thoroughly and you will be rewarded by each student's attention. Long or short— you talk, they listen. Question-and-answer periods should follow.
2. **Resource Presentation:** Textbook reviews relating to subjects under discussion take most of this time in my classes. But use it also to show slides, quote experts, and explain current standards of pertinent techniques.
3. **Show and Share:** Avoid using this time exclusively to show off your samples and work. Encourage students to bring their own examples relating to the class. Invite them to bring works-in-progress, gifts, heirlooms, imported items, and, especially, incomplete projects that students feel unable to continue without help. Use this time for objective sharing of observations. Never criticize or pass judgment. Encourage careful scrutiny of workmanship, design, use of materials, and the purpose of the item.
4. **Individualized Instruction:** This is the heart of any craft class, regardless of media. Allow plenty of time for it because this is the reason students enroll. Recently, I discovered the advantage of using a chair with casters. Preferring to have my students in a horseshoe configuration facing me, I literally roll around from one end of the horseshoe to the other visiting each student. Offer individual tips to each person at their own individual level. Take care to make each person feel that their speed of learning is fine with you. When teaching adults, it is best if the slowest do not feel left behind and the quick learners don't feel bored.
5. **Technique Lesson:** Set aside this time to demonstrate techniques. Students may gather around you to observe technical skills. Paint, sand, glue, or sew, but talk as you work, pointing out the steps involved.

Rare is the group where everyone's learning level is the same. There are several ways to deal with this common reality. Designate those with similar levels to sit together. This can be as simple as having a table for beginners, intermediates, and advanced students. This facilitates small-group instruction.

Consider different projects, manuals, and homework for each level. Announce when you're about to demonstrate a particular technique and at what level. Students from other groups can join if they need to make up work or need review. If possible, have someone assist you. Assign them a particular class level or technique. Two of you can teach simultaneously from opposite sides of the room.

Here are a few more tips:

- Define a lesson as a period of instruction specifically devoted and limited to a particular skill or idea.
- Allow an appropriate amount of time to cover each subject.
- Present new information in logical sequence.
- Remain focused on the subject at hand.
- Check on class comprehension. Periodically ask, "Have I lost anyone?"
- Proceed from known and familiar to unknown and unfamiliar.
- Draft your lesson plans according to students' expressed interest and ability level.
- Encourage measurable achievement: Have each person illustrate his or her new skill; assign and check written homework; have students bring something from home to illustrate understanding; have students repeat back to you or define new information.

Visual Aids

An entire book could be filled with ideas for classroom visual aids. Here's a start:

Shelves of binders, photo albums, magazines, and scrapbooks Students never seem to see enough of these. Use pocket-style plastic pages in binders. Fill them with magazine clippings and small samples of actual work. Photos of works-in-progress and completed projects by the teacher and past students offer excellent reference and stimulation. Make craft trade journals available to students as well.

Project displays Though perhaps more suitable for shops, this method works well in classrooms, too. Create a change-

able display of ongoing projects. Label each project with
the day and time a class will be taught around that project. List the teacher's name, skill level required, and cost of
materials. Note the approximate time it takes to make the
project.

Also consider offering:

A detailed list of materials required
Tuition discounts   Offer to reduce class fees for students
who register early. Consider offering a discount before the
class begins for anyone who brings in a friend.
Kits of materials for class projects   Occasionally, include
some but not all slow-moving inventory. Call it "extra-special
kit price."

Teaching by Correspondence

People study by correspondence for many reasons. Perhaps
they have small children, transportation problems, or not
enough time to attend scheduled classes. Many prefer to
learn at their own pace. Whatever the reason, students who
study at home need instructors who teach from *their* homes.
Why not you? I have taught by correspondence three different ways:

1. I developed, marketed, and sold my own courses through
   classified ads.
2. The community college where I teach offered students
   the option of taking my courses in person or by mail.
3. A national craft organization sponsored my courses.

Established teachers have the advantage of not needing much time to gather information. After all, you are
already putting yours to use regularly in your classes and
workshops, aren't you? Begin by writing a comprehensive
course outline. Describe the complete course concisely.
Explain everything you plan to include. Next, convert your
usual verbal instructions to written form. Be thorough and

precise. Arrange your material so students learn in a logical, sensible order. Group the information into lessons.
Decide how many lessons it takes to offer the student a rich
educational experience. Be exact about what each person
will learn from each lesson in your course.

I prefer to use a formal outline to plan my lessons. That
is, I use Roman numerals to designate each lesson of the
course. Beneath each Roman numeral, I use capital letters
to sketch out the main points contained in that particular
lesson. I have used the outline format throughout this
book. It is invaluable for organizing information.

Remember, you will not be present to determine
whether students have understood your material. To gauge
comprehension, prepare homework essay questions that
cannot be answered with a simple "yes" or "no." Here are a
few essay question examples:

- Have you ever painted before? If so, please describe your
  experience. If not, why not?
- Are there any particular books or patterns that have
  sparked your interest in painting or helped you learn
  more?
- Why have you decided to learn more now? What do you
  hope to gain?
- Did you find my instructions easy to understand? If not,
  what could have been clearer for you?

When satisfied with the contents of your course and
how the information breaks into lessons, focus on each lesson individually. Think sequentially. Students must see your
ideas flowing logically from one point to the next. Start with
beginning techniques. Before adding new ones, show how
they relate to previously learned material.

Make each instruction clear. Choose questions and
assignments that require students to research information
using their newly gained skills. I include a reading list
with each lesson. I also invite each student to tell me
about books they have on the subject just presented. This
tells me about the student's previous experience and
interests.

After completing all the lessons, go over them carefully. Your educational material must be free of errors and neatly arranged and formatted. When you have a perfectly completed document plus a course outline, you are ready to create a flawless original. Computers are excellent for this purpose. If you don't have a computer, pay someone to create your document for you. Each time you sell your course to a new student, make copies from the original. The real work is preparing the course for the first time. It takes me months to complete each course—it is not an overnight project.

When your course is ready to market, approach your supervisor if you are teaching for an adult program or community college. Show him or her your course outline. Suggest the idea of offering your course in correspondence form along with regular classes. Ask to have it included in the class schedules describing regular classes. In my case, the dean agreed that offering my correspondence course would enhance the reputation of the college's faculty while providing teachers additional freelance teaching opportunities.

The college advertised the class in the course catalog and collected the tuition fee. They retained a small percentage to cover advertising expenses. They sent me names and addresses of those who registered. We had previously decided that if three to six people registered, we would consider the idea a success. Nineteen enrolled.

To market your course on your own, target your market with care. Ask yourself which magazines and journals your potential students might read. Select from these to place your first ads. Keep fastidious records when students begin to enroll. Create a file for each person. Record what course each person is taking. Keep track of your students' progress as they complete each lesson. Each time a student returns a lesson, add the information to his or her file before sending the next lesson.

Keep copies of all letters, lessons, and work samples students send in. I photocopy all work students send me for examination. Since I return the original work promptly, the photocopies provide an excellent record of student work.

Take care to send answers, information, and subsequent lessons promptly. I did some market research on the potential of teaching by correspondence. I learned that the main complaint of students studying by mail is unexplained delays getting their work and samples returned to them. To reassure my students, I offer a guarantee. I send a copy to anyone who inquires about my courses. I promise I will *always* respond within two weeks—no delays!

Bear in mind that all expenses from postage to stationery are deductible. Keep your records in good order and increase your income—without leaving home!

Finding Other Ways to Profit

Teaching from a home-studio or shop enhances your credibility as an expert in your field. You may find that other income-earning opportunities from unexpected sources will come your way. Here are a few examples from my experience to illustrate what I mean. Aside from teaching, designing, and writing from my studio, I have been called upon to:

- Provide private consultation on a project that proved problematic for a client
- Appraise needlework pieces for insurance purposes and estate sales
- Repair or restore damaged needlework
- Draw up individualized needlework instruction for others
- Alter clothing and mend quilts
- Dye items others had made by hand
- Finish projects begun by someone else

These jobs, and many others, I classify as "special services." The only sensible way to charge is to determine what satisfies you on an hourly basis. With experience, you will know exactly what to charge, but at first you may need to be a clock watcher. Time yourself as you work on a single project.

Apply this method to anything you do on commission, from a square inch of needlepoint to a square inch of color painting, from decorating a quarter of a wedding cake to setting a single stone on a jewelry project. Keep track of all the projects you work on for a year or two and soon you will have your own personalized timetable to take the mystery out of charging for miscellaneous special services.

To summarize, experienced crafters looking to teach their skills to others can choose from several teaching situations:

- Offer classes in a traditional setting within a craft shop.
- Teach freelance classes from your own home-studio.
- Teach crafts for local parks and recreation programs—an option that is gaining popularity.
- Consider freelancing at community centers and for other local associations and organizations.
- Community colleges offer steady employment to craft teachers.
- Children are tomorrow's consumers. Think about local 4-H groups, Girl Scouts, and junior and senior high schools.
- After gathering some experience, consider teaching state, regional, national, and even international seminars.

Resources

Brodsky, Bart, and Janet Geis. 1973. *The Second Treasury of Techniques for Teaching Adults*. Berkeley: Community Resource Institute Press.

———. 1992. *The Teaching Marketplace*. See address above.

Margolis, Fredric H., and Chip R. Bell. 1992. *Instructing for Results*. San Diego: Lakewood Publications.

National Association for Public Continuing and Adult Education. 1971. *A Treasury of Techniques for Teaching Adults*. 1201 16th St. N.W., Washington, DC 20036.

Carol Carvalho
American School of Fiber Arts
P.O. Box 6554
Malibu, CA 90264
Phone: (310) 457-6999

ENTREPRENEURIAL SPIRIT

Carol expresses a typical entrepreneurial attitude. "I left the security of a well-paid job for the uncertainty of a crafts career. Expressing my creativity became more important than a regular paycheck from a job I no longer enjoyed. I left my job with enough savings to live for one year. My lucrative career did not provide the inner peace I needed.

"Crafts fascinate me," explains Carol. "I yearn to spend all day with them." Carol began her crafts career teaching needlework four to six hours per week while still working full-time as an architectural engineer in the aerospace industry. "I found teaching satisfied an inner need I hadn't recognized before. I enjoyed helping other people grow and learn. Each time I taught a class at our local college, students said, 'I'm so glad you taught this class. I wanted to learn needlework, but had no place to go to learn.' From this expressed need, my idea for American School of Fiber Arts (ASFA) was born."

Carol approached local school districts and adult programs. She urged them to add more fiber classes to their curriculum. They chose not to. Like countless entrepreneurs before her, she spotted an unmet need and filled it. She established her own school of fiber arts.

ASFA provides a classroom setting where novice and professional meet to share ideas and techniques. Carol explains further: "This is a place to learn and grow. We inspire one another to expand our technical and creative horizons and form lasting friendships.

"I dedicate myself to perpetuate fiber crafts, and to provide high-quality education in fiber fields from the best instructors. Accomplished artists, designers, and teachers come ready to share their knowledge and inspire student creativity."

Though classes and workshops provide most of her income, Carol added a small inventory of needlework-related items for sale at her school. Mail-order sales are growing. She is exploring the idea of selling wholesale.

Carol admits that although knitting is her favorite craft, it's not the one in which she works most. "I devote my personal time to knitting, but during work hours, I work at what pays the bills. Even when I work in less favored crafts, I am still happier working in crafts rather than aerospace. Everything cycles. One day my favorite craft will peak and I will be ready."

Crafts Brief

Business founded: 1992

Legal form of business: Sole proprietorship

Home-office? Carol began her business at home, but felt hindered by lack of space and privacy. "I rented a classroom in a converted elementary school used as a community center. I allocated one-third of the 28-by-28-foot classroom for my office/studio. My office contains a desk, computer with two printers, six bookcases, typewriter, phone, three file cabinets, drafting table, two small supply cabinets, and a cutting table. My studio has four sewing machines, a 46-inch loom, and a 4-by-8-foot work table."

Best part of craft career: The freedom and opportunity for creativity.

Least favorite: Paperwork and accounting chores.

Strengths: Problem solving and good organizational skills.

Weaknesses: Time management.

Daily routine: "I fill my day with correspondence, answering phone inquiries, scheduling students who register for classes, contacting teachers, writing lesson plans, and teaching classes myself. Each afternoon, I do banking and post-office errands."

Professional organizations: Professional organizations are important to learn about craft trends. I belong to the Professional Knitting Guild to keep abreast in the knitting field. The Hobby Industry Association keeps me informed on what's happening in crafts in general. I promote myself as a designer and writer through the Society of Craft Designers. I belong to the National Needlework Association as it's the only national organization just for fiber artists.

Professional journals: *Craftrends & Sew Business, Craft & Needlework Age, Profitable Craft Merchandising,* and many consumer magazines.

Goals: To sponsor an annual convention of classes, teach local year-round workshops, develop a mentor program, and develop a comprehensive fiber library.

Advice: "Evaluate your strengths and cultivate them. Stay with what you do well—develop your strengths. Project a professional image! Crafts business *is* business. Others will perceive you as a professional if you project yourself that way. If you create an image of 'happy hands at home with nothing better to do,' the business world will not take you seriously.

"If you plan to teach, take courses in communication skills and classes on how to teach. Being a good craft technician does not mean you will be a good teacher. Abide by deadlines and always keep your word. When you say you will do something, do it and do it on time! A business, school, or magazine cannot concern themselves with your child-care problems or unfinished proposals. They must meet their own, fixed deadlines. They have time constraints to write, edit, print, and distribute. Budget your time. Plan for the unexpected so you can meet deadlines even when crisis strikes.

"Finally, never stop learning. Learn everything you can. Take craft classes. Attend trade shows and read trade magazines even in non-craft-related industries."

CHAPTER 22

YOU AS WRITER

CRAFTSPEOPLE OFTEN THINK the *only* way to generate income from objects they produce is to sell them. Not so! Before you sell an item, you can get paid to write about its design for craft magazines. Then you can further increase your profits by selling the item traditionally. Magazine editors need writers to quench an endless thirst for new ideas and designs for publication. Hobbyists need writers to provide fresh ideas, inspiration, and motivation. Readers learn about the latest trends and techniques from both publications and craft designers.

If you know how to paint, make wooden toys, knit sweaters, design jewelry, or create a host of other handcrafts, consider writing about your skills and designs. Explain them and share them. The more than one hundred craft magazines in print today need craft designers and writers.

Manufacturers of craft supplies also need people who can put their design skill into words. Such companies often provide free materials to crafters who write for publications so published designs will encourage readers to try companies' products. Further, they pay the designer endorsement fees when he or she mentions products by name in articles.

So, what is a freelance craft designer? According to *Webster's Dictionary,* "freelance" at one time meant "a weapon available from a mercenary soldier of the Middle Ages who offered his services to any state or cause that would pay." Today, the term refers to "a person who sells work or services without working on a regular salary basis for one employer without personal attachment or allegiance; one who sells a service to any buyer."

Write about your designs or provide step-by-step instructions so others can re-create them. Dozens of craft and general topic magazines buy designs from freelance designers and writers. Why not you?

If you plan to write articles and instructions for publication, there are several factors to bear in mind. You must write at a professional level if you want to sell your original designs to magazines. Beautiful designs mean little if the writing and instructions are unclear. Strong writing skills are just as important as mastery of the craft you are writing about. To improve your writing, consult the resources at the end of this chapter.

You must be an experienced expert and technician in your craft. This is not the time to learn basic skills or to try to explain a skill you have only recently acquired. Subscribe to the leading consumer and craft magazines. Remain abreast of the current market including trends in style, color, fabrics, raw materials, and methods. Research continually. Train yourself to digest the abundance of information presented in major craft magazines.

You must be able to break down each step of the creative process. Articulate in words what your hands do "automatically." Readers usually are not at our skill level, so we can leave nothing unsaid.

You must develop organizational and priority-setting skills to meet deadlines set by magazines for which you write. Filing, researching, and retrieving information is not possible without an efficient organizational system. Maintain order among your craft resources by using file folders, cabinets, and file boxes to store:

1. Patterns, articles, blueprints, and graphs
2. Catalogs

3. Idea binders
4. Tear-sheet binders
5. Writer's Guidelines provided by the magazines for which you want to write
6. Tear sheets of your published articles/designs
7. Consumer magazines, arranged alphabetically
8. Business/trade journals, arranged alphabetically
9. List of editors, with addresses and phone numbers (preferably in computer database)
10. List of craft magazines that buy designs from freelancers

Magazine deadlines will become a daily routine. If procrastination becomes a problem, either rethink dealing with editors and publishers or change your habits! It is critical that you *always* meet the deadlines set by an editor once you have been commissioned to write a design article. Maintain your Monthly Action List with a time line! Crafters who write on a freelance basis make frequent use of organizational skills and the ability to prioritize. Hang a blackboard in your office or studio to keep current obligations/deadlines visually present. List tasks in priority order. (See Chapter 3 for more about Action Lists.)

When you're ready, follow these steps to sell a design for publication:

1. Select several magazines appropriate for your design. Remember, other magazines in addition to craft publications buy designs. Be sure the magazines you select suit your style. Collect as many as possible, and keep them filed alphabetically by magazine title. This way, when you have an item to sell, you can shop for the best market.

   Magazines such as *Threads* want only the *process* of your design. And *Piecework* magazine, for example, focuses on the *historical significance* of each craft. Other magazines want little to no text, preferring explicit instructions with accurate measurements and materials lists. Traditional magazines may not be interested in, say, your contemporary style, but those focused on modern styles may. Editors of all types of magazines share a common frustration—articles or designs entirely unsuited to their particular publication. Study several issues of the magazine you are considering before submitting an idea.

2. Learn what editors want by writing to magazines of interest and requesting free Writer's Guidelines (always include a self-addressed stamped envelope). Collect guidelines from as many publications as possible, and keep them filed alphabetically by magazine title. Often, *before* you create the project, you can maximize your chances of selling and/or publishing the instructions for a design by studying the magazine's Writer's Guidelines. What does the editor say she wants? Gear your style to the reader's skill level rather than your own level of expertise.

   Magazine guidelines tell you what kind of articles and designs the editor seeks as well as length, format, styling, and other details. Many guidelines tell you the best months to submit seasonal designs. October, for example, is too late for Christmas projects. These must reach magazines in March or April.

3. Prepare the best query letter possible. The intent of queries is to interest the editor in your idea. Queries should be only one page in length. Make your letter crisp, business-like, brief, and grammatically perfect. Two excellent books on query letters appear at the end of this chapter.

4. After completing your letter, enter the information about the design and publication in your records to facilitate tracking your outstanding designs. Keep a design file, organized by project, and include the magazine to which it was sent, the date, and whether it was accepted, rejected, and/or resubmitted.

5. Include a Project Fact Sheet with descriptive details about the project (see Figure 4). At the top of the Project Fact Sheet, include your name, address, telephone numbers, fax number, and e-mail address. Reproduce my blank outline or draft your own.

6. Editors like quality snapshots. Take the time and effort to photograph your finished project. Send an overall shot plus close-ups to show details.

7. Send your informational package together with your business card, résumé, and clips of previous articles in a presentable folder. Include a SASE so editors can

---

Figure 4
Project Fact Sheet

Project Name:

Project Description:

Level of Skill/Experience Required:

Sizes/Dimensions:

Finished Measurements:

Required Supplies:

Other Materials/Notions:

Special Abbreviations, if any:

Special Techniques Used, if any:

Special Notes:

Swatch or Sample Enclosed?

---

return your package to you if they decide not to use it. Write on letterhead stationery to identify yourself as a professional.

8. Wait until an editor asks you to submit the project itself. When they call or write asking to see it along with your instructions, you will know a writing assignment is on the horizon.

9. When you get a writing/design assignment, begin the project according to the specifications agreed upon between you and the editor.

10. Many manufacturers have endorsement programs. This means they may provide complimentary supplies to *qualified* designers. Additionally, when the design appears in print, many, but not all, companies will pay you an endorsement fee if your materials list mentions their product by name. This payment is in addition to the fee paid to you by the editor of a magazine for your design.

11. Prepare a list of manufacturers of products you use. Each time you plan a new design, contact a few companies. See if they will agree to supply you with complimentary materials for the project.

12. Write or call the manufacturer, identifying yourself as a professional designer. Use letterhead stationery to avoid appearing as if you are a consumer looking for "freebies." Write a crisp business letter. If you have a letter of assignment from an editor, include a copy when you request complimentary supplies from a manufacturer. This proves to them beyond a doubt that it's worth their while to send you products and to keep you on their mailing list.

Once you are on the mailing list of a specific manufacturer, you will receive updated information about new and upcoming products. Many companies routinely send samples of new products to designers on their list. This encourages us to incorporate them into future designs.

13. Study endorsement letters you receive. Some manufacturers send complimentary supplies *and* pay an extra endorsement fee when the article mentioning their product is published. Obviously, receiving supplies at no cost in addition to $50 to $125 per article per endorsement adds to profitability for each design article you sell.

From batting to fabric, nails to paint, manufacturers recognize qualified designers as their target market. They know if we support their products, and use and endorse them, everyone wins.

Consumers feel confident when they shop from a materials list prepared by a competent designer. Shop owners find it easier to satisfy customers who know what they want. Designers benefit from the year-round product information mailings each company provides. Learn all you can about the terms of selling your designs. What rights will you sell? All rights? First rights? Publishers and editors usually send you a letter explaining that they want to buy the rights to publish your design. Most also include a contract. Read the contract carefully as it tells you:

- When they will pay you, on publication or upon acceptance
- Which issue of the magazine will contain your design
- How many complimentary issues containing your design will be sent to you when your design is returned

Always save tear sheets from magazines in which your work has been published. Send copies to manufacturers when requesting endorsements and to magazine editors to lend credibility to your status as a designer. Most manufacturers who provide endorsement fees request a tear sheet or photocopy of your article containing proof of endorsement of their product in your list of required materials.

Have your articles been rejected? It happens to all serious writers. Study, date, and file each rejection letter. As with all writing, examine each rejected project. Promptly rewrite and resubmit it to another magazine from your list. Many rejections have to do with the timeliness with which you offered a project or how many similar ideas or color schemes may already be in the editor's hands. Writer's magazines frequently state that if you don't receive rejections regularly, you are not submitting your work to enough publications.

If your resourcefulness extends to both writing and crafting, pair them up! Each motivates the other. Together, they can more than double your income as you market your creativity.

Writing Craft Instructions

Accuracy is absolutely crucial as you prepare instructions for publication. Though at times errors creep in, editors do not like to publish corrections or to call you for clarification. Follow the outline below to eliminate or greatly minimize errors:

1. Create the project. Document your instructions step by step. Leave nothing out. Write as if the reader were making a project from your instructions for the first time. I prefer to fill only a half-page at a time with instructions, line by line, as I work. I keep a tablet with a pencil attached propped beside me.
2. Go to your computer (or typewriter) and type in the instructions, refining them as much as possible along the way. Print out the first draft.

3. Make the item a second time from your instructions, making corrections and clarifications as you go. Type in your changes and print out your second draft.

4. Repeat the process of crafting, writing, typing, and proofing until you have completed the project and finalized a satisfactory second draft.

5. After completing the instructions, distance yourself for a few days or ask someone else to complete the craft project following your instructions. Ideally, another person should make the project from your instructions without asking for your help. Revise, correct, and reword the instructions as needed for the third draft. Can your instructions stand on their own without you to answer questions that may arise during the crafting process?

6. Prepare a *detailed* list of required supplies; measure and calculate accurately. List principal requirements in descending order of amount or importance.

7. Check with manufacturers from which you are collecting endorsement fees to find out *exactly* how they want their products listed and described. Watch for correct usage and inclusion of "Inc.," the ® and ™ symbols, product names, and color numbers.

8. If an item is generic, describe it as such. For example: "white acrylic paint." Otherwise, state the manufacturer if the project requires use of a specific company's product for successful reproduction. List where hard-to-find materials are available. Provide names and addresses of companies. Your editor may include this with your instructions or choose to group company and product information in a specific section of the magazine.

Time a given portion or module of the project to determine exactly how long it takes to complete the item.

When your instructions involve mathematical calculations, get out your own calculator. Go over the instructions from top to bottom. Do all your numbers, literally, "add up"?

Tips for Computer Users

Below, you will find additional tips for writing instructions on a computer:

- Once you have written the first draft and have started on the second, use a split screen to free-flow ideas from the primary to the second draft. Make use of grammar checker and thesaurus functions in your word processing program.
- Use a database program to file payments received, lists of outstanding queries and projects, an alphabetical list of editors and magazines, and designs out on speculation. I have a file called "DESIGNS OUT." It lists projects alphabetically, to whom they were sent, the date, and whether they were accepted, rejected, and resubmitted.
- Use cut-and-paste techniques to reorganize information.
- Maintain a sensible system of subdirectories.
- Keep a separate list for tracking non-design articles.
- Establish an endorsement file of companies whose products you use frequently.
- Make use of search-and-replace features. For example, substitute "rows" for "rounds" throughout a completed instruction.
- Do you need a scanner? Scanners eliminate the necessity of copying information from paper to your computer. Scanners automatically "read" text you want to include in your documents and insert it where you want it.
- When you are designing and writing as you go, there will be times when you do not yet know final mathematical figures. When unsure how many inches, balls, stitches, etc., are required, place a code such as "xxx" in lieu of an accurate count. Print out the first draft. Continue working on the project, following your printout word for word, making changes, counting, calculating, correcting, including every detail. As you prepare to make a second draft, use your computer's search feature to locate xxx. Now, you can enter the correct numbers.
- Signify that information is ready for final draft by inserting bold, large fonts for each completed section edited on the computer. Example: **FRONT NECK.** This signals the instructions are accurate to that point. Begin to refine the next section.
- Try using one screen for free-flow ideas and a second for a primary draft when devising text portions of instructional articles. Condense and restate as you improve the text, moving it from one screen to the other.

- Consider naming second and third drafts individually, in the event that earlier drafts contain information you wish to preserve. Example: "Red-box.art" for the first draft, "Red-box.#2" for the second draft, and "Red-box.#3" for the third draft.

Resources

BOOKS

Brohough, William. 1993. *Write Tight: How to Keep Your Prose Sharp, Focused and Concise*. Ohio: Writer's Digest Books. (Simply the *best* book on creating professional, concise text.)

Burgett, Gordon. 1985. *Query and Cover Letters . . . How They Sell Your Writing*. California: Self-published.

Cool, Lisa. 1987. *How to Write Irresistible Query Letters*. Ohio: Writer's Digest Books.

Dowis, Richard. 1990. *How to Make Your Writing Reader Friendly*. Virginia: Betterway.

Ross-Larson, Bruce. 1982. *Edit Yourself*. New York: Norton.

Zinsser, William. 1994. *On Writing Well*. Ohio: Writer's Digest Books.

WRITING GROUPS AND MAGAZINES

The National Writers Club
1450 South Havana, Suite 620
Aurora, CO 80012

National Writers Union
236 West Portal Ave., #232
San Francisco, CA 94127

The Professional Writer
Box 7427
Berkeley, CA 94707

The Writer
120 Boylston St.
Boston, MA 02116-4615

Writers Connection
1601 Saratoga-Sunnyvale Road, Suite 180
Cupertino, CA 95014

Writer's Digest
1507 Dana Ave.
Cincinnati, OH 45207

Therese (Terri) Nyman
4969 Lerch Drive
Shadyside, MD 20764
Phone and fax: (301) 261-5271

QUILT MAGAZINE EDITOR

Terri Nyman entered the craft industry as editor of *Creative Product News,* a popular monthly craft industry magazine. The trade journal served craft-store owners and other craft professionals. Terri's job was to inform them about the latest craft products on the market. While working at this job, Terri took on the challenge of editing *Quilt Craft,* a consumer magazine for quilters, on a part-time, freelance basis.

Writing and editing brought her such satisfaction that when *Creative Product News* ceased publication, she decided to turn freelance editing into a full-time career. The publisher was pleased with her work. Within nine months, Terri was editing two Lopez publications: *Quilt Craft* and *Lady's Circle Patchwork Quilts.*

The latter, a well-established magazine, became a challenge for Terri. Its more experienced readers expected more than quilting basics. They expressed interest in national and international quilting affairs. They showed an insatiable curiosity about prominent quilt artists and their methods. Fabric news, design trends, and quilting history are also popular with *Lady's Circle Patchwork Quilts* readers.

Editing two quilting magazines with such diverse readership challenged Terri. She describes the need to separate the distinct nature of each magazine. "I must get into a specific mode to work on one publication or the other to keep my perspective," she explains.

Terri takes time working with the freelance writers and designers who contribute to her magazines. She treats them with respect, always open to their suggestions and interests. She has a knack for making her needs for the magazine very clear so a writer/designer knows exactly which path to follow. Thus, she inspires them to produce their best efforts.

Crafts Brief

Business founded: 1992

Legal form of business: Sole proprietorship

Hours: Terri devotes forty to fifty hours per week to editing.

Home-office? Yes, exclusively. From her 12-by-12-foot office, Terri refers to her phone, computer, and fax machine as tools of her trade. Her quilting supplies, books, and work table have taken over her living room. Terri works alone, but hires freelance writers and designers.

Best part of craft career: Scheduling and creative freedom.

Least favorite: Her busy routine leaves Terri too little time for her personal life.

Strengths: Terri lists her organizational skills and writing ability. Determination, organization, keeping an open mind, and a sense of humor are important to her.

Weaknesses: She confesses to procrastination and being less precise and detail minded than she would like.

Daily routine: Interacting with other quilting professionals via CompuServe, an online service, starts her day. Her usual workday consists of writing and editing. At times, she attends quilt shows and meetings or consults on photo shoots for her magazines.

Professional organizations: Quilter's Unlimited, a northern Virginia quilt guild; American International Quilters Association; American Quilters Society; National Quilters Association; American Association for University Women; and Washington Independent Writer's Association.

Professional journals: *Craftrends & Sew Business* and *Craft & Needlework Age.*

Goals: "I want to continue doing what I am doing now while maintaining my integrity and enhancing my skill. I also want to travel more."

Advice: "Research your chosen field thoroughly. Learn about the people, companies, and trade and consumer shows, and take time to attend! Keep your financial expectations modest. Maintain your own work space separate from other activities and people in your home. Keep a sense of humor. Enjoy the interpersonal relationships available within the craft world and always, *work hard!*"

ADDITIONAL RESOURCES

Magazines

ARTS 'N CRAFTS SHOW GUIDE
Box 104628
Jefferson City, MO 65110

CRAFT & NEEDLEWORK AGE
(trade journal)
225 Gordons Corner Plaza
Box 420
Manalapan, NJ 07726

CRAFT SUPPLY MAGAZINE
(bimonthly and annual trade directory)
Box 420
Manalapan, NJ 07726-0420

CRAFTING FOR TODAY
243 Newton-Sparta Road
Newton, NJ 07860

CRAFTRENDS & SEW BUSINESS (trade journal)
6201 Howard St.
Niles, IL 60714

CRAFTS
Box 1790
Peoria, IL 61656

CRAFTS 'N THINGS
2400 Devon Ave., Suite 375
Des Plaines, IL 60018-4618

THE CRAFTS REPORT
300 Water St.
Wilmington, DE 19801

HOME OFFICE COMPUTING
411 Lafayette St.
New York, NY 10003

HOME PC
Box 420213
Palm Coast, FL 32142-0213

INTERNET WORLD
20 Ketchum St.
Westport, CT 06880

NORTHERN LIGHT
(artist's magazine)
1507 Dana Ave.
Cincinnati, OH 45207

ORNAMENT
(wearable art)
1221 South La Cienega Blvd.
Los Angeles, CA 90035

PIECEWORK
201 East Fourth St.
Loveland, CO 80537

PROFESSIONAL QUILTER
104 Bramblewood Lane
Lewisberry, PA 17339

Newsletters

**BARBARA BRABEC'S SELF
EMPLOYMENT SURVIVAL
NEWSLETTER**
Box 2137
Naperville, IL 60567

**CRAFTS FAIR GUIDE,
A REVIEW OF ARTS AND
CRAFTS FAIRS** (quarterly)
Cost: $35.
Lee Spiegel
Box 5062
Mill Valley, CA 94942

FLORA-LINE
(quarterly; for floral and fra-
grance crafters)
Berry Hill Press
7336-CPN Berry Hill
Palos Verdes, CA 90274-4404

GIFTBASKET NEWS
(for entrepreneurs in gift basket
and home accessories)
Cost: $15.

Margaret M. Williams
9655 Chimney Hill Lane,
Suite 1036
Dallas, TX 75243

GLASS ARTIST
28 South State St.
Newton, PA 18940
(215) 860-9947

**HOME OFFICE AND
OPPORTUNITIES
ASSOCIATION NEWSLETTER**
92 Corporate Park, Suite C-250
Irvine, CA 92714

**HOME OFFICE
OPPORTUNITIES**
Diane Wolverton, editor
Box 780
Lyman, WY 82937

INTERWEAVE NEWS
306 North Washington Ave.
Loveland, CO 80537

METALSMITH (quarterly)
Society of North American
Goldsmiths
5009 Londonderry Drive
Tampa, FL 33647

**NATIONAL KNITTING
MACHINE TRADE SHOWS
AND NEWSLETTERS**
Box 8145
Englewood, NJ 07631

Craft Books

Benmour, Linda. *The Bead Directory.* Self-published.

Boyd, Margaret. *Crafts Supply
Sourcebook, A Shop by Mail Crafts
Supply Guide.* Betterway.

Caputo, Kathryn. *How to Start
Making Money with Your Crafts.*
Betterway.

Diamanti, Penelope. *The Bead
Business.* Self-published.

Long, Steve and Cindy. *You Can
Make Money from Your Arts &
Crafts.* Mark Publishing.

McRae, Bobbi A. *Fabric & Fiber
Sourcebook.* Taunton Press.

Ratliff, Susan. *How to Be a Weekend Entrepreneur at Craft Fairs,
Trade Shows, Flea Markets, and*

Swap Meets. Marketing Methods Press.

Rosen, Wendy. *Crafting as a Business.* Chilton.

Business Books

Crawford, Tad. *Legal Guide for the Visual Artist.* Allworth Press.

DuBoff, Leonard D. *The Law in Plain English for Craftspeople.* Interweave Press.

————. *Business Forms and Contracts in Plain English for Craftspeople.* Madrona.

Murray, Shiela L. *How to Organize and Manage a Seminar.* Spectrum Books.

Young, Woody. *Business Guide to Copyright Law.* Joy Publishing.

Research Resources

Gale Research Company
Book Tower
Detroit, MI 48226

Guide to American Directories
B. Klein Publishing
11 Third St.
Rye, NY 19581

Catalogs

CRAFTS

American International Trading Co.
260 Newhall St.
San Francisco, CA 94124

Clotilde (sewing catalog/newsletter)
Cost: Free (20 percent merchandise discounts available).
1909 Southwest First Ave.
Fort Lauderdale, FL 33315-2100

Craft Wholesalers Catalog (florals, needlework, painting, crafts)
Cost: $5 (refundable).
987 Claycraft Road
Blacklick, OH 43004
(800) 666-5858

Zim's Inc. Catalog of Craft Supplies
4370 South Third West
Salt Lake City, UT 84107-2630

PACKAGING MATERIALS

Cheswick Trading Inc.
33 Union Ave.
Sudbury, MA 01776-2267
(800) 225-8708

Robert H. Ham Associates, Ltd.
Box 77398
Greensboro, NC 27417
(800) 334-6975

BUSINESS AND OFFICE SUPPLIES

Business Book from Miles Kimball (office supplies, tools, furniture)
1 East Eighth Ave.
Oshkosh, WI 54906
(800) 558-0220

NEBS, Supplier of Business
Forms for Small Businesses
500 Main St.
Groton, MA 01147

Personal Office Catalog (hardware, software, equipment, office
supplies)
1 Crutchfield Park
Charlottesville, VA 22906
(800) 521-4050

Queblo, The Complete Paper
Source
1000 Florida Ave.
Hagerstown, MD 21741
(800) 523-9080

Quill Office Supplies
100 Schelter Road
Lincolnshire, IL 60069-3621
(800) 789-1331

Reliable Home Office Catalog
P.O. Box 1501
Ottawa, IL 61350-9916

Miscellaneous

ACC Group Insurance Program
(custom-crafted to fit the needs
of artisans and endorsed by the
American Craft Council)
ACC Insurance Administrator
3535 University West, Suite 200
Kensington, MD 20895

American Craft Enterprises
21 South Eltings Corner Road
Highland, NY 12528
Phone: (800) 836-3470
Fax: (914) 883-6130

Association and Society Insurance Corp. (insurance carrier
for crafters)
Box 2510
Rockville, MD 20852
(800) 638-2610

Craft Shop Directory (This is a
list of state shops interested in
consignment or wholesale buying. They specify whether they
are looking for woodwork, fiber,
toys, quilts, pottery, or jewelry.)
Cost: $5.

Archangel Crafts Collective
Twin Forks Office Park
6040-A Six Forks Road, Suite 263
Raleigh, NC 27609

Internal Revenue Service (free
publication list)
(800) 829-4032

National Association for the Self
Employed
2121 Precinct Line Road
Hurst, TX 78054
(800) 232-NASE

Professional Association of Custom Clothiers (nonprofit organization; puts out a quarterly
newsletter)
1375 Broadway, Fourth Floor
New York, NY 10018

INDEX

3.0 for
windows

AOL

1 (800)